S0-CBI-481

San Francisco
LIBRARY
UC
San Francisco
LIBRARY
University of California

Psychology
in Medicine

Psychology
in Medicine

J. E. ORME

B.A., Ph.D., F.B.Ps.S.
Chief Psychologist, Middlewood Hospital, Sheffield
and Honorary Lecturer in Psychology
The University, Sheffield

F. G. SPEAR

M.D., D.P.M.
Consultant Psychiatrist, Middlewood Hospital
and Northern General Hospital, Sheffield
and Honorary Clinical Lecturer in Psychiatry
The University, Sheffield

RC 467
O 74
1971

Baillière Tindall · London

278242

© 1971 BAILLIÈRE TINDALL
7 & 8 Henrietta Street, London WC2 8QE

A division of Crowell Collier and Macmillan Publishers Ltd

First published 1971

ISBN 0 7020 0376-x

Published in the United States of America
by the Williams & Wilkins Company, Baltimore

Printed in Great Britain by
Latimer Trend & Co Ltd, Plymouth

Contents

APPENDICES

Preface

This book provides an introduction to psychology that differs somewhat from the usual academic courses in the subject. We have felt that the latter often put too little emphasis on the practical application of psychology, and that the student may easily lose his way amongst the controversy and criticism that surrounds the various approaches to the subject.

In our organization of the text we have therefore not only presented the principles of psychology to the student, but we have indicated the relevance of this material to his day-to-day experience of behaviour. Thus in some areas, for instance in the relationship of the assessment of intellectual status to psychological theory and to clinical problems, or that between learning theory and treatment, we can relate general principles to practical problems. In other areas, for instance in the discussion on motivation, it will be seen that the links are more tenuous. Elsewhere, for example in the discussion on some rather unsystematised forms of psychotherapy, we have included topics which, though well-known to the clinician, have attracted little systematic investigation.

Psychology in Medicine is written for the medical reader and in particular for the undergraduate who is nowadays expected to have a working knowledge of psychological principles, and for the postgraduate student working for part I of the Diploma in Psychological Medicine. We hope also that students of clinical psychology will find it a useful introduction to the medical application of their subject.

We have felt it important not to be blandly uncritical, but to point out the major difficulties and limitations of the subject. Our emphasis and selection of material are obviously personal ones and may differ from those of other authors. However, we have included a short list of further reading in the various topics discussed throughout the text, and we hope that readers will progress to further selective critical study in this fascinating field.

We are indebted to Dr I. A. Ross Smith and Mr R. J. Wycherley for reading the draft and making many helpful suggestions. We also wish to thank Mrs B. Thickett for her secretarial services.

July 1971

J. E. ORME
F. G. SPEAR

Introduction: The relationship of psychology to psychiatry and the role of the clinical psychologist

A common problem of newcomers to both psychology and psychiatry is found in the definition of their respective functions and interdependencies. Often some statement is made to the effect that psychology is the study of the normal mind and psychiatry the study of the abnormal mind. Such a statement serves to resolve many difficulties but this view is an oversimplification. Many psychologists are unhappy with any suggestion that they are studying the mind, normal or otherwise, and consider that their frame of reference is the investigation of behaviour and the formulation of behavioural laws. To many psychologists, in fact, mind appears to be regarded as an unnecessary hypothetical intervening variable on a par with the luminiferous or imponderable ether which was once invoked to account for the propagation of light through space but which was found when the theory of light developed, to be unnecessary. Mind, they consider, will eventually be disposed of in the same way by the elaboration of a theory which does not need to include it. It has been suggested that such psychologists are better considered as physicists and there is no doubt that extreme behaviourist views are not generally accepted. Some psychiatrists, on the other hand, particularly those whose thinking has been strongly influenced by the hypotheses of the psychoanalytic schools, apparently consider that the occurrences within the hypothetical system that they call mind are paramount and control all behaviour. Many psychiatrists of this type go on to apply their views on individuals to the explanation of behavioural and cultural patterns in societies of all types.

Neither of these extreme viewpoints gives rise to a particularly useful view of the two disciplines. It remains true that psychology is, or should be, a broader discipline (with regard to behavioural and mental functioning) than psychiatry, which should be limited to the study, diagnosis and treatment of mentally ill people, however they are defined. Nevertheless, psychological hypotheses about normal behaviour should also be capable of accounting for the disturbances observed in the patients of the psychiatrist and of providing suggestions for treatment. Indeed, one might suspect the validity of psychological hypotheses used in explaining normal behaviour if they cannot account for individual variations, normal and abnormal. We consider that psychology should become a basic science for the psychiatrist, in fact rather than aspiration. If this proposition is to be true it will also be true that psychology will gain in knowledge from association with the psychiatrist. It may be worth noting that advances in physiology have been related to the study of the abnormal. The deduction of possible methods of normal operation of a system from a study of the ways in which it can go wrong can be a very valuable exercise.

Even if this close relationship can be established, however, it is unlikely that psychiatry will form only a subset within the universe of discourse studied in psychology as it will continue to draw from other disciplines, particularly physiology. In the latter we have a description of a system which is parallel to that of psychology and which has often been more amenable to manipulation. It must be remembered that the ultimate aim of all psychiatrists is treatment and therefore the facility with which a system can be changed will determine which approach is used. The relationship of neurophysiology to psychology is a matter for philosophical dispute raising old, often ignored, but still cogent problems concerning mind and body. We do not propose to discuss these problems at this stage any more than we proposed to discuss the ethical problems which would arise from the development of really effective therapeutic techniques: ethical problems, that is, which would be a natural consequence of being able to change an individual personality effectively rather than merely alleviate symptoms.

It is probably correct to say that those aspects of psychiatry which form a true subset of the universe of psychology fall within the province of the clinical psychologist. Working together as a team, the psychiatrist and clinical psychologist should share a wide knowledge of this aspect of their work, each bringing into the partnership a proportionately greater knowledge of physiology, anatomy and medicine on the one hand, and of general psychology and specifically appropriate scientific techniques on the other. The essence of the partnership must be a mutual, though critical, respect for the contribution each can make. Regrettably, such respect often seems to be lacking on both sides. The lack of respect is not only apparent in the publications of holders of extremely different viewpoints but also, and more importantly, in day-to-day work.

In Britain it is still generally accepted that the ultimate responsibility for a patient's welfare must rest in the hands of a person with medical qualification. Although not often discussed as such, one of the objects of a medical education is to fit the graduate for this responsibility and it is possible that this necessity is one of the weaknesses, as well as one of the great strengths, of medical training. Some psychologists appear to feel that this situation of medical responsibility puts them in an inferior position and they become unduly sensitive about their status. Furthermore, psychiatry has become the major specialty in certain areas where it remains unclear which disciplines have the most to offer. Examples of this are to be found in mental subnormality where what the patients need is not only a psychiatrist but a team specializing in social and educational rehabilitation techniques. The same applies in the area of delinquency where psychology and sociology would appear to be just as appropriate disciplines as psychiatry.

It should be apparent from this discussion that psychology should not be regarded as a subject auxiliary to psychiatry. Psychologists are being increasingly used in hospitals by consultant medical staff who are not psychiatrists. Obvious examples of this are with geriatric and child patients, and with the so-called psychosomatic illnesses. Such hospital deployment stresses that the two disciplines of psychology and psychiatry, although at times intimately related, are not necessarily simultaneously involved, nor is one necessarily auxiliary to the other. In fact, throughout this book, it is worth remembering that the discussion of the relationship between psychologist and psychiatrist could be generalized to that between the psychologist and doctors other than psychiatrists.

Another difficulty in liaison arises when a psychiatrist adopts the view that the psychologist is merely a technician. This technician applies a routine measure to a patient and comes up with a set of results that can be interpreted by the psychiatrist like some laboratory and special examination reports. This belief results in a request to the psychology department for 'IQ' or 'Rorschach' and deserves to result in a psychologist's report in the form of a set of raw scores, neither discussed nor interpreted. The psychologist is not merely a tester but someone who brings his own specialized knowledge, experience and techniques to an interview to provide what should be a specialized service for diagnostic and other purposes. Although doctors are conversant with the requirements for their own training and specialization, they may not know the parallel requirements for a psychologist. A professional psychologist will have an honours degree in psychology followed by particular postgraduate training. For clinical psychologists, this postgraduate training is either a two-year University-based course, or a three-year period of in-service training. He may also possess a higher degree (e.g. MSc or PhD))based on clinical research.

Some psychologists consider medical training to be deficient in its scientific aspects. A psychologist might then word a report so that it would be capable of comprehension by a child of 9 and avoid the inclusion of more complex material for fear that the psychiatrist will misinterpret it. This attitude by the psychologist does not contribute to the psychiatrist's education in the proper use of psychological tests and may reflect the detachment from clinical reality that psychologists occasionally show.

We consider that in most cases the initiative in seeking help in an individual case will come from the psychiatrist or other doctor who will request the clinical psychologist's opinion. (We must add, however, that full cooperation between psychologists and doctors might be indicated when the psychologist asks some of the questions about a patient, as well as only trying to answer other people's questions.) In this situation it is essential that the psychiatrist presents his request in sufficient detail to ensure that he can get an answer to the question he wishes to ask. This in turn implies that he has given thought to the problem, and it is one of the objectives of this book to try to suggest the sort of questions which can usefully be asked. The selection of the most appropriate techniques to use to try to answer the question will, of course, be left to the clinical psychologist, but it is to be expected that in his report he will at least name the methods he used and present a summary of his results. The report would also contain some mention of relevant information from other fields and would conclude by presenting the clinical psychologist's opinion of the problem.

Where treatment procedures are in issue the first report should discuss the choice of methods and express opinion as to which is the best in the present circumstances. It will probably be followed by a consultation at which the method to be used will be decided and the choice made as to who should carry out the treatment. At the end of a course of treatment there should, ideally, be a summary report and a critical evaluation of the results by all members of the team.

A research project may be initiated by either party and each has his particular skills to bring. There can be few investigations carried out by psychiatrists which do not owe much to the advice given by their colleagues in the psychology department on experimental design and the statistical handling of results. Similarly, many psychological investigations are correlated with clinical findings and will benefit from a closer liaison between the psychologist and the psychiatrist.

We hope that this brief discussion of the way in which the clinical psychologist and psychiatrist can work together will serve as an introduction to the general scheme of this book. Our approach will be to consider psychological principles and methods from the practical point of view rather than in the divisions of academic psychology. The book, therefore, differs in its layout from the ordinary text-book on psychology. Some of the standard areas of psychology will be discussed in the first section on diagnosis and assessment. Other standard areas will be discussed in the second section on treatment. By so doing we hope to show how normal psychology extends its ideas and application into the abnormal field. We have not devoted any special section to developmental psychology. It cannot, of course, be overemphasized that the assessment and guidance of any individual requires knowledge of normal developmental changes and what is to be expected at any age. Not only is this true of the years from birth to maturity, but it is also fundamental that the assessor should be aware of the changes in experience and behaviour that occur throughout adult life. As this is an introductory rather than an exhaustive text, we have taken the course of referring to important changes with age in various functions as the function arises for discussion. For further information on developmental aspects, as indeed on all the other matters mentioned, the reader is referred to more specialized reading. No general account of psychology can be comprehensive, particularly when, as here, the account is intended to be orientated towards a particular application. We have tried to cover the appropriate areas of academic and accepted psychology and to indicate other areas of psychological thought which have relevance to the clinician. It is our hope that the reader, whatever his basic discipline, will at some stage in his career be stimulated to help in the exploration of clinical psychology, where at present there is only an extensive history of interesting but untested ideas on the one hand and, on the other, incompletely validated techniques of assessment and treatments derived from experimental situations which are but shadows of clinical reality. The reader should always keep in mind that psychology, like any other field, is subject to fashions which change over the years. He should be wary of any writer's persuasive views as he will almost certainly find, somewhere or sometime, an opposing view made equally persuasively. But although psychology does not as yet contain any really massive accretion of uncontested facts, it undoubtedly contains a large amount of data and opinions. For this reason alone, psychology is a specialized subject, even if it lacks the accepted systematization of the physical sciences.

We have attempted to make this book self-sufficient. The material discussed and the type of discussion should be enough for a general introduction. The authorities mentioned by name are on the whole key figures in the approach to the material being considered. Should the reader require more detail on any topic or authority, he should refer to the three books given as general references and to the more specific references for each chapter. Such further reading will almost certainly give him what further detail he requires. If not, it will provide further references to the topic or authority.

PART I

Diagnosis and Assessment

I

Intelligence and Attainment Testing

The request for a test of intelligence is probably the commonest to be made by a psychiatrist to a psychologist. Perhaps this is largely because the psychologists' views that clinical judgement of intelligence is extremely unreliable have been generally accepted. It is also true that intelligence testing is one of the most highly developed branches of psychology and that reliable and useful results can be obtained. For example, when children are being examined it is of considerable importance to know how their intellectual capacities and achievements are related to those of their peers. In childhood the use of the 'routine' intelligence test may well be justified. Even relatively slight differences between individuals, when combined with personality factors, may be of great importance in determining the pattern of education which will be best for the child. In adults, however, the questions to be answered, although parallel, are not exactly the same.

For instance, the question which is being asked about a child when an intelligence test is requested may be: 'This child is disturbed, he is in an A stream at school and his performance is poor. Is his intelligence such that he can only cope with the pressure of work at this level with great difficulty?' Here, in the setting of a personality which reacts poorly to stress, frustration or failure, quite small differences in intelligence may be relevant. In an adult the question is slightly different: 'Does this patient have such a low intelligence that he is quite incapable of continuing in his present occupation, despite the fact that over the years he has become familiar with its routines?' Now we are dealing with a person in a less flexible situation. Although it is relatively easy to change a child's class at school (even despite parental objections!) it can be a major upheaval to change an adult's occupation. Furthermore, at least at present, many employers are tolerant and work schedules can often be rearranged somewhat to simplify the routine. Nevertheless problems arise in both spheres, because the patient is in a position where more is demanded of him than he can give. Sometimes, of course, too little is demanded of a person's capacities, although such people normally resolve their difficulties without visiting psychiatrists.

Even in these simple examples we can see that there is little purpose in obtaining an assessment of intelligence which is unrelated to anything else. It may seem to the psychiatrist that if he is given the IQ as a figure then he can make a decision. In many cases he probably can, as when a children's psychiatrist knows the approximate ranges of intelligence in the various streams of his local school. To do this he would also, of course, have to be familiar with the particular test used and with its range of variations. With many problems of this type he would still be better advised to follow the course we have recommended and give his psychologist colleague the facts of the problem. If, for instance, the question is of suitability for a particular type of employment, precise studies may have revealed the appropriate IQ ranges as measured by certain tests. Furthermore, given this knowledge of the problem, the psychologist may, if the overall IQ is adequate, proceed to test special abilities and interest patterns related to the work in question (see Chapter 9). It can be seen that an intelligence test is not necessarily a simple procedure and its results may require skill in interpretation. An understanding of the concepts involved in the use of these tests and of the variety of techniques available is essential for their correct employment.

Definition and background

It is not possible to define intelligence to the satisfaction of everybody. A useful but not exhaustive definition is that intelligence is the ability to perform tests or tasks involving the grasping of relationships and reasoning by analogy. The degree of intelligence is proportional to such factors as the complexity or abstractness of the relationships and analogies involved. The degree of intelligence which a person has exercised in the past can be revealed by the extent of his general and specific knowledge.

Although there are basic difficulties in defining intelligence, there is little doubt that intelligence testing is one of the most successfully developed areas of psychology. It is sometimes said that intelligence is what intelligence tests measure. This is not just a cynical observation but a reflection of the practical usefulness of intelligence tests. A definition of intelligence can, in fact, be put in such operational terms.

For practical purposes, intelligence tests started with the investigation of Binet at the turn of the century. His mandate was an educational one to determine the suitability of French children for schooling. He devised a series of intellectual tasks appropriate for infants and children of various ages. It could be seen from a child's performances of such tasks how comparable his 'mental' age was to his chronological age. Some years later Stern introduced the concept of the intelligence quotient or IQ. This was obtained for each child by the computation $\dfrac{\text{mental age}}{\text{chronological age}} \times 100$. With the average child, the quotient will be around 100. For brighter or duller children the quotient will be correspondingly greater or smaller than 100. Although there have been later revisions of the Binet scale (e.g. the Stanford–Binet and Terman–Merrill scales) it is now a rather obsolete test. Its limitations are many: there are statistical faults, an excessive reliance on scholastic attainments and, of course, a lack of real applicability to adults.

Spearman was an important figure in the development of modern techniques of intelligence testing. He claimed there was a general cognitive factor underlying varying kinds of performances and in his work he brought together the observational methods on individual differences of Galton and the correlational procedure of Pearson. Galton had pioneered studies into the importance of individual variations in many aspects of human functioning. He had clearly shown that such individual differences, in perception, ability and so on, were an important factor in the assessment of the individual. Pearson followed by making significant contributions to the development of statistical methods appropriate for examining individual differences among groups of people. From the evidence of his statistical methods of analysis, Spearman's two-factor theory claimed there were two kinds of factor in the quality of human performance. There was a general factor common to all tasks of a cognitive kind (g) and a factor specific to each such task (the s factor). Many subsequent British studies have amply confirmed the existence of g but have also tended to reveal a hierarchical differentiation from this general factor. These group factors are ones common to a kind of cognitive task, falling in between the original Spearman concepts of g and s. P. E. Vernon identifies two main groups; those of the verbal–educational type (v–ed) and those of a more spatial and practical nature (k: m).

American factor-analytical studies, particularly those of Thurstone, at first tended to produce a rather different set of results. A general factor was absent but there were a relatively large number of multiple factors. This difference between the British and American studies is largely a result of variations in the mathematical techniques of factor-analysis that are used. The British method tends to result in uncorrelated factors (orthogonal factors) whereas the American techniques produce correlated (or oblique) factors. When the latter are again themselves factor-analysed, the resulting second-order factors are, in fact, very comparable to the British results.

Somewhat outside this main stream of activity have been the studies of Piaget. He has been particularly concerned with the maturation of intelligence and has made many experimental studies into the nature of the development of intelligence in the child. It is difficult to summarize Piaget's work adequately. He distinguishes the following stages. In the first two years cognitive development is largely of a sensori-motor kind. From 2 to 4 years symbolic thought appears but remains at a preconceptual stage with no use of classification. Between 4 and 7 follows a period of intuitive thought with the individual possessing a largely egocentric view of the world. From 7 to 11 is a period of concrete operations where concepts can be developed in a practical setting. Concepts, of course, enable objects and experiences to be divided into classes by means of what are considered to be their common properties. After 11 years these concrete operations become internalized and adult thinking in terms of hypotheses and propositions develops. Piaget's work, although interesting, has been criticized on a number of points, particularly on the restricted nature of his subjects who tend to be drawn from a rather narrow stratum of society. Another important concept of Piaget's is that of the two-way dynamic processes of 'assimilation' and 'accommodation'. These processes stress how the individual is always relating and incorporating data about the outside world (assimilation) and, reciprocally, moulding and shaping his own psychological organization (accommodation). Such processes stress the fact that an individual is always interacting with the outside world, not only with regard to intellectual processes but also in perceptual and personality processes as a whole. Possibly in the earliest months of life it is usual to find that assimilation is the dominant process but afterwards more of a balance occurs between the two processes. It has been suggested that, in adults, a pathological dominance of assimilation may be found in schizophrenia. It remains to be seen in the future to what extent Piaget's findings can be assimilated into the main stream of knowledge about intelligence and its assessment.

Modern methods of intellectual assessment

The most widely used British techniques are the Progressive Matrices and the Mill Hill Vocabulary Scale, both designed by J. C. Raven, and their derivatives. The former, a set of non-verbal tasks, directly attempts to assess Spearman's three main principles of what he called the neogenetic activity involved by the operation of his *g* factor. That is, they attempt to measure an individual's degree of productive intellectual ability. A vocabulary scale, which estimates a patient's level of word knowledge, on the other hand, is an example of a measure or reproductive intellectual ability. The subject is successful in the latter task mainly as a result of the use he has made of his productive ability in the past. Cattell has distinguished rather similarly the contrasting functions he calls fluid and crystallized ability.

In America, the Wechsler scales for adults, children and preschool children have been the most successfully developed and are widely used in Britain. In these scales 10 or more subtests are computed separately, then added to give a verbal IQ, a performance IQ, and then a full-scale IQ. The verbal subtests of vocabulary, general information and arithmetic are self-explanatory. In a similarity subtest the subject has to elicit the similarity between two named objects. The digit span subtest measures the numbers of digits that can be repeated by the subject after the examiner. The comprehension subtest measures a person's verbal ability to respond to, or understand, certain aspects of social behaviour. The performance subtests include block design (construction of patterns with wooden cubes to match given designs), digit symbol (speed and accuracy of coding) and picture completion (identification of missing parts in pictures). Picture arrangement measures the ability to put a series of cartoon-like pictures into an acceptable story-telling sequence. Object assembly involves the construction of certain items, rather like a jig-saw, from segments. On the whole it might be argued that the performance tests measure productive ability and the verbal tests reproductive ability. This is certainly true of block design and vocabulary respectively. But factor-analytic studies tend to show a somewhat unsatisfactory degree of factor impurity in the other tests. In particular, similarities might be better considered as a performance test and digit symbol as a verbal test.

Both these British and American techniques assess a person's intellectual performance in terms of his numerical position with regard to his own age-group. With the Raven tests, this is based on his percentile ranking. The percentile ranking is the position of his score expressed as a percentage of the scores falling at, or below, that position. With the Wechsler scales a deviation IQ is devised based on the built-in design of a mean IQ of 100 with a standard deviation of 15.

There are, of course, numerous intelligence tests, but it should be apparent that a reputable and generally applicable test should be carefully constructed and standardized on a large number of subjects. The latter should be of different levels of ability and of different ages. Because of these requirements, it can be seen that the number of useful tests available is rather small. In fact the number of techniques applicable to a majority of people, at any age, with really full standardization and norms is restricted to those previously discussed in this section. For rather special kinds of subject more specialized assessment techniques are available. Thus, a number of tests (e.g. the Advanced Matrices and Alice Heim V) endeavour to discriminate more finely among bright adults. For children with special handicaps such as deafness or blindness specially constructed tests are available. For all children of less than five or six, special tests or developmental schedules are in existence. A useful index of the variety of assessment techniques available can be obtained from the catalogue of the National Foundation of Educational Research.

The distribution of intelligence

Modern measures of intelligence are often designed so that their distribution of scores in the general population is normal. It is sometimes argued, therefore, that the normal distribution of intelligence is a statistical artefact. In fact, normality is only used as a criterion because results with various techniques have consistently showed marked trends to normality of distribution without this being a built-in feature. The distribution of ability with modern techniques tends to be a normal one except for some skew towards the lower levels of ability.

It is a statistical property of the normal curve of distribution that 99% of all cases fall in the range of plus or minus 3 standard deviations from the mean. In Wechsler scale terms, with a mean IQ of 100, this range is from 55 IQ to 145 IQ. It should be readily apparent that it is meaningless to give a person's IQ without some knowledge of the standard deviation of the measure involved. An IQ of 190 with a measure possessing a standard deviation of 30 is only equivalent to an IQ of 145 on the Wechsler Scale. It should also be apparent that there are obvious difficulties in the alleged assessments of ability outside the range of 3 standard deviations from the mean, particularly above the mean.

Generally speaking the reliability of a measure of a person's level of ability is high, even over several years. Obvious exceptions to this are subjects who for varying physical, psychological and social reasons are prevented in the first place from achieving their potential level or who subsequently cannot maintain a previous level. A striking example of the former case is the improvement of performance in mentally subnormal subjects after being removed from inadequate environments and spending some time in a more progressive atmosphere. With infants, of course, individual differences in the rate of development as a proportion of the total amount of development are large enough to prevent very reliable (i.e. predictive) assessments of ability.

Intellectual assessment clearly plays an important part in the diagnosis of mental subnormality. It is necessary to point out that no one IQ point constitutes a critical level. Apart from the importance of personality variations, an IQ is only accurate or reliable to about ± 5 points. It is reasonable to argue that intellectual subnormality by itself starts to become a serious handicap when it is more than 2 standard deviations below the mean. On the Wechsler scale this means an IQ of less than 70. Even so, adult individuals within the third standard deviation range (i.e. 55–69 IQ) can still learn to read and write and, granted emotional and social stability, can be satisfactorily contained within the community. The fourth standard deviation range below the mean (40–54 IQ) shows more obvious limitations. Subjects in this range are usually illiterate and tend to need sheltered protection within the community or in a subnormal hospital. An IQ of less than 40 includes what used to be called imbeciles and idiots. Such patients are more satisfactorily assessed on behavioural scales analogous to those used in assessing normal infants and babies.

Although there is much overlapping of ranges of scores, intellectual levels correlate highly with scholastic success and occupational level. To some extent the correlations are reduced either by inequality of opportunity or by the importance of other factors, particularly those of personality. There is at present, for example, considerable debate as to how far high intellectual level can be equated with creative capacity. Some authorities take the view that 'genius' is characterized simply by a very high IQ. Others argue that although the IQ might have to be above average, the essential characteristics that distinguish a 'genius' from others of a similar IQ level are to be found more in non-cognitive factors; for instance, that Terman's study of 'genius' is really a study of high IQ. What is of interest, however, is that Terman's reports show that such individuals, as well as being scholastically and occupationally successful, are also more successful in their personal lives. Although it seems true that a graduate's class of degree is not closely related to his intellectual level one has to remember the intelligence factor has already determined the likelihood of a student reaching University.

In recent years it has been claimed that creative people are those prone to 'divergent' rather than 'convergent' thought processes. Ordinary intelligence tests are said to stress the latter (only one correct answer per problem) and are thus not capable of distinguishing creative people. These creative people are better picked out by specially constructed tests where flexibility of answering can be examined. Although such an argument has some plausibility, there is no real evidence to suggest that there are convergent and divergent thinkers. Furthermore, there is no real evidence to indicate that tests of divergent thinking are anything other than tests of general intelligence. Another difficulty is that any real validation of a test of creativity needs adequate data from subjects who are undoubtedly creative.

The 11-plus examination was a source of great controversy. Psychologists as a whole do not favour a decision made on one examination, particularly at this age. The difficulty, however, is that some sort of selection or streaming is almost always made, even if it is only between the different classes or groups in a comprehensive school. In the past, studies of teachers' assessments have proved these to be extremely unreliable. Eleven-plus examinations, including an intelligence test, are an improvement on such assessments. Selection or streaming of children at school is probably inevitable in most cases. What are required are more flexible divisions and repeated appraisals of a child's attainments and abilities by the best methods available. The occasional school which mixes children of all abilities can only be regarded as experimental and the outsider who has seen the emotions aroused by such changes in the educational system can only be sceptical about the prospects of proper evaluation of such 'experiments'.

CHANGES OF ABILITY WITH AGE

There are marked changes of ability with age not only in childhood but throughout adult life. These changes can be appreciated most clearly in Progressive Matrices and Mill Hill Vocabulary scores. The latter increase steadily through childhood to early adult life, then tend to remain relatively stationary. In the elderly there is perhaps some falling off, but less so in the brighter subjects. With the Progressive Matrices, there is again a steady increase in performance through childhood reaching a maximum well before the age of 25 years. After 25 there is a progressive decline in performance as far as normative data (up to 85 years), are available. Again this decline is perhaps more evident in the duller than in the brighter members of the population.

It is therefore apparent that productive intellectual ability declines relatively early in life. This process is somewhat compensated for by some increase in attainments and experiences as reflected in the changes of reproductive intellectual ability. These results are given a clear practical validation in the studies of Lehman into age and achievement. He found in almost every type of scientific and artistic occupation that the most productive years were the twenties and thirties. Portraits of first rank thinkers and artists when elderly obscure the fact that such people were usually quite young when they produced their most important work. Some elderly people produce work of exceptional merit but this is rather rare.

THE ORIGINS OF INDIVIDUAL VARIATIONS OF ABILITY

Adverse environments of various kinds can clearly depress a person's intellectual development. Nevertheless, in a developed society there is little doubt that the major source of intellectual variation is a genetic one. This view, although becoming fashionable, is still unacceptable to many, but as generalizations go it is as accurate as any. Studies of the intelligence of persons with varying genetic and environmental backgrounds indicate that, in general, environment has surprisingly little effect on the level of performance.

Burt, in a closely reasoned argument, attributes at least 75% of the variance (and possibly 90%) to genetic factors. If to this is added the known effect of varying embryonic conditions it can be seen that, except for an atypical minority, the individual's level of ability, even as an adult, is almost wholly determined by factors present before birth.

It is a mistake, however, to argue that such findings will support views of natural superiority or inferiority of different races. With groups who have suffered from adverse environmental conditions, the latter are probably sufficient to explain any lack of comparability to a population more fortunate and homogenous for these conditions.

There is more support for the possibility of a national slow decline of ability. This is a natural deduction from the known fact that there has been a statistically significant negative association between level of ability and family size. If ability is polygenetically determined and the association with family size continues, it seems logical to expect a slow but inevitable decline of ability with succeeding generations. An attempt to test such a hypothesis was carried out in Scotland by Godfrey Thompson in 1947 with equivocal results owing to the shortness of the time interval (15 years), changes in education and test sophistication. Of course variations in family planning can occur and recently there is some evidence that the negative relationships between family size and ability has declined and even been partly reversed.

Apart from certain verbal features there is no evidence of any natural differences in ability between the sexes, particularly if obvious environmental differences are allowed for. It does appear, however, that from infancy onwards females, as a whole, are superior to males in verbal ability. They speak earlier and at every age are more fluent and know more words. Even verbal defects such as dyslexia and stammering are far less frequent in females than in males. It is well known from life expectancy tables that the male is less robust than the female and certainly it is true in the particular areas of speech and language.

As noted, most psychologists accept that intelligence is a general ability and for most people to be good at words is to be good with their hands, provided that they are sufficiently motivated to learn the necessary techniques. If such similarity in performance cannot be found it is readily explained by lack of interest or relevant experience. It therefore follows that a general measure of intelligence is often the one that is required rather than a test of some rather hypothetical special aptitude. Nevertheless, allowing for the vicissitudes of interest and experience, it is sometimes useful (in either vocational selection or guidance) to measure certain aspects such as numerical ability, spatial ability, clerical aptitude, motor coordination, finger and manual dexterity or mechanical ability. For example, it has been suggested that the most successful students on technical courses tend to be those with high spatial ability and relatively low verbal ability.

ATTAINMENT TESTING

A person's level of verbal ability is itself, as explained, a measure of attainment. From a vocabulary test this will be a very general measure of his attainments. With the Wechsler verbal scale the information subtest level can be related to what is usually called general knowledge. The arithmetic subtest obviously gives some measure of a person's relative level of arithmetic, and comprehension performance of his social knowledge.

Even so, it might be desirable to make further assessment of a person's attainments, whether a child or adult. Such assessments can be useful in a number of ways. For example, one might wish to measure accurately a person's reading and spelling ability or even whether he is literate at all.

Such attainment testing, like intellectual assessment, clearly requires standardized tests which are reliable and valid. Such series have been made by workers such as Burt and Schonell. Assessments with these measures can be made of a person's level in such fundamental attainment areas as reading, arithmetic and English while various diagnostic measures indicate where particular difficulties can be elicited.

The administration of intelligence tests and the assessment of performances

Many intelligence tests appear relatively simple to give. It is, therefore, a great temptation, particularly when trained psychologists are not available, for doctors, teachers, personnel workers and others to make their own intelligence assessments of subjects in whom they are interested. There are, however, two serious objections to such a practice. First, the need to ensure that a subject has performed a test in a standard manner to the best of his ability. This often requires a considerable degree of supervised training and practice on the part of the administrator. Secondly, adequate interpretation of what a particular score really means often requires close familiarity with the formidable body of data on intellectual performance under varying conditions with different kinds of subjects. It is, therefore, very doubtful if non-psychologists should be encouraged to use intellectual measures which are, despite appearances to the contrary, highly technical tools belonging to a rather large and specialized body of information. Perhaps the safest solution to this problem is for the non-psychologist to use simple tests such as in a vocabulary test of the synonym selection type and to restrict his interpretation to a minimum. Such a measure is provided by one of the versions of the Mill Hill Vocabulary Scale.

It is also important to stress, particularly when dealing with clinical subjects, the occasional discrepancy between test result and clinical impression. A subject's social behaviour can, in fact, either at interview or in general, suggest an intelligence level either above or below that of his test level. The latter is usually accurate enough to indicate how much of his behaviour can be attributed to non-intellectual factors such as those of personality and social background. Finally it should be noted that although a person's level of ability might conceivably be potentially higher than his actual test performance at any given time, it cannot be lower. Provided a reliable test has been given by a properly-trained psychologist, the assessed level of ability can generally be assumed to be a reliable estimate.

Intellectual Deficit, Brain Damage and Impaired Functioning

While the questions which the clinician puts to the psychologist in connection with the testing of intelligence can be many and diffuse, those concerning the possible presence of organic disease of the brain tend to be few and more precise:

1. Is there evidence of organic brain disease?
2. Does the evidence suggest that organic brain disease accounts for most, or for only a little, of the clinical picture?
3. Do any of the psychological test results suggest that the brain disease is in any way localized?
4. To what extent is the patient impaired, especially with regard to cognitive functioning?

The first question may be asked in regard of any patient of any age in whom the psychiatrist suspects that organic processes are related to the patient's condition. We must emphasize that patients of whom the question can be asked may well be young people suffering from brain tumour and further that there may be very slight evidence of disorder on normal clinical examination.

Any competent doctor should be able to detect gross dementia and where a patient presents with such a state he will not ask our first question, although he may ask the other questions. This detection depends on knowing what can be expected say, from, the normal healthy old person or from a younger person of subnormal ability, but the deviations from normal are such that they can be detected unequivocally on clinical examination. We do not accept, however, that it is possible to diagnose early dementia or other mild brain damage unequivocally at a clinical examination. It is equally true that psychological testing is still an imperfect instrument for this task, but we think the evidence suggests that it is at least as sensitive.

Some psychiatrists make a practice of obtaining tests for intellectual impairment as part of their routine investigation of their patients. However, for most medical consultants, especially neurologists and geriatricians, psychological services are not in sufficient supply to do this. Moreover, from all points of view, effective screening would be a preferable procedure. Basically, the selection of patients for referral depends on the clinical observation of memory disturbance as one of the fundamental signs of organic impairment. Inability to recall the day, month and year, name of the examining doctor after being told it, name of the Prime Minister and his predecessor, to recall a name and address or a series of numbers and to subtract serial sevens may all be tested clinically. But at present the weight attached to the findings of such an examination is based on a subjective judgement of the physician after taking his other observations of the patient into account. It is on the basis of a suspicion resulting from this type of questioning or on certain inconsistencies in the patient's history that the psychologist's opinion is sought.

Our second question is asked when the clinical evidence for the presence of organic brain disease is fairly convincing but where the patient also shows signs of mental disorder, either neurotic or psychotic. Here there are two objectives: first to modify the prognosis in a less favourable direction where a depressive or other illness is complicated by dementia; and second, and more important, to ensure that where the major factor in causing the patient's present state is, say, an endogenous depression, the appropriate treatment is applied. In all cases of organic brain disease the psychiatrist is concerned with the problem of possible treatment. Where this arises there are two possibilities: first, that general impairment of function is the result of an external removable factor, for instance an infection of a deficiency state; and second, that it is the result of a local lesion, for instance a tumour, within the skull. In both these situations psychological assessment can contribute to the diagnosis.

It is generally accepted that intellectual activity is particularly associated with cortical activity. Studies such as those of Lashley tended to emphasize the generality of function of the cortex. A falling off in performance tends to be related to the amount of cortex damaged rather than to the specific area impaired. Such findings tend to be easily, if loosely, related to the concept of the general cognitive factor which we have described. Hebb postulated intelligence A, the innate capacity of the brain for development, contrasted with the measurable intelligence B, the actual capacity of the brain after development has occurred. Heredity sets the limits of potential ability but these limits may not be achieved owing to the vicissitudes of development.

Any temporary or permanent impairment of the organism by physical or psychiatric illness will tend (but not universally) correspondingly to impair intellectual functioning. This is inclined to be more apparent on tests of productive rather than reproductive intellectual ability. Psychotic patients, particularly schizophrenics, may show such intellectual impairment. If the illness is long-standing, it will also tend to affect reproductive level as there will have been a limitation of attainments. Language disturbances are fairly common in schizophrenia and organic states. Where these occur, verbal performance will clearly be impaired. There is also some reason to believe that the distribution of ability in psychiatric illness is basically rather inferior to that in the general population. This might be explained by arguing that initial limitations of ability inevitably lead to greater difficulties in dealing with emotional difficulties. Only in the rather rare condition of obsessional neurosis is there any evidence that a particular psychiatric category of people possesses a range of ability superior to that of the general population. There is also some evidence that psychopaths may show a level of reproductive intellectual ability inferior to that of their performances on productive tests. This perhaps reflects their inadequate socialization and limited conformity to the society in which they live, whatever its cause.

With generalized cortical damage, ability on tests of productive ability tends to be inferior to that on tests of reproductive ability. Thus tests involving the ability to solve new problems (block design, Progressive Matrices) will be inadequately completed compared with performance on tests involving simple recall of knowledge (vocabulary, general information). Such contrasts in performance form the basis of Weschler's Deterioration Quotient. Of the Weschler Scale subtests some are relatively impervious to impairment (Vocabulary, Information, Picture Completion and Object Assembly) and are called Hold Tests. Others are sensitive to impairment (Similarities, Digit Span, Digit Symbol and Block Design) and are called Don't Hold Tests. With a subject's age scaled score equivalents

$$\text{Deterioration quotient} = \frac{\text{hold} - \text{don't hold.}}{\text{hold}}$$

But there are limitations to such assessments using standard intelligence tests. One can only exclude 'false positives' at present at the expense of having an appreciable minority of 'false negatives'; that is, if the cut-off point used is one where no non-organics are classified as 'organic', then a proportion of 'organic' cases will be classified as 'non-organic'. With regard to cerebral localization, a number of studies have indicated that laterality (and possibly lobe location) results in characteristic deficits on certain intellectual tests. Left-sided lesions possibly result in poor performance on tests involving verbal material. Right-sided lesions tend to affect performances dealing with visuo-spatial material.

Apart from the use of standard intelligence tests, material has also been designed specifically to test for intellectual deficit, and here the picture is clearer. Where the intellectual deficit is due to brain damage, the most successful tests have been those involving memory and learning. The most commonly used memory tests are those where a simple design is viewed for 5 to 10 seconds, followed by the subject then recalling the design and drawing it. A number of such designs are attempted and brain-damaged subjects tend to be readily distinguished from non-brain-damaged subjects by their greater inaccuracy. Such memory tasks have to be rigorously standardized against the usual variables of age and general intelligence level. The best-known series of designs are those of Benton, Graham-Kendall, and Bender. It is important initially to check if such tasks distinguish between brain-damaged patients and psychiatric subjects rather than between brain-damaged subjects and normals. Such a check not only concentrates on the direct effects of brain damage (rather than inattention) but also makes sure the test will be able to answer the kind of question that is asked in practice. For example, the question usually asked is: 'Is this 75-year-old man, who is clearly ill, suffering from brain damage or depression?' not 'Is this man either brain-damaged or normal?'

Verbal learning tasks where the subject has to learn pairs of words or meanings to words which are now new to him, have also proved to be equally efficient discriminators of brain damage as memory tasks. But with all these measures, the brain damage has to be damage that is having some generalized cortical effect. Such a proviso might be criticized on purist grounds by the neuro-pathologist but this does not do justice to the importance of the query as exemplified earlier, 'Is this patient dementing or is he depressed?' Examples of verbal learning tasks are those of Walton and Black (The Modified Word Learning Test), Hetherington (The Neologism Learning Test) and Inglis (Paired Associates).

Attempts have also been made to measure more specific kinds of intellectual impairment that have been postulated to be of primary importance in schizophrenia. Interesting studies have been in terms of over-inclusive thinking and of thought disorder. Even these studies, however, only identify a proportion of schizo-phrenics. Usually only the paranoid or the non-paranoid sub-groups are identified, and it is even conceivable that the tasks used are only identifying the effects of the personality variable of extraversion–introversion in a psychotic group. Psychiatric illness in general also seems to produce a non-specific intellectual im-pairment, including a reduction of psychomotor speed. Other techniques, such as the Vigotsky test of concept formation and the Goldstein object-sorting test, have also proved disappointing in the attempt to identify schizophrenic subjects. Tests of concept forma-tion and abstract thinking present a subject with a number of objects, coloured, shaped and marked in various ways. The sub-ject then has to classify the objects in as many ways as possible, using the colours, shapes and marks to do so. The Goldstein object-sorting test has much the same purpose only using a collection of real life articles. The difficulty with such tests tends to be that they turn out to measure general intelligence and its impairment rather than some specific cognitive ability or disability. A par-ticular difficulty is then that both brain-damaged and schizo-phrenic patients find such tests difficult. Furthermore, these kind of tests frequently have only an inadequate degree of validation data available.

More recent contenders in the field of schizophrenia are measures derived from repertory grid technique by Bannister and Fransella. This technique is used for the investigation of individual patterns of beliefs and attitudes. Bannister has suggested that in thought-disordered schizophrenics such patterns of belief would be relatively loose and inconsistent. In a repertory grid experiment he has provided evidence to substantiate this hypothesis. It is of interest, however, that the non-thought-disordered schizophrenics are basically the paranoid schizophrenics and the latter are not

C

loose or inconsistent. Although it would be unwise to condemn what is an interesting technique, it is possible that this technique is only measuring a non-specific intellectual deficit.

One test that does appear to measure something else in addition to general intelligence is the Porteus Maze test where something like forethought and planning capacity is required. This test consists of a series of mazes of varying difficulty. The subject has to trace his way successfully from a start to a finish and the task is like finding a way between two places on a street map. Important in success is the ability to plan ahead and thus avoid wrong turnings. Delinquent groups tend to perform less well than non-delinquent groups. This deficit is attributed to the psychopath's characteristic inability to plan and control his behaviour in real life for a future objective. Porteus Maze studies also indicate a deficit of performance after prefrontal leucotomy. Such findings are in contrast to the usual findings with standard intelligence tests showing no permanent decline once immediately post-operative effects have ameliorated. This deficit on maze performance was considered to reflect the characteristically uninhibited behaviour of the post-leucotomy subject. It is perhaps of interest, however, that recent long-term follow-up studies of leucotomy subjects have indicated a more general intellectual deficit with subjects eight or more years after the operation. Similar long-term studies seem indicated for the effects of repeated E.C.T.

The Porteus Maze test is nevertheless highly associated with general intelligence, and recently Gibson has devised a Spiral Maze where intellectual level is unimportant in performance. The subject has to trace a line round a spiral which contains obvious obstacles and he is urged repeatedly to go faster. Performances, therefore, contrast speed (time) and accuracy (errors of touching lines or obstacles) so that the two are negatively correlated. Gibson has shown that delinquent groups tend to be relatively quick and inaccurate. It might well be that the division between this kind of group and the opposite type, those who are slow and careful, reflects the effect again of the introversion–extraversion variable.

In a more general way, reaction time and psychomotor speed tend to be affected by mental illness. Speed of work normally declines with increasing age from the 20's onwards and also with decreasing intelligence. But over and above this any psychiatric illness tends to impair speed of performance (with the possible exception of the psychopath as already noted). The greater the severity of the illness, the slower the individual's reaction time, so that in general neurotics are slower than normals, and psychotics slower than neurotics. This factor itself accounts for a certain amount of the intellectual deficit shown on intelligence tests as time taken is often a scoring variable. But even on psychomotor tasks where variations in ability are unimportant, speed of reaction is reduced in illness. More complex studies of speed and error, such as those involving distraction or vigilance are also being made in mental illness. Such tasks slip over into the field of perception and its relationship to personality.

3

Perception

Whether or not intelligence is treated as a general factor with an array of subsidiary factors or whether the view is accepted that there are several factors which one cannot separate, there are occasions when certain specific abilities need to be tested. These arise where the patient experiences great difficulty in certain tasks but where the apparent level of general intelligence should be adequate to cope with them. Some of the best examples of this type of problem arise in dealing with children, where a variety of specific defects may have wide-ranging behavioural consequences. Many of the defects require adequate medical diagnosis, but it may be that they are first detected or isolated during a psychological test procedure. These defects are often perceptual in nature.

Difficulties in development may be caused by a variety of conditions, any of which may give rise to a generalized disturbance. The location of the original problem may be a matter of some difficulty. Thus, although the grossly spastic child may be easily recognizable, minor degrees of anoxia at birth may give rise to minor defects of function which are very difficult to detect. The danger that the delays in walking and later clumsiness may be put down to low intelligence is even greater here than in the case of the overtly spastic child, where at least the coexistence of gross physical disturbance and intellectual normality is recognized. Similarly, although a totally deaf child may well have its disability recognized early and appropriate education be started, those children who suffer from partial deafness, for example from the form of deafness where there is adequate hearing of low frequency sounds but deafness for high frequency sounds, may be regarded as subnormal. This difficulty will arise because, although the child passes its normal milestones at the appropriate times, it will have great difficulty in learning to speak. It will imitate the sounds it hears, mainly vowel sounds, and the resulting attempts at communication will be quite incomprehensible. Such a difficulty, once the possibility has been considered, can be investigated audiographically using conditioning techniques in which a picture is revealed if a button is pressed after a tone has sounded. At first the button pressing response to a loud noise is established and then the child is tested with pure tones at varying intensities. If the conditioning is adequate the button-pressing behaviour will delineate the appropriate auditory thresholds. The technique is now obsolete and of theoretical interest only as it has been found that earlier diagnosis is possible by measuring physiological responses to sound, e.g. changes in heart rate.

A more complex condition is that known as congenital dyslexia, the inability to learn to read despite the presence of apparently normal intelligence in other areas. Investigations of this condition have become more frequent of recent years but even so the aetiology or prognosis for each individual case remains unclear. The evidence as yet does not confirm the viewpoints that dyslexia is either a result of a cerebral abnormality or a result of faulty education. Evidence is also lacking on its response to attention of various kinds.

It has been argued by Piaget that the child's ability to think is not solely a gradual increase in intelligence as measured by tests of the Stanford–Binet type, but also contains various step functions in which a change takes place allowing the child to solve problems of a qualitative type which were previously impossible. Raven has argued that such qualitative changes occur and can be seen in the success with which different kinds of problems are tackled on the Matrices test. These changes in perceptual processes would appear to have some similarity to the sudden solution of a problem by the emergence of a *Gestalt*. At least in theory it should prove possible to test these functions and derive normative data. We should then have a series of tests which are complementary to the normal intelligence tests and which assess development of this type.

Abnormalities of perception are related to many psychological disturbances and perceptual changes in the major psychoses have been the subject of much research. Little use has been made so far of the information gained, but it may be that tests of complex perceptual functions will become more commonly used in future. Simple perceptual functions are often tested by the physican. Indeed, they are often regarded as physiological functions and regarded as parts of the physical examination, although they are not necessarily carried out as a routine. This situation has probably arisen because the commonest difficulties in simple perceptual tasks arise as a consequence of disease of the sensory organ rather than centrally and even when there is central disease it is often of gross structural type. At this stage we should try to define what we mean by sensation and perception. This is a problem of some difficulty, which may be unresolvable. It is possible to regard the terms as belonging to different universes of discourse and to say that sensation is a physiological phenomenon while perception is psychological. Unfortunately this distinction is so contrary to common usage as to make the division impractical. Further, it tends to imply that the terms are coextensive within their own fields and this, too, would be unacceptable to most people.

If we regard both these terms as being psychological, they may be distinguished on the grounds of the amount of organization involved, that is, on the number and complexity of factors which have to be added to the input to the organism to change a sensation to a percept. It has been argued that a sensation must be perceived to be recognized but this conjures up unlikely concepts of one part of the system examining another. Such a process can be repeated *ad infinitum*. Furthermore in certain circumstances a sensation is experienced, not perceived. Such linguistic manipulation may seem trivial but it does perhaps help our understanding of the concepts. Sensation may be regarded as the awareness of an input modified only by the modulating activity of the sensory end organ (we shall carefully avoid the even more difficult problem of defining awareness!), while percepts arise when these inputs are modified centrally by the processes resulting from previous sensations and their integrations. This implies that perception only occurs as a result of learning and can be differentiated from sensation on this basis although in practice such a differentiation would be very difficult and can only be maintained on a quantitative not a qualitative basis.

In practice it is not surprising that the differentiation between sensation and perception is made arbitrarily. The neurological examination carried out by the physician tests phenomena which are regarded as sensory rather than perceptual despite the use of such phrases as 'perceives light'. Sensations of touch, pain, vibration, movement, temperature, smell, vision and hearing are all normally examined by the clinician. More complex phenomena, for example two-point discrimination and stereognosis, may also be tested but here we are dealing with discriminative processes which should perhaps be regarded as perceptual. Tests of vision and of hearing almost always involve perceptual processes in that they require reporting and interpretation of the situation as in the Snellen chart. The conditioned 'peepshow' audiogram mentioned above is an exception to this difficulty.

Colour vision, however, is often regarded as a perceptual process and it is discussed as much in textbooks of psychology as of physiology. It is commonly tested by the use of the Holmgren wools or Ishihara's plates, the latter being a set of composites of coloured dots in which numbers are shown by the use of contrasting colours. Where colour blindness is present either the number is not detected or an erroneous number is perceived. Although such plates are a useful screening device, really efficient assessment of colour vision and its deficiencies can only properly be ascertained by precise instruments such as an anomaloscope. Further tests of colour vision are made in patients who have difficulty by using various coloured light procedures such as the Eldridge–Green lantern. The object of this further testing is usually to determine whether the subject is 'red–green' safe for certain occupations. More complex investigations of perception are usually carried out by the psychologist. It would seem useful at this stage to discuss perception and its basic sensation as viewed by the psychologist as these processes, being closely linked with awareness and the self, are clearly basic to the organism's functioning and might well prove to be important in the investigation of abnormal states.

Sensation

Sensation results from the stimulation by physical energy of receptors associated with a sense organ. No organ is infinitely sensitive to the energies to which it responds. Every sense has an absolute threshold which is the minimum stimulus energy to which it can respond. The smallest difference in stimulus value that can be differentiated is known as the differential threshold.

Historically, five sensory modalities were recognized, namely, the two 'higher' senses of sight and hearing and the three 'lower' senses of touch, taste and smell. Such a classification is too simple. For example, what was originally called 'touch' is now subdivided to include the rather specific senses of pain, itch, heat, cold, touch and vibration. A more modern system of classification introduces the conception of exteroception, interoception and proprioception. Exteroceptors include the five traditional senses, interoceptors give information about internal bodily states and proprioceptors enable the individual to perceive the position of his limbs and related data. In passing it is worth noting that the higher senses, sight and hearing, were perhaps called higher because of their dominance in man. With some other animals, smell and touch are clearly more important.

Much confusion has arisen in the discussion and investigation of sensation because of the semantic difficulties which surround the subject. These in turn are related to philsophical questions which may be unresolvable, in particular the relationship between mind and body. We propose to take an empirical monistic view and regard the relationship between mind and body, physical and psychological science, to be that of identity, the difference being in the mode of approach employed. Some aspects of the system may be better described in physiological and others in psycho-logical terminology. The two systems of descriptions do not mix. Thus what travels along nerve fibres is an electrochemical change with a varying distribution in space and time, not, for instance, a sensation of heat. It does not matter where these changes occur in the nervous system, but when they occur in, hypothetically, a certain place and in a certain way they *are equivalent to* a sensation of heat.

On the physiological side the sensory apparatus is composed broadly of receptors, sensory nerves, sensory tracts in the spinal cord and sensory areas in the brain. More complex processes occur in the brain but they are, as yet, ill understood. Much of the physiological aspect of sensation has been questioned recently, particularly with regard to pain, and what has for many years been thought to be a comfortable body of established fact is now an area of intensive research and speculation.

Both physiologists and psychologists have concerned themselves with the measurement of sensory experience. Methods for doing this in general involve an attempt to equate the intensity of a measured stimulus with the subject's responses to it. The first measurement to make for any sensation is the threshold and a variety of techniques have been evolved for measuring thresholds in the various sensory modalities. Most depend on the subject reporting that he experiences the sensation being tested although this is not essential. The peepshow audiometer (p. 23) is after all only a device for making a series of threshold measurements.

Measurement of intensities of sensation above threshold value has tended to follow two main techniques. The first and oldest rests on the concept of the *just noticeable difference* (jnd). This is the minimum difference between stimulus intensities which can be differentiated by the subject. For example, the ear can detect differences in the pitch of tones, but when the difference becomes too small there is a point, the difference threshold, when it is no longer possible to discriminate. A scale is then set up based on the number of jnd above threshold which equates with a given stimulus. The other approach depends on getting the subject to make an estimate of the intensity of the stimulus in relation to an arbitrary standard. Thus, in assessing auditory intensities the subject may be presented with a standard tone and told that this is to be taken to represent 10 arbitrary units. He is then presented with a series of other tones and asked to grade them on this arbitrary scale. Work using this technique by Stevens has led him to modify Fechner's original and classical law of psychophysics. Fechner, as had Weber before him, had tried to show that there was a precise mathematical relationship between the jnd and the strength of the physical stimulus. Fechner originally postulated that

$$\psi = k\,\phi$$

where ψ = psychological sensation
and ϕ = physical stimulus
and measurements of ψ are in jnd's.

This is sometimes called the Weber–Fechner law. But Weber's law, which is the earlier of the two 'psychophysical' laws states that:

$$\frac{\delta\,\phi}{\phi} = \text{a constant, for the jnd}$$

and even this formula, from which Fechner's law is derived, is only thought, by experimental psychologists, to be true under certain circumstances.

Stevens, using his different method of measurement, suggests that a better expression is:

$$\psi = \phi^k$$

where the value of k varies with the sensation. In general from his results $k < 1$ but the exceptions, the sensations of electricity, pain, and direct stimulation of the auditory nerve where $k > 1$ are of interest in that they tend to support the hypothesis that modification of input starts at the sensory end organ.

Specific aspects of sensation have been studied in more detail sometimes as 'sensation' and sometimes as 'perception' for, as we have remarked earlier, the distinction is not always easy to make in practice. For instance, colour vision is often regarded as a perceptual phenomenon although we have elected to consider it briefly here.

THEORIES OF VISION AND COLOUR VISION

The duplicity theory of von Kries attempts to explain the phenomena of light and dark adaptation. Von Kries suggested that the rod cells are responsible for vision under conditions of low illumination (scotopic vision) while the cone cells are responsible for vision at normal illumination (photopic vision). As the dark-adapted eye appears insensitive to colour it appears that the rod cells are only sensitive to brightness. Such a theory helps to explain the Purkinje phenomenon that the light-adapted eye is most sensitive to the yellow region of the spectrum, the dark-adapted eye to green. This suggests that the point of maximum sensitivity of the rods is the green and of the cones the yellow area of the spectrum. The duplicity theory also explains the fact that perception of objects at night is better when they are looked at peripherally than directly. The fovea contains no rod cells but there are relatively few cones in the periphery. Night blindness may be due to factors affecting the rod cells, especially lack of oxygen or vitamin deficiencies. A converse defect of the cone cells leads to day blindness where the patient sees normally in twilight. Although there are many proofs of the duplicity theory, some amendments are necessary. Limited dark adaptation of the fovea has been demonstrated as has some sensitivity to colour of the retina's cone-free periphery.

The perception of colour is often associated with feelings of pleasure or displeasure. Indeed, with the Rorschach test, the person's use of colour is held to parallel his mode of emotional reactions. But such reactions to colour might be learnt and culturally determined. Cultural differences and nomenclature might also account for apparent differences in the perception of colour by different peoples. Colours (hues) vary in brightness and saturation (degree of admixture of white and coloured light). Colour also varies according to whether it is seen as 'surface' or 'film' colour.

The basis of colour perception is complex. The retinal cells, particularly the cones, behave as if three mechanisms were involved, related to the red, green and blue areas of the spectrum. Yellow can be produced by a mixture of spectral red and green, but these and blue are 'primary'. They cannot be made by mixing other colours. Simultaneous contrast is the name given to the observation that the perception of one colour tends to give rise to its complementary colour. Thus a surface adjacent to a red surface will appear to be tinged with blue-green. Any two colours which produce a neutral grey are said to be complementary. Successive contrast is the name given to an allied phenomena. Thus, observation of a red surface replaced by a grey surface will result in the latter appearing tinged with blue-green. If a bright red light is observed in a dark room and then switched off, alternating patches of red and blue-green appear in front of the eyes. These phenomena are known as positive and negative after-images, respectively.

About $7\frac{1}{2}\%$ of British males suffer from some form of defective colour vision (dichromatism). This is usually a defect in the way red and green are perceived, but less commonly blue is involved. Colour defects are rare in women and it appears that such defects are sex-linked, hereditary characteristics. Colour blindness (achromatism) is rare. Sufferers are not only colour blind but are dazzled by strong light and have poor visual acuity. These defects are due to the subject being dependent on rod vision.

There are a number of historically interesting theories of colour vision. The three best known are those of Newton, Helmholtz and Young, and Hering. These three theories each tend to postulate three types of colour receptor. The range of colours perceived can be explained by supposing varying degrees of differential stimulation. It is in fact true that systems of colour television, for example, work perfectly well on such an assumption. Nevertheless it has not been possible to identify clearly three different colour pigments in the retina. More recently Land has suggested that all that is required for a complete range of colour perception is sensitivity to light of two wavelengths, one relatively short and one relatively long. These, it is argued, can carry all the required information. Such an explanation avoids some of the difficulties of the Young-Helmholtz theory. On the other hand the Hering theory is to some extent supported by micro-electrode experiments on the colour units of the retina. These experiments suggest there are four colour cone types with maximum sensitivities in the blue, green, yellow and red regions of the spectrum respectively.

Similarly to vision, the other special senses have their perceptual aspects closely involved with the basic sensation. For instance Broadbent has been a leading advocate of the need to study auditory sensations and perceptions with their important implications for studies of speech and communication. In hearing, the subjective loudness of a sound is determined by the number of impulses generated and propagated down the auditory nerve to the brain. A theory of pitch is more difficult. The telephone theory likens the cochlea to a microphone and the auditory nerve to a telephone wire. Pitch is determined mainly by the distribution of impulses travelling up the auditory nerve. But studies indicate that such a theory can only be true for low frequencies. For the rest of the range, the Helmholtz resonance theory appears to give a reasonable degree of help. This theory asserts that the fibres of the basilar membrane of different length resonate to different frequencies in much the same way as the strings of a piano. In the higher brain centres there is some evidence that different areas represent different areas of the cochlea. If the harmonics of two tones fit together, they will probably sound harmonious and consonant. If they do not fit, dissonance may be experienced. Even so, other factors, particularly experience and learning, affect the experience of consonance and dissonance. The direction of a sound is perceived by differences in the sound as it arrives at the two ears. These differences are of time of arrival, intensity and phase. Cues to distance depend only on one ear and are largely of intensity and of frequency composition (i.e. high frequencies become absorbed by low frequencies with increasing distance).

The chemical senses of smell and taste are difficult to study precisely. Hemming's smell prism of 6 basic odours accounts for most phenomena, but Crocker has postulated a simple fourfold classification. Studies of taste have suggested four basic qualities of saltiness, sourness, sweetness and bitterness. In practice, however, it is difficult to separate taste and smell. Smell is far more acute than taste but both adapt rapidly to continued stimulation.

Less work has been done on the internal sensory capacities of the body and these data are to be found in physiological works and scattered throughout the literature. Much of the input from the body's internal sensory system appears to be processed automatically and cannot really be regarded as sensation unless something has gone wrong. For instance, the only time vestibular function manifests itself as sensation is when the individual is in highly abnormal circumstances or when there is something wrong with the apparatus.

This characteristic is even more true of pain. It has been held by Merskey that pain can be operationally defined as 'an unpleasant experience which we primarily associate with tissue damage or describe in terms of tissue damage or both'. Although many may disagree with this definition it has the advantage that it emphasizes the psychological nature of pain, an emphasis which is becoming increasingly important as the complexity of the subject becomes more apparent.

Certainly from the point of view of the physiologist the simple view of pain as a specific sensory modality with its own anatomical and physiological apparatus involving discrete end organs and neural tracts is, as we mentioned (p. 26), no longer accepted. Wholly psychological views have been put forward, notably those of Szasz who maintains that pain is the sensation experienced when the body, regarded as an object of the ego, is threatened or damaged. This theory is obviously based on the psychoanalytic model but there is some independent evidence (Merskey & Spear) which suggests that of the hypotheses currently available it is probably the most generally applicable. So far other sensory modalities have been subjected to very little psychological, as opposed to 'psychophysical' examination.

Perception

Perception is not just a reproduction of the sense data presented. It is creative, not just reproductive, and it is strongly influenced both by previous experience and by non-cognitive factors. This lack of identification between perception and sensory stimulation will be constantly apparent in the rest of this chapter. However, simple but compelling examples of this principle as demonstrated in visual perception are illusions and reversible figures (Figs 1, 2).

Gestalt theory is important to any discussion of perception. Wertheimer found that if two adjacent lights were switched on and off at different time intervals, perception varied. When the interval was sufficiently long, two lights were perceived. But if the interval was shortened one light would appear to move. He named this effect the phi phenomenon. From these and other studies arose the basic principles of *gestalt* theory. In particular, *gestalt* theory asserted that the whole configuration of stimuli determined what was perceived. This whole or *gestalt* was not simply the sum of the individual parts. Such principles and their demonstration were an important feature of the *gestaltist's* attack (led by Wertheimer, Koffka and Kohler) on nineteenth-century associationism.

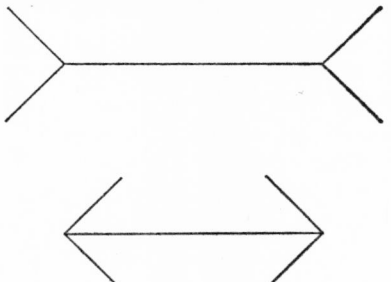

FIG. 1. An example of perceptual illusion:
the Muller–Lyer arrow-head illusion.

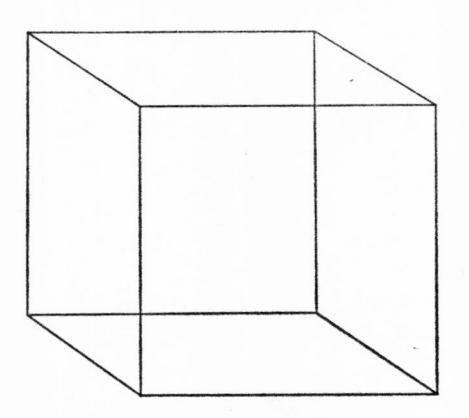

FIG. 2. The figure–ground phenomenon:
the Necker cube reversible figure.

The latter assumed that perceptual data could be analysed into component sensations and was in fact, nothing more than the sum of these. *Gestalt* is a German term which in English means 'form' or 'pattern'. The *gestalt* school of psychology believed that behaviour could only be understood in terms of its natural complexity. Any attempt to break down molar behaviour into a molecular study of sensations and actions was doomed to failure.

Even ordinary perceptual phenomena could readily be demonstrated to be the result of a complex organizing activity. *Gestalt* psychology remains a development particularly associated with perceptual phenomena. Although the *gestalt* psychologists assumed that perceptual organization was innate, other workers have tried to account for similar perceptual phenomena by learning, or as features of the stimulus pattern itself.

The main *gestalt* principles of perceptual organization include the following:

1. The figure–ground phenomenon (Fig. 2). People, houses, trees and so on tend to be perceived because of their contours as a figure against a less important background. With the reversible figure diagram, for example, there is always a perception of a figure against a background.

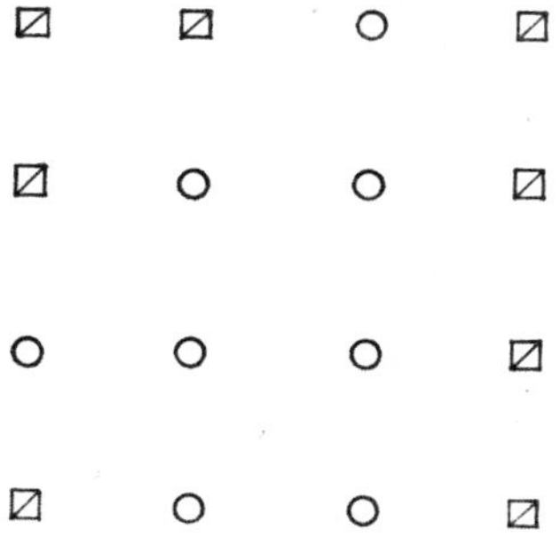

☑   ☑   O   ☑

☑   O   O   ☑

O   O   O   ☑

☑   O   O   ☑

FIG. 3. The principle of *pragnanz* or good figure.

FIG. 4. The principle of closure.

2. The principle of *pragnanz* or good figure (Fig. 3). Perception tends to be in the direction of stability and simplicity. Regular and continuous figures are more readily perceived than irregular and discontinuous ones. The difference in the elements making up the square is disregarded.

3. The principle of closure (Fig. 4). There is a tendency to perceive figures as 'closed' even though gaps are present in the contours.

4. The principle of proximity (Fig. 5). The closer the elements, the stronger the tendency to perceive a *gestalt* from the elements.
5. The principle of similarity (Fig. 6). Elements which are similar are more readily perceived as forming a group.

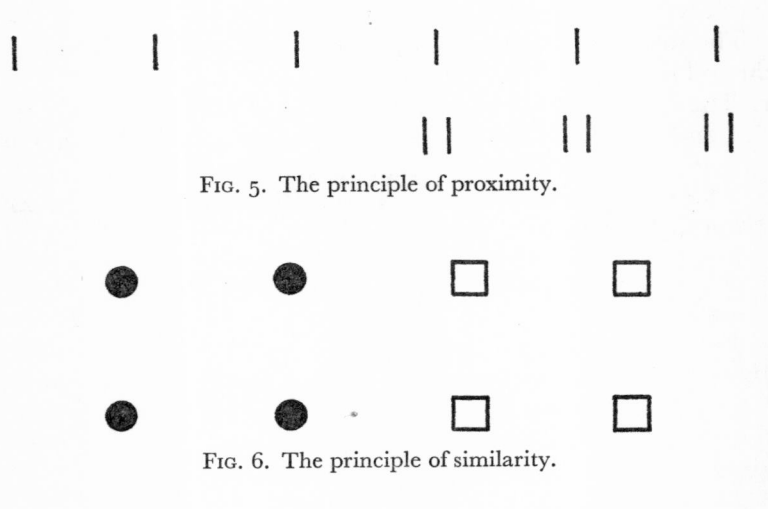

FIG. 5. The principle of proximity.

FIG. 6. The principle of similarity.

The *gestalt* theorists thus made important contributions to the study of perception, particularly visual perception. In passing it might be noted that auditory phenomena had given the classical example of *gestalt* of the melody. A melody is more than the sum of its individual notes and when the last note of a melody is sounded, the whole of the melody is, in a sense, still present. But the attempts of the *gestalt* school to extend their views outside this field have not been so successful. A case in point was the hypothesis of isomorphism which attempted to explain the perceptual facts on the grounds that a cortical pattern directly paralleled and caused the perception of *gestalt* phenomena. It is also clear that the *gestalt* theorists pay little attention to the importance of past experience in determining what is perceived. Kohler, however, has studied what is called the figural after-effect. This is the effect of an immediately preceding stimulus upon a subsequent perception. For example, a subject fixates visually on a small cross to the left of which is a circle. After 5 minutes he then looks at a cross on another presentation, on either side of which is a square. The square to the left will appear smaller than the one on the right. This shrinkage is due to satiation or inhibition and shows marked individual variations. Throughout the whole of *gestalt* theory is the use of concepts of fields and forces of energy that reach and maintain an equilibrium. By such are the phenomena of perception explained. The resulting *gestalt* tends to be of sufficiently strong organization as to resist analysis.

Apart from such data made peculiarly their own by the *gestalt* workers, other important perceptual phenomena are as follows. If a small light is viewed in an otherwise dark room, it may after a time appear to wander about. This is called 'autokinetic' movement. It is perhaps due to the fact that the eyes have no visual-spatial 'framework' to which they can anchor themselves. Slight tremors of the eye muscles cause them to lose their fixation, resulting in perception of movement of the point of light. Now if the light is surrounded by a luminous rectangular outline which is moved, the light will appear to move and the rectangle to remain stationary. More complicated examples of this phenomenon occur spontaneously to people when on board ships or aircraft. Individual variations exist in the degree to which subjects are susceptible to such phenomena.

Other experiments have been made in which observers have worn spectacles inverting the field of view. After a time behaviour becomes reasonably coordinated but the field of view still appears inverted. But when the spectacles reverse the field from left to right, the surroundings begin eventually to look normal.

The perception of depth depends principally on 'retinal disparity' as the images on the two retinas are unlike. This can be effectively demonstrated by means of a stereoscope. Depth perception appears to begin spontaneously in the first six months of life. At longer distances where disparity does not operate, varying details of shape and surface texture are important cues. Monocular clues to depth also include those of linear perspective and of the accommodation of the lens. But perception of depth or distance depends to some degree on expectation, as demonstrated by the Ames 'distorted room'. An observer looks monocularly at a large structure made like a room. The floor, ceiling and end wall are actually sloped but the retinal image on a single eye results in the perception of a normal room. The erroneous perception is so stable that if a child and a man are placed in opposite corners, the child actually looks larger than the man.

D

Such experiments tend to be associated with perceptual theories stressing the probability factor. That is, we tend to perceive the 'world' so that it is maintained as far as possible by the perceiver as he has known it in the past. It can be noted that various learning theories have in fact attempted to explain perceptual phenomena in their terms. but at present no practical synthesis of learning and perceptual phenomena has been made.

Perception of movement is not produced primarily by the movements of the images of objects across the retina. The eyes, in fact, are themselves constantly moving even when regarding stationary objects. The perception of movement is determined mainly by the change of position of objects in relation to their background.

A common example of apparent movement is, of course, in the cinema. The after-effect of seen movement occurs frequently. If we stare at a quickly moving river and then look away at the bank, this may appear to move in the opposite direction. Michotte showed by experiments how causality may be inferred in a compelling way from the perception of the contact of moving shapes. This inference occurs even when no solid object actually strikes another one.

Constancy of shape and size are striking perceptual phenomena. If a subject is asked to judge the size of an object at a considerable distance from him, his judgement will not conform to the size of the image projected on his retina. It will be more like the size of the object he would see if the distance was a more usual one. It is only when objects are more than a quarter of a mile away that they begin to look smaller. Thus the size of an object tends to remain relatively constant within certain limits, whatever its position in space. Constancy of shape also occurs so that with a tilted square or circle we perceive a shape between that of the 'real' shape and the shape projected on the retina. Colour constancy frequently occurs—grass still looks green at twilight. Brightness constancy is also common. Perceptual constancy helps us to perceive the world as a stable world.

ATTENTION AND PERCEPTION

Perception is selective according to the direction of attention of the perceiver. Attention appears to divide the field of attention into a focus and a margin. Attention also fluctuates, as can be seen especially in the perception of reversible figures. Such an effect has been attributed to satiation and is probably more due to central than peripheral effects in the nervous system. It is of interest that after subjects have undergone sensory deprivation, they often complain of perceptual impairment. At the time they are deprived, they tend to lack concentration and may even experience hallucinations. It should be remembered, however, that sensory deprivation experiments vary greatly in their details, and there is controversy about which of many factors, for instance sensory deprivation, social isolation or expectancy, are crucial. 'Subliminal' perception is the name given to indications that people may perceive things without ever being conscious that they did so. What is less clear is whether such 'subliminal' perception may seriously influence people's ideas and actions. Such an influence, of course, has been suggested as a mode of political indoctrination and also to induce the buying of certain products. For example, at the cinema or on the television, pictures may be flashed on for too short an interval to reach the conscious threshold of perception, yet such data may be perceived at a subliminal level and influence subsequent behaviour. However, evidence for such an effect is not convincing.

The span of apprehension of attention has been variously studied. A common method is to find how many dots on a card can be correctly apprehended when exposed for a limited time. A usual result is 4 or 5 but such experiments are clearly affected by *gestalt* organization.

Certain physiological processes intensively studied in recent years are of particular relevance to the psychology of attention. Sensory impulses from the sense organs in various parts of the body are transmitted by the main sensory nerve tracts, through the brain stem and the nuclei of nerve cells at the top of the brain stem, to the cerebral cortex. The optic thalamus and the reticular formation have important roles in the regulation of sensory input. The reticular formation is important in arousal from sleep and in the perceptual processes of waking life.

THE IMPORTANCE OF MEANING

The relevance of meaning to perception is important. A time interval might elapse between something and apprehending its meaning. This process of understanding and classifying perceptual data is sometimes called apperception. Experiments show, in fact, that previous knowledge or emotional state may strongly influence what is perceived. Such a process, of course, is very akin to that of projection and the assumptions underlying projective techniques of personality assessment. It is clear also that previous experience, interests, motivation and emotional states play a large part in the selectivity of perception. At its simplest they determine what is perceived as figure rather than ground. A particular example of the tendency to perceive in terms of what is familiar can be seen in experiments on the effect of naming on the reproduction of shapes. Different names given to the same stimulus affect what is produced. For example, two circles joined by a horizontal line may be 'named' as 'spectacles' by one subject or as 'dumbells' by another. Their subsequent reproductions of the shape will tend to be distorted in the direction of a drawing of the object named.

SYNAESTHESIA

Synaesthesia is the name given to the phenomenon of experiencing imagery of one sense with perceptions of another sense. A favourite example is an image of colour accompanying auditory perception (chromothesia). The 'scarlet of trumpets' is an example. Although it is possible to learn many such examples, spontaneous occurrences are far less common. Perhaps in young children, synaesthesia is relatively common and certain examples of this persist into later life as learnt associations. In fact, individuals reporting frequent and varied examples of synaesthesia are often epileptic or suffering from other forms of brain disease.

It is always important to remember, however, that the different senses rarely function in isolation. Even if we are primarily engaged in visual perception data from other sensory channels will influence our percepts.

THE DEVELOPMENT OF PERCEPTION IN CHILDREN

In the earliest years it is clear that shape discrimination, for example, requires time and experience to develop. The more complex the shape, the older the child is before he perceives it like an adult. Similar difficulties are apparent in the child's estimation of size, distance, movement and colour.

What is more difficult to investigage is to what extent such perceptual processes are a result of learning rather than of maturation. Hebb is inclined to believe that even the simplest spatial percepts and *gestalts* are only slowly learnt and automatized. He relies heavily on the data of Senden. Senden studied the acquisition of visual perception in subjects congenitally blind but subsequently enabled to see. Senden's patients, after successful operations, did not immediately perceive in a normal manner but took months or even years to perceive in the immediate way we take for granted. Hebb also argues that what appear to be innate, *gestalt* ways of perceiving are similarly only the product of a long period of learning that normally occurs in infancy. From these studies and other studies of non-humans the development of perceptual processes appears to be a product of long periods of learning. Nevertheless, the role of maturation has not been precisely quantified, particularly as many of the relevant Hebb studies possibly involve subjects with a defective visual apparatus. Hebb's position can probably be viewed as another example of the heredity versus environmental learning controversy concerning behaviour. His view, for example, would probably be questioned by the ethologists.

Hebb's view can be considered an associationist one which is, of course, the traditional pre-*gestalt* view. He views perception as an additive, serial process depending on a series of excitations from the parts of the stimulus figure. In the normal adult this has become such a rapid and unconscious process that the *gestalt* workers were convinced that *gestalt* percepts were immediate. Nevertheless there are probably important species differences. Probably in birds or rats for example, space perception depends more on maturation than it does in the chimpanzee and man. The evidence for the data in this field rests on observations and experiments concerning the development of perception in various species particularly where the amount of experience and learning is controlled. There is also work on non-human animals suggesting that there might be visual analysers in the optic tracts. Such analysers would, for example, detect horizontal or vertical at a pre-cortical level.

THE INFLUENCE OF NON-COGNITIVE FACTORS

It has already been observed that attention and perception can be influenced by non-cognitive factors. Motivation and emotion have important effects on what is attended to and what is perceived. The concept of perceptual defence has been noted elsewhere (p. 72). These effects can be short-term or longer-term in the reflection of values and interests. Important studies illustrating the effect of non-cognitive factors are found in work on social relationships, especially racial prejudice. Photographs of people of different races are viewed in a binocular stereoscope so that a member of one race was presented to one eye and a member of a different race to the other eye. Each race appears most accurate in picking out its own members but Afrikaaners differentiated their judgements more sharply into Europeans or Africans. Comparatively few intermediate judgements of Indians or Coloureds were given, that is, the differentiation by Afrikaaners between whites and Negroes was exaggerated.

If there are such persistent individual variations in perception these variations could conceivably be related to personality types or traits. Thus the alleged 'synthetic' and 'analytic' methods of perceiving, or 'objective' and 'subjective' types, could be related to the personality variable of extraversion–introversion. Eysenck has also claimed such an association via the medium of cortical inhibition. Eysenk's suggestion is in fact merely a version of his learning theory account of personality. But studies in perception tend to give little support at present to such a generalized hypothesis and perceptual measures of various kinds do not correlate highly with each other in any one person.

Nevertheless it seems reasonable to suggest that perceptual phenomena could well indicate the effects of emotions and motivation. For example there is evidence to suggest that the pupil of the eye dilates when looking at pleasurable or interesting material and contracts when looking at distasteful material. With male subjects, dilation occurred most when looking at a picture of a nude female. Less dilation occurred with a nude male person and still less with a mother and baby picture. Female subjects showed most dilation with the mother and baby picture, followed by a nude male and then a baby picture. It has been suggested that homosexual males do not show the normal male's pupil response to nude females.

There is little doubt, however, that more perceptual studies of various groups of subjects, particularly in the psychiatric field are needed. For example, it has been claimed that there are differences in classical perceptual phenomena such as illusions, figure-ground and constancies, between normals and schizophrenics. In fact, the study of perceptual phenomena in various groups may even throw light on the basis of certain of their group characteristics. It is possible that certain of the emotional and personality features peculiar to certain diagnostic groups may result from abnormalities of certain perceptual processes.

Petrie has recounted an interesting series of studies on the modification of perception by experience. It appears that the subjective assessment by touch of the width of a block of wood is different if the fingers have been stimulated by rubbing a larger or smaller block for a period of time from the assessment when they have been rested for a considerable time. The individual variation is considerable and may be normally distributed but has been divided by Petrie into people classed as augmenters, moderates and reducers. This experiment is closely related to Kohler's pioneer work on figural after-effect in visual perception. It is also apparent that individual variations with regard to figural after-effects would be related by Eysenck to the extraversion–introversion variable. Augmenters tend, after stimulation of the fingers, to increase significantly the perceived size of the block and reducers significantly to reduce it, while moderates show no significant change. The work is of interest in that it demonstrates a perceptual aspect of, and perhaps a basis for, the psychological dimensions of extraversion–introversion (p. 49) with reducers tending to be extraverted and augmenters tending to be introverted and with relationships to the tolerance of pain (poor in augmenters) and of sensory deprivation (poor in reducers). A third category, that of people whose perception changes are conditioned by whether the stimulating block is larger or smaller than the block to be measured, seems to be related to some degree to organic brain disease, delinquency or immaturity.

Perceptual anomalies in mental illness have long been appreciated. Hallucinations, an important feature in severe psychopathology, have important links with both perceptual and memory processes. As a phenomenon, they show some resemblance to the striking experiences that may occur in falling asleep or in waking up. These striking images, so real at the time, are respectively called hypnogogic and hypnopompic images. Hallucination is a term that should be restricted to experiences occurring in a waking state. Some workers see hallucinations as a disturbance of normal perceptual processes, where the perceptual input bears little relationship to the output of the bodily systems involved, either in quantity or quality. Other workers stress how the hallucination often seems to be an involuntary but convincing recall of certain memories. Hallucinations are not, as it were, completely arbitrary or meaningless. Apart from studying perception in naturally occurring illness, perceptual phenomena are often reported in the abnormal states produced by sensory deprivation, sleep deprivation and hallucinogenic drugs such as mescalin and LSD (lysergic acid diethylamide). Perception tends to restrict itself (probably for historical reasons) to visual phenomena, although in recent years auditory perception (influenced by information theory) is being increasingly studied. It seems reasonable to note again, however, that perception not only includes touch, smell and taste but also the important areas of both pain and time. Time factors are integral and basic components of life and behaviour. Many writers, particularly William James in his discussion of the 'sensible present' and the 'stream of consciousness', have indicated that a time dimension is necessary to any description or understanding of human psychology. A person's behaviour is inexplicable unless the unity between past, present and future is considered. One word of warning is required. Perception, like learning theory, is so fundamental a psychological process that a discussion of such a process can quickly become a treatise on the whole of psychology, normal and abnormal. Such tendencies must be resisted otherwise one's viewpoint becomes unrewardingly biased towards the assumption that all behaviour can be explained in terms of perceptual processes.

4

Personality, Personality Assessment and Differential Diagnosis

We have already discussed the problems involved in the psychological assessment of organic brain disease. In this chapter we shall be concerned with the use of psychological tests to differentiate between patients who have mental, emotional or behavioural disorders which are not related to gross disease of the central nervous system. In any consideration of this type we are at once faced with the difficulty that many objections have been raised to the reliability and validity of the commonly accepted psychiatric diagnoses. It is a curious phenomenon that many of those who raise such objections continue to conduct psychological investigations in which they relate their observations to these same diagnostic 'entities'. Some investigators (such as Lorr or Foulds) have preferred to use their results to set up parallel systems of classification. Such parallel systems are still in the early stages of development. They may well have great potentialities for further investigation, but for the time being it is unlikely that they will be used in normal clinical work. We shall, however, present some consideration of one or two of these schemes.

Despite the objections to which we have referred, the vast majority of psychiatrists use diagnostic categories which involve the same technical terms and which have a fairly well agreed meaning. Where a group of psychiatrists have roughly the same background it has been found by Kreitman that there is reasonable agreement in their use of a classification scheme. This agreement is, in general, better for the more severely ill patients. Our discussion in this chapter has to consider that the clinical psychologist will be asked to help in classifying the patient into one of the very broad categories described below.

Patients who come or are brought to a psychiatrist can be broadly classified as suffering from mental subnormality, organic disease of the brain, functional psychosis, neurosis, personality disorder or various combinations of these. The first two groups have been considered in Chapters 1 and 2. Functional psychosis in this context covers the two diagnoses of schizophrenia and manic-depressive psychosis, discounting at present the problems of subclassification and including the agitated depressions within the framework of manic-depressive psychosis. It has been suggested that neurotic and psychotic depressions cannot be separated. It has also been claimed that these two types of depression respond differently to drugs but this claim is not always supported. Factor-analytic studies by workers such as Hamilton suggest that these illnesses can be separated and their responses to electroplexy appear to differ. We therefore accept that a differentiation between these illnesses and neurotic states needs to be attempted.

Although the neurotic illnesses are usually subclassified into anxiety states, hysteria, depressions and obsessional illness, this differentiation is less reliable than the separation of psychoses and it also seems probable that the syndromes are less stable over time. When longitudinal studies are carried out, many patients with neurotic illness show a varying pattern of symptoms which will result in their being classified differently from time to time. Symptoms which seem neurotic may, however, arise in association with an underlying psychotic illness and it is in this type of situation that psychological testing is frequently used to try and sort out the complexities.

The term 'personality disorder' can be used to describe various conditions, mainly behaviour disorders, including psychopathic personality as defined in the Mental Health Act, 1959, and sexual deviations. The application of psychological tests and methods in these conditions poses the same problems as the application to any particular groups, normal and abnormal. Only by controlled studies of the appropriate groups can group characteristics be obtained. This rule applies whether the study is a fact-finding one or one in search of validity for a particular hypothesis.

A common problem with which the psychiatrist is concerned is the detection of early psychotic illness in a patient who presents with symptoms of a non-specific or even misleading nature. In the majority of cases it might be considered that the results of the clinical examination will point fairly clearly in one direction or the other and the psychological investigation is required only to provide confirmatory evidence. Of course, occasionally it does not provide this evidence but raises doubts instead and may then be of great value. At times, however, the clinical examination is quite equivocal and considerable reliance will be placed on the results of the psychologist's assessment. Unfortunately, on these occasions the psychologist's opinion might also be inconclusive. But where the psychiatrist is unable to make a diagnosis within his own system of classification it is unreasonable always to expect the psychological investigation to add more than a few grains of evidence to put in the psychiatrist's diagnostic scales.

Diagnosis inevitably carries implications for treatment so there is bound to be some overlap between the problems considered here and those which we discuss in Part II. At present we shall limit our discussion to those psychological tests which might contribute to useful, or potentially useful, separations between patients, particularly with regard to the use of physical treatments. We shall defer until later consideration of the problems of selection of one or other of the various psychological treatments available and the use of tests to guide and assess such treatments.

With the diagnostic scheme we have adopted, the diagnosis of psychotic illness implies that physical treatments will almost certainly be used. This is not to decry the value of the intensive rehabilitation programme nor, indeed, the interest of psychotherapeutic methods, both 'behavioural' and 'analytic', but in present circumstances none of these are of universal application and most depend on the initial use of some physical therapy. At present the physical treatments in common use are drugs of various types and electric convulsive therapy (ECT). Rarely, patients may be subjected to various brain operations. These various forms of treatment have different effects and although their use is largely empirical it is desirable to develop some form of prediction of efficacy in individual cases.

The primary diagnosis of a psychosis as either affective or schizophrenic will be the main determinant of the type of drug used, particularly as their effects are largely symptomatic. However, although antidepressants and tranquillizers are used separately, they are also used together commonly in both types of psychosis. The indications for this usage are almost entirely clinical and determined by the psychiatrist. As far as the various antidepressants are concerned, this is also true for the selection of the individual drug. Some clinical indications for this have been suggested but are not wholly accepted.

Where schizophrenia is concerned the position is rather different. Evidence is now accumulating to suggest that the different drugs used, in particular various members of the phenothiazine group, are effective for different types of schizophrenic syndrome. For instance, some drugs appear to be preferable in the treatment of apathetic, withdrawn patients, others in those who are aggressive and paranoid. Obviously much of this differentiation is made clinically by the psychiatrist but the development of scales like those of Lorr and Foulds using both clinical interview and psychological test measures may lead to greater refinement and efficiency in treatment.

When the diagnosis of neurotic illness has been made we again have to consider the possibility that there are complicating factors, particularly in the form of an endogenous depressive component, and testing may reveal these. Although it is commonly believed that neuroses are best treated by some form of psychological treatment it remains true that with the present availability of therapists, most patients are treated symptomatically with drugs. In this situation, effective selection of patients who will respond to the more time-consuming methods is of great importance. Whether such effective selection can be made is arguable as methods of treatment themselves are far from being regarded as effective by all. Little attention has yet been paid to the question of individual responses to drug treatment in neuroses. It may be that physiological rather than psychological tests are required. For instance, it has been speculated that ability to taste phenylthiouracils may be related to response to therapeutic drugs.

The assessment of personality

In all forms of work with patients their personality constitutes the background against which their pathology is studied and treated. Occasionally there is no predominant foreground characteristic and the distortion is in the personality itself as judged by comparison with other personalities and the cultural norms which surround the individual. In our introduction we discussed the possibility that some problems which are largely dealt with by psychiatrists could equally be treated by people without a specific medical training. The pictorial analogy introduced here (i.e. to the figure–ground perceptual phenomenon) may perhaps help to clarify this. Localized disturbance within the foreground features may correspond with the traditional view of illness as a pathological process super-imposed upon an organism or system which has in other respects developed in a normal way. This foreground distortion may, of course, result in a secondary disturbance in the background. The psychotic illnesses can be easily (if not necessarily correctly) viewed in this way, while most neurotic patients show specific symptoms which will correspond to our foreground distortion. On the other hand, where the background (of social functions) is disturbed, this corresponds to a disturbance of the type regarded as personality disorder which may result in antisocial or socially incompetent behaviour of long duration. Problems of this type may perhaps be primarily educational or sociological. Thus although the distur-bance may be causally related to an 'illness', its definition in the first case is often based on the fact that the features described repre-sent the extremes of normally distributed characteristics or have been regarded as undesirable by those who lay down the value systems of the community, or both. Illness, on the other hand, is a departure from a hypothetical ideal, although whether it requires or receives treatment may be determined by individual or social factors. Our demarcation, however, can by no means be regarded as absolute, both because the psychology and sociology of illness will arouse interest in and be of importance to those who start off working with the 'background' and because psychiatrists, like all physicians, are interested in prevention of illness and will inevitably concern themselves with the whole picture.

If we look at personality in this way we are clearly dealing with features of the individual which change only slowly over time. In-deed, clinically, rapid changes in personality are regarded as symptomatic of major illness. A distinction is often made between personality and character, normally with the implication that per-sonality is a term applied to the readily apparent features of a per-son's behaviour while character is the group of fundamental factors which controls this.

Although we have said that personality changes only slowly over time, nevertheless it does change. Some features of personality may be inborn. For instance, Cattell claims that the trait which he describes as 'threctia' (a trait of shyness and timidity) has a large hereditary loading, but many other traits are largely learnt. In both cases gradual changes will occur as a consequence of further learning or of maturation. Clearly, therefore, an understanding of personality implies an understanding of its development. As yet no

such understanding is agreed upon and there are numerous conflicting theories. The use of personality tests is complicated by the
fact that some of these have been constructed to measure variables
predicted by the theories, while others have been constructed in the
first instance to explore, using factor-analytic methods, the dimen-
sionality of the hyperspace required for a model of personality.
Others purport to measure personality variables which might perhaps be better regarded as sub-clinical manifestations of psychiatric
illness. Different tests are often not comparable in any way
at all. We propose to discuss personality and tests of personality
in a general sense in relation to the appropriate theoretical
structures.

PERSONALITY

The popular conception of personality is usually of a person's social
stimulus value. It tends to be reserved for well-known or striking
people. Psychologists sometimes define personality in a similar way,
as being the effect of one person's appearance and behaviour on
another. But usually more complex definititions reflecting the
general complexity of personality studies are given. In this way
personality might be defined as the integrated organization of an
individual's total psychological and physical attributes in so far as
they are manifested in focal distinctness to others. It will be
appreciated that such a global definition suggests that personality
studies cover an extremely wide range of phenomena.

Apart from personality as such, the related concepts of temperament and character are often used. Temperament may be described
as the affective attributes of a personality. Character tends to be
reserved for the moral attributes of a personality. Another and even
more difficult concept is that of the self. This is perhaps a unifying
factor that occurs through all a person's experiences, memories and
habits, traits and values. It is elusive and difficult to define, but not
really eliminated by a behaviourist approach.

A trait is an aspect of personality that is reasonably characteristic
and distinctive. If a dictionary is examined a large number of words
can be extracted describing how people act, feel and behave. Many
of these words are either synonyms or are rare. In fact, if such a list
of words is studied by appropriate techniques they can be reduced
to a limited number of personality traits which are relatively independent of each other. It is more difficult, however, to know whose
final list is the best and, of course, there is no guarantee that a dic-

tionary will automatically do one's initial work of isolating all the important variables.

It is sometimes postulated that a number of personality traits can be subsumed under a simpler ordering of personality variation called a typology. If only two types are postulated, this is an example of a dichotomous theory of personality. The best-known of these is Jung's extraversion–introversion although it is an error to summarize Jung's typology as a straightforward dichotomy. Among many other dichotomies have been those of Kretschmer who distinguished cyclothymia–schizothymia as a less marked form of the distinction between the affective disorders and the schizophrenias. Janet distinguished psychasthenia from hysteria in terms of his concept of dissociation. William James described his distinction between tough- and tender-minded personalities. It is sometimes suggested that all such dichotomies are basically the same, but they have marked differences which cannot be easily dismissed.

FACTORIAL STUDIES

Of recent years, the factor-analytical studies into personality by Eysenck and Cattell have attracted considerable attention. Working mainly with psychiatric patients, Eysenck claims to have established factors of neuroticism, extraversion–introversion and psychoticism (and in the social attitude sphere, radicalism–conservatism and tough–tender-minded). Cattell, on the other hand, working mostly with non-psychiatric subjects, obtained at least 16 primary personality factors. As with American studies of intelligence, however, such factors are oblique (that is, they are still interrelated) and can be further analysed into some 5 or more second-order factors. The more important of these are extraversion–introversion, anxiety–integration, sensitivity, egotism–maturity by frustration and constitutional adaptability.

There are similarities between the Eysenck and Cattell factors, but these similarities might be more apparent than real. For example, in the Cattell system, introversion is linked with Janet's dissociation theory and Cattell's neurotic introverts will tend to be hysterics. Eysenck's introversion is linked with Jung and here it is the neurotic extraverts who are alleged to be typically hysterics.

It must be appreciated that the terms extraversion and introversion have become so widely used that they can be defined in dissimilar ways. Generally speaking, the extraversion characteris-

tics stress sociability and outgoing behaviour, sometimes impulsive
and uninhibited. Introversion stresses the reverse—greater tendencies to introspection, conscious anxiety, inhibition and control.
It might be reasonable to question how far these characteristics
really go together, how unrelated they are to emotional maladjustment, and how far they really give a true description of what
Jung originally had in mind for his extraversion–introversion
typology.

Jung's system is in fact exceedingly complex. He postulates the
two general attitude types of outgoing extravert and inward-
looking introvert but maintains that these conscious attributes are
always opposed by compensating unconscious attitudes. That is,
not only 'in every introvert there is an extravert trying to get out'
but also 'outside every extravert is an introvert trying to get in'!

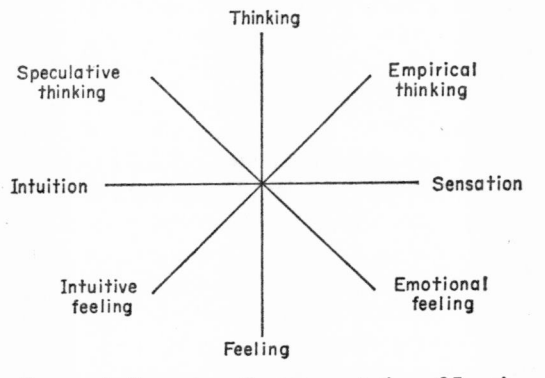

FIG. 7. A diagrammatic representation of Jung's
typology (after Crichton-Miller).

People can also be subdivided according to which of four psychic
functions are dominant. These are regarded as two pairs of orthogonal polar dimensions and compromise forms between adjacent
types are possible (Fig. 7). Again that which is consciously dominant
is unconsciously opposed. Thus, even on pure forms Jung describes
8 basic personality types. These can be extended even further as
Jung considers that a second function, the co-function, can also be
developed in consciousness—it cannot be the polar opposite—and
may be introverted or extraverted regardless of the attitude type
of the primary function.

With both Cattell's and Eysenck's systems, practical usefulness is
perhaps the most important criterion of judgement. The Maudsley

Personality Inventory and its successor, the Eysenck Personality Inventory, do not distinguish easily between the neurotic groups, nor is neuroticism confined to the neurotic groups. Also, if a wide variance of scores is obtained, neuroticism and introversion are not independent but are virtually identical (as Freud suggested). Cattell's 16 PF questionnaire has been little used with abnormals. But available results have led Cattell to state that the most important finding is the importance of a general factor of a 'lack of psychological strength'. Cattell's acceptance of this seems more realistic at present than Eysenck's attempt to rationalize the results which disagree with his original theory.

Both Cattell and Eysenck publish so much that other and often earlier factorial work in the personality field tends to be forgotten. In 1915 Webb, a pupil of Spearman, published evidence supporting the notion of a general factor of personality stability or persistence. Later on Burt published data indicating the existence of both a general and bipolar factor of personality rather similar to Eysenck's neuroticism and extraversion–introversion. Yet it is unfortunate that factorial students of personality seem remarkably prone to reify their results as though factorial methods were a mode of creation of new ideas rather than a classification of already existent data.

BODY BUILD AND BODY SIZE

For many centuries various relationships between physique and personality have been suggested. It is with Kretschmer, however, that modern studies begin. He distinguished three main physical types—the asthenic (frail and linear), the athletic (muscular and vigorous) and the pyknic (plump and fatty). Kretschmer's studies indicated an association between pyknic build and manic-depressive psychosis, and an association between schizophrenia and the asthenic build. He also believed psychotic states to be continuous with normal behaviour. This developed into the schizoid–cycloid theory of personality which was also held to be associated with body build, in a way similar to that of psychotics. Many criticisms of Kretschmer's work are possible. Manic-depressives tend to be middle-aged and because of this more pyknic than schizophrenics, who are younger. Yet it would appear that if these are allowed for there still exists some association between body build and type of psychosis in psychotic patients.

Sheldon devised a more elaborate technique of physical typing

E

using three components of endomorphy (soft and rounded), meso
morphy (hard and muscular) and ectomorphy (thin and lightl
muscled). Sheldon derives these three components from the initia
developmental layers of the embryo. Each individual is measured
on each of these components and given a rating from 1 to 7, with
as a minimum. Sheldon suggests that endomorphy and meso
morphy are more common in females and males respectively
Sheldon claims that there are three types of temperament (viscero
tonia, somatonia and cerebrotonia) associated with the three
physical components. Viscerotonia is characterized by love of com
fort and sociability, somatotonia by physical vigour and adventure
and cerebrotonia by restraint and inhibition. Sheldon's high corre
lations between physique and temperament have been criticized on
methodological grounds. There is also a difficulty in determining
how much of the association in any case is due to social expectation
and values towards people of different physical types. At its simplest
if one is fat, one is expected to be jolly. Nevertheless, an undoubted
relationship does exist and has obvious affinities with that of the
Kretschmer studies. Investigations into delinquency for example
reveal a significant incidence of mesomorphy. Studies of college
groups reveal important differences in somatotypes between diff
erent specialities and between the attainment of various classes of
degree.

Taken as a whole the available evidence including factor
analytic studies indicates a significant association between physical
and psychological attributes. The correlations, however, are
generally of a low order. This might be a fault of technique, or
simply through not knowing as yet the correct physical and psycho
logical attributes to measure. It might be that, in any event
physical typing has at best only a small association with psycho
logical attributes. Furthermore, on the psychological side so many
variables ranging from frank psychosis through neurosis and
psychosomatic disorder to healthy subjects have been used that it is
perhaps surprising so many positive results have been reported
This itself does suggest the role of common genetic factors in
physical and psychological make-up. Clearly, more refined studies
are needed in what seems a promising field. Yet it does seem possible
that the various relationships claimed between body build and
personality could all be explained by arguing that extraverts tend
to be relatively thick in body build and introverts relatively thin
With psychiatric illness, the extraverts tend to develop hysteria i

neurotic, paranoid schizophrenia if schizophrenic and mania in the affective disorders. The introverts tend to develop one of the remaining groups, i.e. neurotic anxiety or depression, non-paranoid schizophrenia or melancholia.

Apart from the distinction between different types of body build, many studies indicate that overall body size (regardless of body type) is a factor showing important links with personality. Large body size appears to be related to more emotionality, small body size to less emotionality. In neurotic subjects, large body size has been associated with activity and aggression, small body size with a weaker and more timorous mode of expression. The latter finding does not match with the ideas of Adler who suggests that physical inferiority is compensated for by aggressiveness.

Finally, other physiological associates of psychiatric illness may be discovered. If such items turn out to be consistent physical correlates of schizophrenia or even of some schizophrenics, psychological tests may help to clarify the particular cluster of symptoms involved. Such a possibility might well happen in the field of affective disorder where mood changes appear to be related to abnormal changes in electrolyte balance and total body fluid. Even where such correlates seem firmly established, precise measurements, including psychological testing, will be imperative if prediction of the degree and kind of change occurring in a particular individual is to be possible.

PSYCHOANALYTIC PERSONALITY THEORY

Psychoanalytic ideas have so permeated our culture that psychoanalysis is often identified with psychiatry and psychology. Yet it would not be exaggerating to say that neither discipline, as practised, would be radically different if psychoanalysis had never existed. Discussion of psychoanalysis in more detail will be left to the section on therapy but a brief outline is given here of its personality theory.

Freudian theory conceives of personality as being a three-part structure. The *id*, which is unconscious, is the store of libidinous motivation. Sex and aggression are its principal motives and its goal is pleasure. The *ego* (part conscious, but part unconscious) bridles the id into socially acceptable channels. That is, the ego works in consideration of the reality principle. Thirdly, the *super ego* consists of restraints, also with conscious and unconscious parts, imposed by introjected standards derived from other people. This personality structure develops in the earliest years in the infant's relationships with his mother and father. Particular attention is paid to the alleged stages of infantile sexuality—the oral, the anal, the genital and the oedipal. Psychoanalysts claim that Freudian theory is necessary to understand the adult personality. Many psychoanalysts believe they find validation of this theory in their clinical experience, but empirical verification of Freudian principles has only been mildly positive at the best. Even then, there is great doubt how far the child's experiences are not so much causal to the adult's make-up, but rather early expressions of inherited characteristics. In addition, modern learning theory tends to claim a simpler and more scientific view of the same data that the psychoanalysts study (p. 117). It must also be noted that the psychoanalysts tend to view their subject in a closed 'religious' manner which is at variance with modern scientific attitudes. Recently there has been an increasing tendency to accept psychoanalytic personality theory only in so far as it has been empirically verified. This is an enormously difficult task. The work of Newson and Newson, for example, stresses that we cannot possibly know the effects of child-rearing practices on the adult as we even lack data on the type and incidence of child-rearing practices in our society. Many people would also judge that personality develops or alters in later childhood, adolescence and adulthood, suggesting the first few years are not all important. However, the psychoanalyst might well argue that the basic attitudes acquired then are still basic whatever change is observed in their particular manifestation. It is of interest that psychologists studying perceptual processes or the effects of learning tend to argue that the earliest years are important in their fields and it is generally agreed that emotional organization in the individual starts in the earliest years. Such arguments are still a long way from supporting the very definite theory of psychoanalytic personality development. It has also been argued that there is really no evidence to substantiate the belief that learning in childhood has a necessarily massive effect on subsequent behaviour.

PERSONALITY MEASUREMENT

Each person is a unique individual. One person may be, for example, exactly as extraverted as another person. But the way he manifests his extraversion will be qualitatively different in that any expression will be a function of his unique personality structure.

Allport stressed that the importance of such individual structures is a major obstacle to scientific personality studies. This was because the latter essentially deal with what people have in common and not in their very personal individuality. Nevertheless, Allport went on to discuss essentially nomothetic (group derived) techniques and Eysenck for one has persuasively argued that individuality and general principles are not irrevocably opposed. Every bridge, for example, is unique, but is built according to general principles.

It must be accepted, however, that personality measurement lags far behind intellectual assessment with regard to validity and usefulness. In the psychiatric field a great source of difficulty has been the tendency to describe personality in terms of psychiatric symptoms. At its worst such a practice tends to describe normal persons as being in effect, mild versions of psychiatric patients. Thus, for example, the schizoid personality is regarded as a person who is some sort of sub-clinical schizophrenic. Remarkably little reliable work has been done to establish the nature of the pre-morbid personalities of psychiatric patients as distinct from the early stages of their illness. If the premorbid personality of a schizophrenic is not necessarily a schizoid one, it would be useful and perhaps revealing to obtain any suggestions of typical associates of personality phenomena. Attempts have recently been made, as by Foulds, to show the need and the value of distinguishing between psychiatric illness and personality variants.

Personality and its measurement is a complex and difficult field whose limitations are only too apparent. Sometimes criticism becomes heightened at particular points, such as the propositions of psychoanalytic theory or the use of projective personality measures. In the whole field it can be safely said that no one theory or method of measurement is clearly better than another. Even traditional psychiatric groupings are all too easily open to criticism of the very need for their existence. Clearly, reliable and valid methods must dominate in the long run although it cannot be said at this stage which these are liable to be. At present it can only be accepted that personality evaluation remains an individual art, whatever the particular trappings the personality assessor uses. Even more than in the assessment of intelligence, the psychologist assessing personality must be a specialist diagnostician rather than a psychometrician.

The personal interview is the oldest method of personality measurement. It is obviously subjective and attempts to objectify it have not been conspicuously successful. On the other hand, questionnaires and inventories in particular objectify verbal material at the expense of structuring the areas examined. In addition, falsification (deliberate or otherwise) and a lack of insight or understanding render these techniques open to criticism. Nevertheless, modern inventories involve (or should involve) far more than the compiler sitting down and drawing up a list of items which he judges to be appropriate. Many recent studies emphasize the problems, for example, of what is called response set. Different people, for example, appear to complete inventories from the point of view of social desirability, others tend to answer 'Yes' or to give extreme opinions, whatever the items concerned.

One interesting example is the Runwell Sign–Symptom Inventory of Foulds which consists of 81 items. These 81 items are a list of what might be considered key statements in describing the most typical features of eight standard psychiatric categories. Eight categories, each with 10 items (11 for one) for anxiety state, neurotic depression, mania, paranoid state, obsessional, nonparanoid schizophrenia, hysteria and melancholia, make up the inventory. The administrator interviews the patients with these items to elicit whether they apply or not. The inventory is scored not by simply adding up the 'scores' on each category but by contrasting various category scores and groups of scores. With his standardization data, Foulds claims an impressive level of differentiation (a) between psychiatric patients and normals, and (b) between the major psychiatric categories used. Foulds argues that his results also indicate that it is valid to consider psychiatric illnesses (personal illness is his term) as lying along a continuum of increasing degree of failure to maintain or establish mutual personal relationships. Next to normals are psychopaths whose difficulty is only one of personal relations. Then come the neurotic states who are in addition personally ill. Further along the continuum is the psychotic who in addition may be integrated or non-integrated. Foulds's inventory and its system, as he points out, should be of use not only diagnostically but also in studies of aetiology and treatment.

Another important aspect of Foulds's work has been his consideration of the need to distinguish between personality traits and psychiatric symptoms. Foulds stresses that a confusion between these two (the one normal and enduring, the other a sign of illness and malleable) leads to serious errors in diagnosis, aetiology and treatment. For example, if an extravert becomes depressed, he might be wrongly thought to be a hysteric because of obvious extravert traits in his behaviour. Foulds prefers to call this personality variable hysteroid–obsessoid although his measure of it tends to correlate highly with measures of extraversion–introversion.

The Maudsley Personality Inventory (and its modified form, the Eysenck Personality Inventory) has not been shown to be useful in differential diagnosis. This relatively short inventory contains items measuring either 'neuroticism' or 'extraversion–introversion'. The tendency to score introverted and neurotic appears to be common in all categories of neurotic and psychotic. This perhaps indicates that the inventory only validly measures a general factor of emotional instability. Therefore, perhaps its only real use would be as a screening device between the stable and unstable. But if so, shorter measures and equally efficient ones are available.

Similar criticisms can be applied to the longer Cattell 16PF personality inventory. Scoring of this inventory leads to a personality profile based on individual scores on Cattell's sixteen personality factors. It can be seen readily from the profile which of an individual's sixteen scores depart most from the norm or average and hence indicate his strengths and weaknesses. This inventory should, at face value, be capable of differential diagnosis but there is little evidence so far that it can reliably do this with any validity. Whether the measurement of Cattell's more limited number of second-order factors can be shown to be of use in psychiatry is also a task for the future. It is surprising that inventories like the Maudsley and the Cattell are so disappointing after the rigorous arguments that have been repeatedly made by their designers over so many years.

Possibly the only inventory in common use that has any claim to be valuable in differential diagnosis is the MMPI (Minnesota Multiphasic Personality Inventory). Even so, this is only because the MMPI has tried to keep up with the times. When originally published in 1941 by Hathaway and McKinley, a fairly straightforward match was expected between diagnosis and the appropriate score on the clinical scales (hysteria, depression, hypochondriasis, psychopathy, masculinity–femininity, paranoia, psychasthenia, schizophrenia, mania, social introversion). These clinical scales are largely derived from the classical descriptions or attributes of the diagnostic categories. There are also various scales measuring different aspects of validity and test-taking attitudes.

Such obvious matches are infrequent, at least in ordinary inventory practice, though, as we have noted, Foulds claims something not far removed with his inventory. Subsequent refinements of scale groupings, personality profiling and coding, together with many new scales, have tended to keep the MMPI very much a live test. Nevertheless, if one leaves out the more clinical interpretation of a particular record, there is doubt as to how far these scoring refinings objectively match with differential diagnosis. In addition, the length of the inventory (566 items), together with its verbal requirement, reduce its applicability to only a proportion of psychiatric patients.

A number of scales originally derived from MMPI items have been published for various special purposes. One of the best known is the Taylor Manifest Anxiety Scale which has been used in many research studies as well as individual diagnosis. As this scale correlates highly with scales usually labelled 'neuroticism', it is doubtful if it measures anything more specific than emotional instability. Sandler has devised an inventory (Tavistock Self-assessment Inventory) which he has used in conjunction with a factorial technique to establish personality correlates of various psychiatric symptoms. His technique is interesting but there may be doubts about reliablity and validity. Laing and Philipson have evolved a questionnaire which attempts to measure an individual's assessment of how others see him. These are only examples of the proliferation of inventories available. Unfortunately few of them are generally useful and those few overlap considerably.

Another inventory sometimes used is the Edwards Personality Preference Schedule. This involves a choice between motives and needs, yielding a score on 15 personality scales, supposedly unaffected by social desirability. These personality scales or needs are derived from H. A. Murray who devised the TAT which will be described later. Workers like Edwards believe that it is as important to measure an individual's motivational system as his personality structure. Cattell, as a result of factorial studies, has provided the MAT (Motivational Analysis Test) which aims to measure his postulated list of basic human motives. It can be argued that the abnormal or unusual features of a particular personality at times are to be found more in the motivational field than in its structure. On the other hand the distinction between structure and motivation may be rather arbitrary. Allport, in a classic analysis of the nature of personality, argues strongly for regarding personality as being essentially an individual organization. To regard elements within it (of structure or motivation) as being too discrete is to deny the global organizational properties of personality.

It seems to us that a theoretical point of interest is implied in many personality tests, particularly noticeable in inventories. This point is that inventories usually endeavour to measure a trait, typology or diagnostic category by eliciting in how many ways an individual shows certain characteristics. Yet in practice and clinical observation measurement would rather be made by noting the degree or intensity or only one or two items. For example, a clear case of fugue lasting days would receive a far greater diagnostic weighting at interview than it would as only one positive item on an inventory scale measuring hysteria. An obsessional neurotic may spend all day washing his hands, but not answer positively to many other items of an obsessional kind. At present, the interview would register this intensity but not the inventory.

In the occupational field, the Strong Vocational Interest Blank and the Kuder Preference Schedule have been relatively successful. By covering areas of ground not directly related to the occupation in question, they nevertheless show a certain degree of validity in distinguishing what might be called various occupational types. These have some use, particularly in rehabilitation problems with psychotic and other patients, but it is doubtful if they contribute as much as a combination of intellectual assessment with observation in a work situation. With the Rothwell–Miller Interest Blank, occupations are considered to group into twelve broad categories. The subject ranks various occupations in terms of his preferences. This ranking is carried out for a number of blocks of occupations. The blank is so scored that consistent occupational preferences are clearly apparent, together with particular examples of the preferred occupations.

A rating scale simply extends the usual questionnaire answer range of 'Yes' or 'No' to particular items. Five- or seven-point ratings are commonly used. Although such scales are simple and useful they have at least as many sources of unreliability and invalidity as questionnaires. A number of such rating scales have been more widely used than others, perhaps because they are better designed. Two of the most well known are the Fergus Falls Behaviour Rating Scale and the Wittenborn Psychiatric Rating Scale. Also in this area is the work of Lorr and his associates. Using a rating scale technique known as the IMPS (In-patient Multidimensional Psychiatric Scale) and factor-analytic methods, these workers report five dimensions of psychosis. These dimensions are labelled disorganized hyperactivity, schizophrenic disorganization, paranoid process, anxious depression and hostile paranoia. Such instruments, when carefully used, yield useful data in areas of psychiatric illness where formal personality tests have, as yet, little applicability.

Projective techniques are so called because they assume that ambiguous stimuli will be structured by a person, through projecting on to the stimulus some of his personality characteristics. Such tasks always involve perceptual processes and thus indicate the basic importance of perception in individual psychology. The best known projective technique is the Rorschach test. Ten ink blots of varying hues and shapes are responded to in terms of 'What might this be, what impression does it give you?' Although a person's responses are scored objectively the final interpretation is more impressionistic and subjective. The scoring of Rorschach ink blot responses is complex and is carried out by an inquiry with the subject after he has given his responses. Although his type of response may be important (e.g. responses involving sexual, anatomical or aggressive material) the scoring pays even more attention to other aspects. These aspects particularly include the location and determinants of his responses in the blot material. Each response's score contributes to a final overall Rorschach psychogram and it is from the latter that the most important personality descriptions are obtained. Attempts to validate the test have been limited in success. The Rorschach technique is probably a special kind of interview rather than a properly scientific tool. Such reservations probably apply to all projective methods. Even so, until personality tests reach the sophistication of intelligence tests, there seems little doubt that projective methods, when used by an experienced psychologist, often prove of value. Although actual Rorschach scores are hard to establish from the point of view of validity, assessments derived from Rorschach records often match with diagnosis to a much greater degree. This particularly applies if dichotomic decisions such as neurosis–psychosis are studied. With further subdivision, one must always remember that agreement between psychiatrists is often poor. Where diagnostic reliability between the diagnosticians is poor, a psychological test has little chance of validating itself as an efficient yardstick does not exist. Developments of ink blot methods such as that of Holtzman have been made. Here there are 45 blots where only one response is required to each blot. Such a technique controls the amount of responsiveness but at the same time ensures that subjects respond to all the aspects of the blots. Even so, it is doubtful whether such techniques will really supplant the Rorschach. Disadvantages are present as well as advantages in any new technique and in addition they lack the impressive background literature and experience.

The second best known projective method is Murray's Thematic Apperception Test (TAT). This consists of 20 ambiguous pictures to which the subject has to make up what he considers an appropriate story. As with the Rorschach, but to a lesser degree, attempts have been made to objectify what has still remained a clinician's technique. Various scoring systems are available—some designed to measure specific needs such as achievement and some which simply count up the frequency of various types of themes and content. Such a straight-forward procedure as the latter has been surprisingly neglected.

A less structured (i.e. vaguer) series of pictures than the TAT is Philipson's Object Relations Technique (ORT). Although this technique can be used as an alternative to the TAT it has rather a different composition. The TAT sets out to measure responses to certain key situations (man–woman, adult–child, etc.) and certain drives (aggression, sex). The ORT studies response to one-, two-, three-person and group situations in three varying degrees of reality presentation. Although it has theoretical affiliations to the psychoanalytic writings of Klein and Fairbairn, such a background is not necessarily required of the user.

Although the TAT contains a number of pictures for children, it is generally conceded that Bellak's Children's Apperception Test (CAT) is a more appropriate instrument for the young child. With this test, animal pictures are utilized on the hypothesis that young children respond more to them than to pictures of humans. There is also a version of the CAT for older children, replacing the animal figures by human ones, but keeping what are considered to be the key situations depicted. Raven's Controlled Projection, a version of the sentence completion technique, is also useful with children. The child fills in a story outline and in so doing is able to project his own personality. The Raven technique is also useful, in that a picture made by the child during the story telling is an extra bonus in the personality data obtained.

With children, their stories and drawings and their use of play material are often used as a way of assessing personality. Indeed, formal interviewing and inventory completion might be useless. It is usually assumed that the child's play with toys—whether structured as with dolls or trains, or unstructured as with Plasticine or paint—is a way of expressing or projecting his personality and its difficulties. A child's drawings of people are often informative of his personality and his drawings and paintings in general might be useful clinically. Again one must add that although the experienced assessor appears to derive much of importance from such techniques it is very difficult to objectify (or validate) what are alleged to be the key elements.

A number of techniques have been devised for investigating the individual personality as it is structured within itself rather than in how it compares with others. Such techniques usually require a great deal of statistical analysis and were impractical in pre-computer days. Whether they justify by results the amount of work still required is an open question. At present, three techniques in particular (semantic differential, repertory grid, and Q sorting), all loosely related, are producing a great deal of interest.

Before these three techniques are discussed, mention must be made of the word-association technique which is perhaps their historical predecessor. The word-association test simply involves getting the subject to respond with a word to a stimulus word, the response word, the time to respond being noted. Refinements might be added by measuring the subjects psychophysiological response to various stimulus words via pulse and breathing rates, galvanic skin response (sweat gland activity) and so on. Although there is some value in picking stimulus words that are thought appropriate to each subject, a standard list with available lists of common responses is probably more scientifically useful. Delays in response, unusual associations, and emotional reactions all indicate what is of emotional value to the subject. Some techniques in fact were early used (as by Jung) to uncover areas of neurotic 'complexes'. In addition, trends in the performance of psychotics, especially schizophrenics, have been used to study thought disorders—as seen in association disturbance. Bizarre ideas, fragmental thinking and loose associations are all thought to be evident in word-association performances with schizophrenics. Such primary thought disturbances have been claimed to be the basis of the more elaborate disturbances of hallucination and delusions.

The semantic differential of Osgood is a relatively sophisti-

technique. The subject takes a concept such as 'mother' or 'sex' and the concept on a seven-point rating scale. Such scales (as we will discuss under emotion) tend to cluster in three modes of emotional variation. A subject's profile of ratings of a concept will clearly indicate his attitudes to such concepts. Furthermore, his profiles of ratings of different concepts can be compared so that the similarity (or otherwise) of the concepts to him can be elicited.

Kelly's repertory grid test is so flexible that this flexibility is either claimed to be its source of value or of worthlessness, according to one's viewpoint. In a way it is a close relative of the Osgood semantic differential technique. A common set of people (or more correctly, verbal concepts of such people) are taken, such as mother, wife, father, teacher. Each of the people (or elements) are compared with one another with regard to a construct (such as kindness, strength, cleverness). The precise elements and constructs used are chosen to fit the individual case and problem. The resulting grid of elements and constructs can best be factor-analysed by a computer. The results can be described in terms of the dispersion of the elements in the construct space, or of the dispersion of the constructs in the element space. It is thought that such grids may prove helpful in guiding psychotherapy and measuring the effects of treatment as much as in diagnosis. Another use of repertory grid technique has been in schizophrenia where Bannister has derived measures characterizing thought disordered patients. Particularly important appears to be a measure of 'loosened construing' shown in a weakness of correlation between constructs in repertory grid measures. Bannister has suggested such looseness of construing in schizophrenia is related to the 'double-bind' phenomena described by Bateson (p. 165). Furthermore he suggests that a 'psychotherapy' of schizophrenia might be advanced by deliberately setting out to tighten up a schizophrenic's way of construing events. But as we have noted (p. 19) this measure can be criticized as measuring only a non-specific intellectual deficit.

Both the semantic differential and the repertory grid have much in common with Stephenson's technique. Statements about the self (usually 100) are sorted into different categories by the patient. These categories include a self sort (degree to which the statements resemble him), an ideal sort, and so on. These can be compared with sorts made by other people about the patient. Such sorts can be done at various stages of therapy, or between children and parents, husbands and wives. Such Q sorts can also be quantified and a matrix of correlations analysed to produce factors of personality types. These compare with the ordinary correlation matrices described (many people on a large number of measures) and with Cattell's P technique (one person on the same number of measures on a number of occasions).

These three related ways of studying the individual clearly involve verbal constructs, and are often described as involving studies of meaning and conceptualization. It is quite clear, however, that they are very much techniques of investigating personality, particularly from the point of view of emotional and motivational factors. Other attempts to measure personality lead to a consideration of the important factors of emotion and motivation in personality. Such studies range from the simply physiological to the psychologically complex. At present many of these behavioural and psychological studies are largely of a research nature and have little precise to offer in the way of individual classification and prediction of behaviour. But it is probably true to say that such studies on a long-term basis may turn out to be more successful than most present standard techniques of personality investigation.

This account of personality testing has confined itself to mentioning the most common types of techniques. Personality tests are legion and almost anything the organism does has been used at some time as a test. The fact that such techniques do not become widely used perhaps reflects that they show little sign of general validity and applicability. In psychiatric diagnosis the main task of personality assessment has been directed to categorization in the following way: Is a person's performance normal or subnormal? If abnormal, is it neurotic or psychotic and which sub-category is the best fit? But obviously, personality assessment can be related to many other ends, such as aetiology or the assessment of therapy. Studies of particular groups, such as athletes, artists, parents and children, husbands and wives, physically ill groups, psychosomatic patients and so on, are clearly valuable for various reasons. The more valid personality assessment becomes, the more useful it will become in many spheres apart from that of differential diagnosis.

5

Emotion

Disturbance of emotion

Psychiatric illness frequently involves a marked disturbance of the emotional life. This disturbance might even be a primary feature of the illness. The close link between psychiatric illness and emotional disturbance can be seen in the names of important psychiatric illnesses such as anxiety state, depression, melancholia and mania. Classical descriptions of other conditions, such as hysteria, psychopathy and schizophrenia, usually stress the importance of certain emotional characteristics. The emotional abnormality may be in the direction of a blunting or inappropriateness of emotional expression as well as in an undue intensification. It is also true to say that much psychiatric therapy of various types is evaluated in terms of an improvement in the patient's emotional state.

The concept of psychosomatic disorder also involves an association between certain physical illnesses and persistent emotional disturbances. Diseases such as asthma, peptic ulcers, colitis and many others are claimed to be linked with personalities characterized by persistent emotional difficulties. It is less easy to show the precise nature of these links—whether they are simultaneous aspects of a general syndrome or whether there is a causal connection between them. Almost every kind of illness has, at some time, been claimed to be associated with emotional disturbance. Adequately designed studies with objective measurements are clearly required together with the ability to examine the results in an impartial manner. Such requirements are needed for example, in examining the relationships between lung cancer and tobacco smoking. A number of studies would suggest, for example, that the relationship is not a simple causal one.

It is of interest that much work on emotions deals only with unpleasant emotions, often with neurotic and psychotic subjects. To a great extent such emotions are disruptive and this might lead to the impression that emotions in general are disorganizing and even pathological influences. It might be that emotions of great intensity tend to be maladaptive but moderately intense emotions are a normal and necessary part of motivation.

There are, of course, a wide range of pleasant and positive emotions such as love, joy, reverence and security. Such emotions are organizing rather than disruptive and play a large role in normal adaptation. McDougall and Lewin, for example, stressed the place of emotions as a basis for the direction and motivation of behaviour. Modern behaviour theories stress the importance of emotional factors by the prominence they give to such concepts as drive reduction, reward and reinforcement. Even classical contiguity learning is generally considered to take place by the involvement of some affective state. Learning theories are discussed in detail later in association with behaviour therapy (Chapter 9). Here we merely note that common fears (snakes, mice, insects) and phobic states can be explained by supposing the setting-up of a conditioned emotional response of fear to a basically neutral stimulus. Such fears often act as examples of avoidance learning. As the organism always 'avoids', there is normally no chance of the response being extinguished. Suitable behaviour therapy techniques have been claimed to be an efficient approach to such conditions.

Apart from such pathological examples there is a widely held belief that emotion tends to have a disorganizing effect on behaviour. It is often stated that reason and emotion are opposite poles so that any increase in the one results in a decrease in the other. The psychoanalytic viewpoint tends to oppose reason and emotion, perhaps reflecting certain aspects of some cultural beliefs in the nineteenth century. Such a division is perhaps true for certain intense emotions but it is also true that reason is facilitated by a certain degree of emotion. There are, for example, many accounts of emotional excitement that appear to parallel genuinely creative activity. In fact, emotions and their disturbances are part of everyday life. Everyone knows what emotions are but their analysis, definition and measurement are difficult.

Definitions and classification

Emotions can be defined as a complex state of the organism usually involving (1) bodily changes of a widespread character, and (2) psychological features such as a state of excitement or perturbation, marked by strong feelings, with tendencies to definite forms of behaviour.

Emotions, feelings and moods are categories that inevitably overlap. Feeling is an inportant aspect of emotion, but only one aspect. All experience has some type and degree of feeling tone. Emotion is considered to occur when the degree of feeling tone becomes relatively intense. Emotions must also be distinguished from moods. The latter are essentially emotional mental sets. Moods predispose the individual to experience one kind of emotion rather than another. Affection is a general term that is often used for the feeling and emotional aspects of experience.

Typical examples of emotions are joy, fear, anger, pity, shame, compassion, amusement, gratitude, disgust, sorrow, disappointment. Although emotions are affective states, they have important cognitive and conative aspects as well as physiological and motivational features. One of the oldest divisions of mental states was the tripartite one of cognition, affection and conation. Care must also be taken to distinguish emotions from even more complex psychological organizations known as sentiments, attitudes and opinions.

Feeling has long been considered the affective aspect of experience. All behaviour and experience contains an emotional component. Care must be taken not to identify the emotions with the passions or intense emotions. Partly because of the latter mistake, and partly because of its experiential aspects, accounts and studies of emotion tend to be somewhat unrewarding or unsatisfactory. In recent times, indeed, many writers have suggested that it is more practical to classify behaviour than emotion. This involves rejecting the traditional concept of emotion and suggests that behaviour usually subsumed under this heading should, for example, be placed along a continuum of energy mobilization. This would involve, perhaps, the assessment of the degree of arousal which is particularly accompanied by activation of the sympathetic nervous system.

The classification of emotions and feelings has often been attempted. Wundt, a pioneer of experimental psychology in the

F

nineteenth century, considered that emotional experiences varied in three dimensions. These three dimensions were (1) unpleasant to pleasant, (2) excitement to calm and (3) strain to relaxation. Much subsequent work has resulted in agreement or disagreement with Wundt's three modes. Most agreement seems to be about the variable of pleasantness but with more argument on either the need for, or the precise nature of, other modes of description or measurement.

Two workers more recent than Wundt have produced empirically derived modes of emotional variation rather similar to those of Wundt. Schlosberg derived three areas of variation from a study of judgements of the facial expression of emotion. These were (1) pleasant–unpleasant (love–anger), (2) attention–rejection (fear–disgust) and (3) level of activity (sleep–tension). Osgood in his semantic differential studies derived three major modes of variation from factorial studies of adjectives. These can be listed as (1) good–bad (evaluation), (2) strong–weak (potency) and (3) fast–slow (activity).

It must be stressed, however, that even when studies such as the above produce a measure of apparent agreement this does not necessarily give generally applicable information on emotional variations. For example, the expression of emotion varies a great deal in extent and type between the social groups of different classes and cultures. Another problem involved in the judgement of emotions is the importance of knowledge of its antecedents. Sherman as long ago as 1927, for example, found that observers disagreed a great deal about the precise emotion expressed by children when the observers had no knowledge of the stimulating conditions.

Another general difficulty follows any attempt to study emotions if the subject's own assessment is involved. Introspective accounts vary in clarity and accuracy and are difficult to bring under experimental control. Yet subjective experiences are important in the usual definitions of emotion. To leave them out might make for better experiments but it must always be remembered that to do so is to move away from the traditional concept of emotion.

Emotional development

Whatever the variety of adult emotional life, differences of opinion also exist according to how much of this variety is primary (and innate) or secondary (learnt variants and blends).

J. B. Watson postulated three innate emotions, which were further limited by being only produced by characteristic stimulation. Thus fear was produced by loud noises or loss of support, love by bodily stimulation and rage by a restriction of bodily movement. Only by subsequent learning is the range of emotion and stimulating situations extended.

A major difficulty in studying emotional development arises from the fact that what is innate may not be present at birth but may only appear with later maturation. Bridges in 1932 put forward a developmental theory of emotion. She claimed that the baby up to 2 months of age shows only an undifferentiated emotional excitement. But by 3 months a positive emotion of delight and a negative emotion of distress have appeared. By 6 months, fear, disgust and anger have differentiated. Further differentiation occurs throughout childhood and adolescence. Each emotion, even the original undifferentiated one, is said to persist throughout life as well as its subsequent differentiations. Bridges suggests that both learning and maturation are necessary to account for emotional development. Her theory is somewhat similar to that of Freud who maintained that the affect at birth is one of undifferentiated pain/anxiety (*unlust*).

The emotional pattern of an individual clearly begins with hereditary factors. There are, for example, marked differences in emotionality between species of wild and domesticated animals. Wild species of animals are generally so intractable that even when reared in captivity from birth they rarely remain tame by the time they are adult.

To study such phenomena experimentally two kinds of rat were cross-bred—the white gentle rat and the grey wild rat. Savageness appeared linked with hair colour. The grey rat has two colours of hair intermixed, a light tan and a very dark brown. The cross-bred offspring included those with light tan hair only, some with very dark brown and some with white. The very dark brown will become tame like the white rat but the tan coloured will be savage. A later study reported that the inbreeding of emotional rats produced offspring more emotional than their parents, a trend noticeable even in the first generation.

Biochemical factors may be important. Two distinct hormones have been found in the adrenal secretions of man and animals.

More aggressive wild animals, such as the lion, are thought to have an excess of noradrenaline in contrast to a supposed excess of adrenaline in a timid animal like the wild rabbit. It has also been claimed that the direction of anger is related to adrenaline and noradrenaline. Anger directed outwardly is associated with a noradrenaline-like substance whereas anger directed inwardly and anxiety is supposed to be associated with an adrenaline-like substance.

Relevant studies in humans are uncommon. But the alleged general factor of 'neuroticism' might be a measure of emotionality if it is considered to be the inverse of the earlier Webb and Burt factors of emotionality and strength of purpose. The evidence concerning such a general factor would tend at present to suggest a strong hereditary influence, though environmental factors are still of importance.

It is not possible, however, to say that inheritance can always account for emotional difference. Infancy and childhood are often considered a source of emotional characteristics, especially emotional disturbances. Empirical studies are few and those which have been done tend to throw doubt on more observational and impressionistic views, such as those made by psychoanalysts. An example of this is the maternal deprivation in infancy hypothesis. Where positive results are forthcoming, they tend to indicate a more complex picture than that previously imagined.

Harlow experimented with monkeys taken from their mothers shortly after birth. Some were raised singly in cages with either 'wire' model mothers or 'cloth' model mothers, and some in cages with both kinds of mothers. Each 'mother' was fitted with a nursing bottle. The observed preference for the cloth models suggested that the comfort of contact may be more important than the simple satisfaction of hunger. Even those monkeys fed by the wire mother spent more time with the cloth mothers. These results appear to parallel observations of infants and children.

The holding of soft blankets or cuddly toys seems to provide emotional support at night or at other times when fear might be present, and there is little doubt that such provision is a common feature of our child-rearing practices. Evidence on the handling of young rats also points in this direction. Much work has been done experimentally on the effect of stroking the skin of young laboratory rats. Animals stimulated in this way or by handling for a few minutes each day grow more quickly than controls which are left alone. Again, experimental animals do not eat more than controls but they appear to make better use of the food they eat. There is generally higher rate of development, for example; both the cholesterol content of the brain and hair growth are increased and there is an improvement in learning ability. A handled animal, on being put in an unfamiliar open space, will confidently explore, whereas a non-handled animal tends to show signs of 'emotionality'. Handling is most effective if done before the rats are 20 days old. The handling may activate the hypothalmic–pituitary–adrenal system so that later in life the animals have a more effective response to stress.

One aspect of emotional development concerns the problem of emotional control. This is usually supposed to increase throughout childhood and adolescence. Common emotional reactions during these periods would be considered immature and maladaptive if they appeared in the adult. The temper tantrum period of infancy and the quickly changing emotional attachments of adolescence are examples. Although it is easy to give generally acceptable statements like this, more normative data are required.

Emotions, like other aspects of experience and behaviour, must necessarily be viewed as integral parts of the organism. For example, the limited time perception of the infant might be an important factor in his intense emotional reactions. It is difficult to control an intense emotional reaction if there is little appreciation that it will end.

Psychoanalytic writings imply a marked link between emotion and the unconscious. The latter is said to be non-rational (i.e. emotional) and the two primary groups of instincts (sexual and aggressive) are generally thought of as being basically affective in nature. To some extent modern man is seen by the psychoanalyst as fighting a continuous battle against the powerful emotional bases of his nature. As soon as consciousness relaxes, as in dreams or free association, the links between the varying contents of experience become clearly emotional rather than rational. In the earliest years the lack of rational control contrasts with the later years and the development of various defence mechanisms. These mechanisms, such as repression, reaction–formation, sublimation and so on, keep the affective unconscious under some kind of control.

Jung also stressed that an increase in emotion went hand in hand with a contraction of consciousness, but of recent years psychoanalytic concepts and their derivatives have rightly been subjected, where possible, to empirical verification. Relevant examples of this are the many recent studies of perceptual defence. These studies revolve around observations that negatively toned words require a long exposure time (as for example in a tachistoscope), before they are identified than more neutral words. Some subjects, however, show a reverse or sensitization effect as if they were fascinated by sexual and aggressive impulses.

Theories of emotion

A classic theory of the emotions is the James–Lange, put forward by two psychologists independently. Here emotion is identified with the awareness of physiological changes. Emotion is, as it were, parallel to, or even an aftermath of, bodily activity. This theory is rather at variance with the layman's view of experienced emotion as being the cause of the physiological changes. The Cannon–Bard theory held the hypothalamus to be the emotional centre. Experiments showed that bodily changes could take place without experienced emotion. Masserman in 1946, working with cats, showed that electrical or drug stimulation of the hypothalamus results in such reactions as 'sham rage' or 'sham fear'. Masserman considered such reactions to be 'pseudo-affective', differing significantly from ordinary emotional states, in particular, in the presence of motivational aspects. In other words, it might be misleading to identify such reactions with normally occurring emotions. Both the James–Lange and the Cannon–Bard theories illuminate some important aspects of emotion, but neither is fully able to account for all aspects.

Darwin's theory of the expression of emotions is of importance in stressing the continuity between man and other animals. Darwin supposed that to understand emotional expression in man attention must be paid to the natural conditions under which they originally served a directly useful purpose. Thus, in the principle of serviceable associated habits, the emotional expression originally involved a useful activity, as for example in drawing back at the sight of a snake. Such actions relieve or gratify certain states of consciousness. The principle of antithesis economically supposed that opposite emotions involved an opposite set of reactions. Sobbing, for example, involves opposite reactions to those of laughing, as they are opposite emotions. The third and general principle was of the added direct effects of the action of the nervous system generated by the emotion. Such effects would not be specific to any one emotion but would help to build up the bodily state of emotional excitation. Much of what Darwin supposed, of course, can be attributed to learning rather than to innate patterning. Some cultures and nations are very expressive (the Italians, for example) whereas others, like many American Indians, are characteristically unexpressive.

The physiology involved in emotions includes that of (1) the sympathetic and parasympathetic autonomic nervous systems and (2) the endocrine glands, both being connected with the central nervous system. The meaning or conscious side of emotion is centred more in the cortex which thus can control the hypothalamus. But with an increasing intensity of emotion, the hypothalamus feeds more and more impulses to the cortex. The sensory feedback results in increased activity and biochemical changes until the hypothalamus is more free of cortical control. In strong emotion, behaviour is perhaps organized more in terms of the neural patterns of the lower centres than in the learned patterns of the cortex. Sympathetic, parasympathetic and endocrine effects all combine and interact to produce a response. This makes it difficult to classify emotions by morphological systems considered in isolation. The following paragraphs indicate recent suggestions rather than definite statements on emotional centres.

It is believed that the thalamus plays a decisive role in the perception of pain. Pleasure centres appear to be scattered throughout the brain, particularly in the hypothalamus. Rage and fear have been produced by electrical stimulation of the amygdala. Experiments by Delgado and others have suggested that adjacent areas in the amygdala are associated with hate and love. Such experiments, using electrical stimulation of these areas, suggest that one of these emotions might easily pass into the other. Such a change of course is frequently observed in human relationships. The amygdala has an important role in sexuality. If it is removed or diseased, excessive sexuality may be observed. Other experiments by Delgado and others with Rhesus monkeys indicated that stimulation of the caudate nucleus made the animals unusually gentle instead of fierce.

Electrical stimulation experiments by Olds and others of non-cortical areas have revealed a number of points associated with pleasure, some of them specific pleasures such as food, drink and sex. Sometimes a more complex response is produced, perhaps by stimulating more than one pleasure centre at the same time. This complexity is possible as such centres are often packed closely to gether in the brain. Such centres have been located in cats, dogs monkeys, apes and dolphins. Relatively few opportunities occur for similar studies with human subjects but the data available suggests the same type of findings. Nevertheless, as Masserman indicated these centres do not function in isolation and, above all, the regulatory role of the cortex is of great importance.

Measurements of emotion

Physiological reactions associated with emotions have been frequently studied in attempts to measure emotions. An example of this is the polygraph, often used as a 'lie detector', which records simultaneously changes in the galvanic skin response (i.e. changes in electrical resistance due to sweat gland activity), pulse rate, breathing rate and blood pressure. Visceral changes, in fact, appear to accompany emotional changes not otherwise detectable.

Basal levels have not generally been found to be of much significance; it is rather the amount of change, particularly under conditions involving a degree of stress. It is also doubtful whether the different physiological measures recorded correlate very highly. It is not possible to say what emotion is being detected, only that there is an emotional change.

Another point of interest is that it seems possible to record physiological evidence of emotion, without there necessarily being any awareness of emotion. Such a finding again raises the problem of defining emotion without regard to any experiential content. It is of interest in this respect that Arnold considers physiological reactions as not being truly 'emotional' but more a sign of an 'impulse to action'. She notes as an example that one of the strongest galvanic skin response stimuli is the sound of one's name. The arousal reaction is the reaction by which an organism attends to new stimuli and mobilizes itself to deal with them. It is similar in scope to what the Russians call the orientation reaction. Although it is characterized by muscular, EEG and autonomic nervous system changes, certain studies question whether such a reaction is a simple one. It would certainly appear that attempts to measure it by only one variable (for example, the galvanic skin response) are unlikely to succeed because of variations between individuals and within one individual over time.

Studies using psychophysiological reactions have indicated an important association of the degree of reactivity with general ratings of behavioural stability and discharge success in psychopathic patients. It was found that the latter, compared with controls, contained more over- and under-reactors. For example, the galvanic skin response in a standardized experiment tends to be more or less marked in such patients. These abnormally reactive subjects were those rated the most unstable in ward behaviour and had the worst prognosis on discharge. But once again the lack of comparability of patients from one hospital to another or in the same hospital at different times makes generalization difficult.

Empirical measures of emotion are commonly derived from many standard psychological techniques such as questionnaires and inventories, Rorschach responses (particularly the type and extent of response to the colour and shading of the ink blots) and responses to stimuli such as Thematic Apperception Test. It can readily be appreciated that possible measures of emotion can cover a wide range of material ranging from physiological reactions to introspective accounts of emotional experience.

Word-association techniques of various kinds have a fairly long history in the measurement of emotional factors, especially in the investigation of emotional problems and 'complexes'. As we have noted the person is given a word and asked to reply with the first association that comes to mind. Lists of common associations are available so that it can be readily seen if a particular association is an unusual one, possibly of emotional significance. Even if the associations are common ones, emotional significance might be inferred by a delay in responding or by some physiological reaction such as a galvanic skin response or an increase in pulse rates. Such word-association techniques have long been applied in the so-called lie detection methods.

It is clear that emotion is rather an unwieldy concept and attempts have been made to limit or discard the concept altogether in order to render experimentation more precise. Nevertheless, any attempt to discuss emotions in entirety must still include the complex variations of experience, physiological systems and behavioural manifestations as noted here. Although the field contains many detailed experiments, particularly with regard to physiological responses and to learning theory, generally applicable explanatory concepts are few. Until emotion has been satisfactorily delineated in this way it has to be admitted that we are far from adequate understanding and measurement.

This state of affairs is most unfortunate for the psychiatrist, who spends much of his time dealing with emotional disturbance. He may come to redefine some terms and has to some extent already done so, as when he considers anxiety responses in terms of learning and the appropriateness or otherwise of stimuli. It is unlikely that the concept of emotion can be displaced from its fundamental position in the consideration of affective psychoses unless the hopes of the use of a physiological model are realized. Even then, primary diagnosis may continue to rest on observation of the emotional state. In such states at least the emotion experienced by the patient is appropriate to his behaviour even though both are inappropriate to circumstances. A far more difficult problem, particularly for those psychologists who maintain a wholly behaviourist view, is posed by the affective incongruity shown by some schizophrenics. Redefinition at present seems unlikely to resolve this problem, nor is there any satisfactory explanation or methods of measurement of the phenomenon beyond simple observation.

6

Motivation

Disorders of motivation

Motivational change is rarely considered to be an important feature of illness but it has a considerable place in the folklore of disease and may be worth more serious consideration than it sometimes gets. The lassitude and disinclination for any effort which arises in the course of many illnesses is well known and cannot always be accounted for solely in terms of disease process. Further, common usage implies that some patients 'fight back' while others 'give up' and die. Such observations, if they could be substantiated, would indicate a profound change in individual motivation which would be worth intensive study.

Changes and disturbance of motivation arise in many psychiatric illnesses. The patient with a depressive illness may become motivated to kill himself. Schizophrenic patients often show marked apathy. Indeed, a method of intensive treatment of schizophrenia by activation and socialization has been called re-motivation. A number of studies have in fact given some support to the theory that schizophrenics are poorly motivated and that this can account for many of their symptoms and characteristics in different spheres. The cause of such undermotivation is frequently said to be in the early social relationships of the schizophrenic within the family group. But studies of motivation in schizophrenia do not as yet indicate that in fact undermotivation is a cause of the condition. Far less support has been established for the viewpoint that schizophrenics are overmotivated, usually by excessive anxiety

In the neuroses it is often argued, especially by the psychoanalytically orientated, that symptoms are a result of frustrated or distorted motives. To the psychoanalyst, the neurotic is suffering basically because of being unable to achieve satisfaction of the basic types of motive, the sexual and the destructive. The sexual deviant is even more clearly someone who is deviant because an important motive is not satisfied in a socially acceptable manner. In psychoanalytic theory the sexual motive can be expressed in directions which would not be considered sexual by the man in the street. Eating, drinking, religion, art, in fact, almost any object of personal motivation (and its disorders) may be said to be versions of the sexual motive. Even if such an argument is an invalid one (at least as a general principle) there is little doubt that any area of motivation clearly also has its concomitant of possible motivational difficulty. Anorexia nervosa could perhaps be considered an uncommon specific motivational disturbance. It is complemented by the even rarer condition of bulimia.

There may be some profit in considering some of the varieties of psychopathy in terms of motivation. Psychopathy is used here to mean that group of conditions characterized by an apparent inability of the individual to be guided by the long-term consequences of his actions. This often results in a relative predominance of affective biological drives with immediate hedonic satisfaction over socialized drives where any satisfaction is delayed. Such difficulties may arise either from excessive biological drive strength or a defective learning process. It will be appreciated that there is considerable scope for further investigation into motives, particularly human motives. Both psychoanalytic and learning type therapy obviously have to consider motivation and its disturbances. This subject will therefore be further mentioned in the discussion of psychotherapy.

Motives may be defined as those factors within an organism which determine and direct behaviour over extended periods of time. Their study is required in all aspects of psychology as the precise motivation of the subject is a fundamental variable in any investigation. All behaviour can be held to be motivated, but the term motive includes a variety of biological phenomena as well as the many types of intent discovered introspectively and labelled as motives by the layman. The criterion of extension in time is included in the definition to exclude, for example, simple reflexes from discussion. Such an exclusion would not be accepted by all psychologists.

When the term motive is used in this way it may be applied to both physiological and psychological data. It might be added that a discussion of motivation in physiological or psychological terms is often related to the opinion that the motive under consideration is genetically or environmentally determined. This dichotomy cannot always be maintained.

Heredity and environment

Although the importance of hereditary factors in physical characteristics of all species is generally accepted and many behaviour patterns in lower animals are regarded as innate, there is reluctance to accept that human behaviour can be genetically determined to any large extent. Controversy over the relative importance of genetic and environmental factors in behaviour has been continuous. Experimental or observational support is difficult to obtain. The studies which have been made have all been subjected to criticism whatever their standpoint.

Much of the prejudice against accepting the influence of heredity in human behaviour can be related to the belief that such behaviour is rigidly determined while plasticity of behaviour is alleged to be one of the most marked characteristics of the human organism. But animal studies do suggest that hereditary behaviour can be quite variable in at least the details of its expression. For example, the general pattern of a spider's web is species specific, but the details of individual webs in individual situations are highly variable. Furthermore, the studies of animal behaviour of Tinbergen and others suggest that many behaviour patterns are determined by both hereditary and environmental factors. For example, young chicks and ducklings appear to go through a period in which they will follow a relatively large moving object. The process is called imprinting as it appears to have a more or less permanent effect. In their normal environment this process results in the young birds following the mother. But a change of environment during the critical period can result in the birds following their owner or any other regularly recurring moving object.

The application of such concepts to human behaviour is difficult because of the problems involved in transferring experimental results from one species to another. This is particularly true with regard to humans because of their greater plasticity of behaviour and the relatively limited information-carrying capacity of the genetic apparatus. Even the influence of heredity on general intelligence has been doubted, while its effects on personality development are so interwoven with the effects of environment that it is at present impossible to disentangle them. But when quite minor details of physical structure are clearly genetically determined it is improbable that the neural organization determining behaviour is not similarly influenced. Amongst educationists it is common to believe in a period of 'readiness' for various scholastic tasks. Similarly, the difficulties of acquiring perceptual skills relatively late in life, which have been noted when sight is restored in people who have been blind from birth, suggests that certain periods of development may be critical for various functions. It is conceivable that some mechanisms akin to those of imprinting and innate releasing mechanisms are important to man.

Despite these controversies it is useful in the general discussion of motivation to consider general biological factors which are clearly influenced by inheritance and psychological factors which tend to be more readily related to the cultural and social patterns of the environment.

Biological factors in motivation

Sweeping generalizations are common in this field. It may be said that all organisms have primary drives for self-preservation and for sexual behaviour which ensure the perpetuation of the species. Parental drives, such as a maternal instinct in the female, or social drives, such as an instinct of gregariousness, may be alleged to be primary innate motives. Much behaviour can certainly be grouped under such headings but they have little value as explanatory concepts. The terms instinct, drive and need are used almost interchangeably but they are also used in somewhat more limited ways in the discussion of motivation. The following can be used as guides but different workers tend to use the same words rather differently:

Instinct: This term is best used as a descriptive label, designating complex patterns of behaviour that are specific and universal to a species, innate, requiring no learning and have biological value.

Drive: This term has been given a considerable variety of meanings. It is essentially an hypothetical concept of broad application. In the present state of this field the most acceptable definition is probably that drive is an organically (physiologically) based state which leads to the development of goal-directed behaviour. Such drives may be innate (primary) or acquired (secondary).

Need: In the present context need is essentially a sub-category of drive. It refers to a variety of specific organic deficit states, e.g. thirst, leading to behaviour resulting in a rectification of this deficit.

INSTINCTIVE BEHAVIOUR

At one time in the development of psychology, due largely to the influence of McDougall, the concept of instinctive behaviour was all-embracing. Any phenomenon (for example, sentiments and attitudes) no matter how complex was reduced to instinctive patterns. In the case of human instincts a counter-movement inevitably arose. It became unfashionable to postulate instincts as causes of behaviour (especially in man) and the term fell into relative disuse. The difficulty remains that when the term instinct is discarded, complex patterns of behaviour with an innate basis which should be studied as such tend to be ignored or examined with false premises regarding their mutability.

Important work in the field of instinct has been carried out by Lorenz and Tinbergen, among others. Their studies are concerned with the factors determining complex behaviour in animals. The example of following a moving object by young chicks described earlier is an example of imprinting. The term imprinting implies that certain patterns of innate behaviour can only appear at a certain stage of development of the organism. The behaviour may persist for the rest of the organism's life or, if not initiated by an appropriate stimulus at the right time, never appear. There may be different stimuli for releasing and for directing a response. When the response or series of responses is released there is said to be an innate release mechanism (IRM) for them. Thus very young thrushes will gape in response to tactile stimulation. Later they will gape in response to visual stimulation. The direction of gape appears to depend on the visual form perceived, as the bird's mouths strain towards the small end of visual forms having both a larger and smaller end. Many varieties of such innate responses to perceptual forms are known. The direction of flight of a silhouette may arouse an escape reaction according to whether it suggests a hawk or not. In the human baby at a certain age, it has been found that a smiling response will occur when approximations to a face (such as a mask) come into its peceptual field.

An interesting feature claimed of much instinctive behaviour is its direction to a goal. Whatever the goal, the act of attaining it is termed the consummatory response. If patterns of behaviour motivated by hunger or thirst are described this response is, obviously, eating or drinking. Other consummatory responses may be less clear-cut but are still definable, as the completion of a web or the establishment of a territorial claim. The end attained is fairly constant and characteristic of the species, but the moves made in its attainment may be highly variable and moulded by environment. The behaviour cannot be always regarded as a predetermined series of motor reflexes but must be controlled by factors in the animal's perceptual organization. Apparently the organism persists in its endeavour until some sort of matching with a predetermined pattern occurs, i.e. until the structure 'looks right'.

Increasing attention is being paid to human behaviour in the light of the ethologist's ideas. Some psychoanalysts, for example, feel that concepts such as imprinting might have an important bearing on the psychoanalysts' beliefs regarding the primary importance of the infant's behaviour. Nevertheless, it might be the ethologist himself who will have to make the more original and provocative observations in the field of human behaviour. We will later mention Lorenz's contribution to theories of aggression but Desmond Morris has made a more general claim that human behaviour cannot be understood without a consideration of its evolution. Morris suggests that evolutionary man lost his hair when he became a hunter, which involved periods of exertion resulting in heat production which had to be dissipated. Even so, Morris feels that the change from herbivore to carnivore must have involved other genetic changes. Increased sexuality might be related to the need for providing a mechanism by which partners would keep together through their offspring's lengthy period of dependance. He emphasizes that female breasts, far from being simply related to suckling, are undoubtedly sexual signals in the true sense of the word. It is also useful to reflect to what extent man's work and occupation are sophisticated developments of hunting behaviour. As such they may, therefore, be an end in themselves and not be related to consummatory acts. As with all primates, grooming behaviour is important and in man this grooming behaviour includes much conversation whose purpose is simply social consolidation. The ethologist, in fact, is now providing a probably necessary counterbalance to the views of both the learning theorist and psychoanalyst. A major limitation to both these approaches in understanding human behaviour has been their belief (explicit or implicit) that human behaviour is almost infinitely flexible in its

esponse to environmental factors. The ethologist on the other hand
tresses the importance of studying behaviour under natural con-
litions. Captive animals may well behave in an abnormal, stereo-
yped manner.

PHYSIOLOGICAL DRIVES AND NEEDS

Drive, though currently a more fashionable term than instinct, is
open to just as much misuse. If it is possible to say that any pattern
of behaviour can be due to instinct it is equally possible to attribute
it to a drive. However, the term does tend to be restricted to states
of physiological deficit. Clearly there are basic drives for food and
water but more specific chemical drives have been postulated.
Furthermore, observations of animals who feed themselves a
balanced diet when given a free choice of food and of cravings for
salt in adrenalectomized subjects suggest that drives for single
substances may develop.

Such specific drives or needs have been related to Cannon's
theory of homeostasis. It has been argued that the goal of all such
motivated behaviour is to maintain physiological homeostasis.
This, however, is not necessarily so. Some deficiency states, for
example avitaminosis A or D, do not give rise to specific hungers,
nor is sexual behaviour clearly related to an organic deficiency
state. Hungers may also develop for specific non-nutritive, possibly
harmful substances like morphine or alcohol. Here the development of a physiological dependence, which may, in the absence of
the drug, be equated with a deficiency, has been postulated. However, there is no convincing evidence for such an explanation.

Sexual behaviour is often considered to be related to a physiological drive but in many respects its characteristics differ from
those of other physiological drives. Sexual deprivation does not
result in death, nor indeed in injury. Furthermore a correction of
the deficiency underlying other organic drives results in restoration
to an optimal physiological condition, but unlimited sexual activity
after deprivation is said to result in exhaustion. In many ways it is
more reasonable to regard the sexual drive as similar to drives for
sweet stuffs, being stimulated by many environmental factors.
Nevertheless, experimental evidence suggests some dependence of
sexual behaviour on hormonal factors and on reflexes mediated by
primitive neural circuits. For example, castration of rats results in
a dimunition of sexual activity while genital reflexes survive cord
transections in mammals. This dependence on inbuilt mechanisms

G

is greater in the female than the male and diminishes as th
evolutionary scale is ascended. Nevertheless, in higher mamma
and man there is little association between hormones and sexu:
arousal and activity. Castration after puberty does not lead to
loss of sexual desire.

SATIATION AND AROUSAL

It is characteristic of behaviour motivated by a physiological nee
that when this need is satisfied the behaviour ceases. This is calle
satiation but the mechanism by which satiation occurs is nc
clearly defined. Early workers, especially Cannon, considere
that the physiological deprivation was reflected in local change
in the sensory receptors making the organism more sensitiv
to the presence of the substance it requires. Correction of the de
ficit results in correction of the local change. Subsequent exper:
mental work has made this theory untenable. Although sensor
denervation results in a failure to correct such physiological defici
this is probably due to a loss of discrimination, as electrical record
ing from sensory nerves shows that there in in fact no change i
sensory threshold.

Satiation may well be an internal phenomenon as it has bee:
found that individuals whose satiation is disturbed are able t
differentiate between their pathologically dry mouths and thirst
This differentiation could be made by postulating a central chemi
cal change. Alternatively the mechanism may still be periphera
but complex. Again some experiments have suggested that thirs
may be satiated without fluid entering the body if an oesophagea
fistula be set up. Possibly the repetitive motor acts of swallowin;
are the stimuli involved in producing satiation.

It appears that activation of any drive system involves a simila
pattern of physiological arousal. This consists of electrical activit
originating in the hypothalamus and of activity in the sympatheti
nervous system. Increasing arousal has an energizing effect whicl
at first improves performance but later disrupts the pattern o
behaviour. The more complex the task the lower the optimun
level of arousal for the most effective performance.

Electrical motivation

Stimulation by electrodes implanted in the brains of animals ha
been found to result in both positive and negative motivation

Electrodes implanted in the vicinity of the medial lemniscus and postero-ventral nucleus of the thalamus of the cat can be used as 'punishment'. To avoid this 'punishment' the cat will learn. Similarly, animals will learn to activate electrodes placed in other parts of the brain. The septal area has been found most effective for the rat and the caudate for the cat. These brain parts are related to the diencephalic systems which are known to play a part in motivation. All these factors are considered to be integrated by a central excitatory system, located in the diencephalon and probably in the hypothalamus. This system is considered to be controlled by an inhibitory system, while both are influenced by a variety of internal and external factors.

It is apparent that there is a close relationship between the 'rewarding' and 'punishing' aspects of motivation and emotional responses; the latter are discussed elsewhere (p. 113). Further consideration of motivation will now involve the introduction of more clearly psychological factors, amongst them pain and pleasure, reward and punishment. These factors may often be derived from the primary biological drives by learning processes. Therefore it is to be expected that they may show considerable variation between cultures and between individuals. We propose to classify all these factors as psychological. One of these factors differs from the rest in that it overlaps both groups and will be considered separately.

Incentives

Incentives are defined as factors external to the organism which determine behaviour that bears a directional relationship to them. They may be positive or negative. Many incentives interlock with corresponding drives. Thus where thirst is the relevant drive, water is the incentive. Activity has been shown to be related to the relevance and quantity of the incentive. Furthermore it has been shown that rats will learn to run to a large reward even when they should also have learnt that they will be unable to obtain much of it. This is perhaps relevant to the effect on the human of the large reward on the Treble Chance. A large but unlikely reward is more effective in determining behaviour than probable but small rewards. Football pools winners, of course, obtain money, a commodity with little intrinsic value but a symbol which can obtain many things. We learn to respond to symbolic incentives and they can also be used with higher animals, like chimpanzees, as well as in man.

Negative incentives, like electric shocks, have been used in producing avoidance learning in animals. It has been found that the avoidance reaction may become conditioned to the experimental situation, and avoiding behaviour induced by features of the experimental room. Affective arousal is associated with these phenomena and it has been claimed that this is the learning process which results in neurosis in man.

In man incentives may be purely verbal. The use of praise and blame to motivate and control behaviour is a standard technique in all human societies. Verbal praise or reproof may be reinforced by physical techniques in childhood but in adequately socialized adults such reinforcement is not usually necessary. Some experiments have been carried out on the relative efficacy of praise and blame. In general the results are found to vary from individual to individual and from setting to setting. Early work showed that with schoolchildren praise was more effective than blame but that any comment at all was better than none. If a choice had to be made between consistent praise and consistent blame, praise appeared the most effective, but not invariably so. Children who feel inferior are said to be more highly motivated by praise, whereas self-confident children may be more stimulated by reproof.

Psychological factors in motivation

Incentives have been shown to stimulate any type of motivated activity, whether due to biological or psychological needs. Biological drives and needs have been discussed. We will now turn to the more personal and cultural motives. This division is admittedly rather artificial, particularly as it is difficult to determine which should be regarded as primary. Most psychological motives are said to be learnt, the pattern to be learnt being determined by the environment. Obviously those motives respected by the culture will be taught and may well determine many facets of the individual's motivational structure. For instance, our present-day culture places a high value on material success. It is possibly a consequence of this that an 'achievement motive' can be defined. Small sub-groups of our culture may not rate this type of success so highly. Their aims may be religious or humanitarian. It is apparent that many of our highly qualified but poorly paid workers in the social services accept a different value system from that of other groups in the community. They, too, may have an 'achievement motive' but it may be difficult to assess by ordinary standards of achievement. The different direction of their motivation may be determined by differences in the sub-culture in which they were brought up.

On the other hand, changes in the pattern of culturally approved motives may arise as a consequence of changes in individual motives or their mode of expression. Before the 1939–45 war and perhaps more strongly recently, we see efforts made by people who are motivated by self-preservation (among other things) to undermine the culturally accepted motive of patriotism. Similarly, some of the recent changes in attitude to certain aspects of sexual behaviour may be related to the influence of personal motives. An important motive or set of motives, at least in our culture, which often determines many activities, is that pertaining to the self.

SELF-ESTEEM

Self-esteem is perhaps the most important of the complex of attitudes surrounding the concept of self. This concept is built up by the consequences of social interaction and the beliefs incorporated in it change and develop with experience. The maintenance of an acceptable system of beliefs about the self may well be an extremely powerful motive for action. Indeed, it has been said that a useful way to view the syndrome of depressive illness is as a failure of this motive or its replacement by a system based on self-denigration. The motivational structure modifies both perception and behaviour. While in the normal person events are, in general, perceived in relation to a satisfactory self concept, tending to confirm it, the position is reversed in depression, all events tending to reinforce the conviction of inadequacy and uselessness. Adler based much of his theory of individual psychology on the need to preserve an adequate self concept. For example, feelings of inferiority might be compensated for by the development of a persistent will to achieve. Failure in such an attempt may be a source of emotional disturbance.

Examples of the difficulties produced by attacking the self concept are also shown in various industrial and social situations. Strikes have been called because the status of workers has been undermined or the name of the task suggests that it is done by those who are good for nothing else. Similarly it may be that part of the controversy over the eleven-plus examination was a result of its efficiency rather than the reverse.

Freudian theory, too, has relevance to the problem of the preservation of self-esteem. Here the ego or self is viewed as keeping the balance between the mainly biological motives of the id and the socially approved motives which have been learnt and incorporated into the super-ego. The ego must reconcile the claims of id, super-ego and external environmental forces. Failure in this task is claimed to result in anxiety, guilt, depression or other psychiatric symptoms. Many topics in psychotherapeutic interviewing develop into discussions of the self. A questionnaire known as the IPM (Interpersonal Perception Method) has been evolved in an attempt to examine the self's view of the other's view of him. Similarly some of the more complex tests of individual personality structures (p. 63) have been concerned with examining the way the patient sees himself with respect to others and in relation to his own self ideal.

HABITS AND FUNCTIONAL AUTONOMY

Many behaviour patterns, whatever their origin, become modified in various ways by learning but eventually cease to change. The final pattern is so well learnt that it can be performed without conscious thought. Habits are well known examples of such patterns although they are not well understood. Common examples of habitual behaviour are waking in the morning at a fairly specific time, the choice of a regular route from one place to another and the eating of poultry at Christmas. A very large amount of behaviour is habitual and forced changes in habit patterns commonly produce a certain amount of disturbance, emotional and sometimes physical.

Allport has extended the idea of habit into his concept of functional autonomy. He considers that all human behaviour is so modified by the environment that it is pointless to consider biological drives. Instead he argues that patterns of behaviour, once thoroughly learnt, become self-perpetuating and highly individual. These patterns become autonomous desires which persist for long periods, perhaps indefinitely.

DEPENDENCE AND DOMINANCE

Most children reveal a pattern of dependency on their parents, perhaps diminishing when they start school. Such dependency is particularly shown by the very young, especially on the mother, and might be related to bodily needs such as feeding. Harlow's classic study of the rearing of baby monkeys indicated that the need for bodily contact was more important than food (p. 70).

With human babies it is also important to stress the importance of bodily contact as in cuddling.

Individuals always show dependence or submission to others at some time and there are obviously individual variations. Dominance is the opposite to dependence but these two can be closely related. The so-called 'authoritarian' personality is dominant to people of less power and status, but submissive to those of greater power and status. Dominance includes the need for power and people strong in dominance will struggle for position. It might be argued that natural selection has favoured the survival of dominance. In most known human societies and in monkeys, males are dominant and the injection of further male sex hormones produces more aggression and dominance. Despite this there are important learned aspects to dominance. Children identify with their parents, who are dominant figures by virtue of their role, their greater knowledge or simply their greater physical size.

AGGRESSION

Cultures as well as individuals vary enormously in the amount of aggression they show. For example, murder (and suicide) vary in incidence. As with many motives, aggression is thought to result partly from instinctive origins and partly from childhood experiences. Children are thought to show more aggression if they receive physical punishment. Boys appear more overtly aggressive than girls whatever the cause.

Lorenz stresses that aggression has to be distinguished from predation. Lorenz feels that aggression is closely bound up with the defence of territory (but is also a defence used by a cornered animal). Territory defence is associated with mating and the implication is that the related patterns of aggression are genetically determined. Within a species capable of harming each other, the aggressive behaviour patterns connected with territorial defence become ritualized and non-harmful. But in man, as a primate, aggression was not so ritualized as he was not capable of instantly harming his fellows. This distinction can be seen throughout the animal world. Thus there are built-in inhibitions on a wolf's behaviour but not that of an animal like a hare who normally is non-aggressive. Therefore it is animals like hares who kill each other when under abnormal conditions such as captivity. In man, the abnormal condition is the development of tools and weapons which render him a dangerous animal. Lorenz argues that modern man is, therefore, one in whom there are no built-in inhibitions to aggression, although he is now a dangerous animal. It is in such a context that aggression in man, including wars, has to be examined, as much as in the context of cultural determinants and individually acquired motives. Man's sexual prowess contributes to population explosions, and it has been noted that mammals, when reaching a population density similar to that in human cities, often suffer from massive breakdowns in behaviour.

ACHIEVEMENT AND AFFILIATION

Although probably arising from the need to maintain a positive self concept, an achievement motive has been described. Extensive research has been done on this, particularly by McClelland and his associates. The main importance of this is that some progress has been made in measuring the need for achievement. Such a need is probably an important one in Western culture, especially the United States.

Schachter has considered the psychological effects of an hypothesized need for affiliation. He maintains that man is unable to tolerate social isolation, is strongly motivated to establish relationships with others, both individual and in groups, and suffers frustration when this need is denied. This may be related to the introversion–extraversion dimensions of the individual personality structure if extraversion is defined in terms of sociability.

Group motivation

The motives of a group cannot be considered simply as the algebraic sum of the motives of its members, except possibly when the numbers are very small, as on a committee. Even then it is well known that the motives of a committee may be those of its most dominant member. In larger organizations a certain degree of autonomy will develop. Furthermore, the group develops motives directed towards the group's preservation such as loyalty and conformity. Such motives can be derived from personal motives directly while the motives of the whole group can at times be best examined if the group is regarded as an individual entity with its own goals. Thus, willingness to die in war is a triumph of motivation to preserve a group as an entity over the individual biological motivation to survive. Group phenomena will be discussed more fully later.

The measurement of motivation

It is fairly easy to make some form of measurement in animals of those motives which we have classified as biological. There are four main methods. First, a general measure of undirected drives is the assessment of gross bodily activity. This may be either general, as when rats run in a rotating drum, or restless activity assessed from the movements of a device such as a spring suspended cage. A systematic relationship has been found between activity and drive. Thus, until limited by physical impairment, activity increases steadily in rats deprived of food or water. Other factors like environmental temperature or diurnal variation in activity complicate the picture so a careful control of the conditions of measurement must be maintained if this method is to be successful.

The second method is to measure the magnitude of the consummatory response. This will measure the intensity of the pre-existing drive directed to that goal. It has the advantage that it is not affected by physical impairment but its measurement is not always easy as the consummatory behaviour is often interrupted by pauses which become longer and more frequent as the need becomes satiated. Furthermore in some cases it is difficult to specify the response, for example, in the avoidance of various stimuli. In some cases it may be specified in terms of the 'innate reflex pattern'. Thus in the male rat the consummatory sexual resonse may be measured in terms of latency and frequency of mounting, pelvic thrusts, intromissions and ejaculations.

Third is the obstruction method. Here the animal has to pass some barrier, either simply mechanical and demanding work or punitive as an electrified grid. The degree of obstruction necessary to stop the animal is then the measure of motivation. Some of the results with this technique differ from those in the first two, particularly in the case of hunger or thirst, where the level attained at first falls off quite rapidly. It may measure a different aspect of motivation. Despite these discrepancies the obstruction method is a valuable standard test.

Similarly, with people, it is clear that they vary in the degree to which they pursue the various goals of sex, food, affiliation and so on. But it is obviously difficult to make the same kind of studies just described in work with animals. It is, however, possible for friends to rate a person for his strength of motivation. Questionnaires and inventories have also been constructed which have been validated against reported behaviour. Projective methods can also be used to estimate the strength of various motives. Here difficulty arises. First, is the indicated motive conscious or unconscious? Second, is the motive expressed only in fantasy and not in actual behaviour? A further point worth stressing about motives is their tendency to be organized in a changing, hierarchical manner. A drowning man will probably not be concerned with his sexual motivation. If he is rescued, his motivation and its organization will change. Such a hierarchical but changing organization of motives is characteristic in behaviour. Yet again, more complication is introduced where behaviour at any one time is determined by an interacting complex of motives.

Fourth, the performance of a learned response is closely related to motivation. Rather surprisingly it is not the rate of learning that is affected. When the asymptote of learning is reached, however, the latency of the new response, the number of errors made and the strength and frequency of the performance are all related to the degree of motivation and incentive.

Measurement of the psychological factors in motivation is really in an early stage. Some progress has been made with the assessment of the achievement motive. Despite the difficulties noted above, fantasy activity is used as one means of assessment of motivation and can be tapped by means of projective tests such as the Thematic Apperception Test (TAT). An attempt at a more general assessment of motivation has been made by Murray who lists some thirty psychological needs and has developed techniques of ordering them according to their importance to the individual. Freudian and other psychotherapeutic techniques are often concerned with the explanation of motives and the assessment of their relative importance but work in this field remains mainly descriptive.

Cattell has made an interesting factor-analytic approach to the study and measurement of motives. He claims that such studies have established ergs (or ergic drives) of sex, gregariousness, parenthood, exploration, escape, self-assertion and super-ego. These are considered to be basically innate in origin and it is interesting that they compare well with the lists of instincts that were drawn up at the turn of the century. All of Cattell's instincts, for example, are listed by McDougall with the exception of the last one, which is Freudian. Environment and learning go on to produce meta-ergs (or sentiments) which, of course, are potentially infinite in number. Cattell describes a few which he has studied and which tend to be fairly universal, such as religious interest or self sentiment. Whatever the particular motive, Cattell has again produced factor studies concerning the source of the strength of the motive. Primary factors here are labelled id, ego, super-ego, unconscious physiological interests and interests from repressed complex sources. These five first-order factors reduce to two second-order factors; first a factor of 'integrated, self sentiment interests' (involving the first three); the second a factor of 'unintegrated, unconscious interests' (involving the last two).

Cattell's study of motive often produces rather negative feelings in psychologists, probably because he seems to be attached to a rather obviously McDougall–Freud mixture. On the other hand, the appearance of such motives from his studies may only serve to confirm the impressions of these earlier writers. Moreover, one is now being given the chance to measure a more scientific looking motivation system. Cattell in fact envisages the psychologist as rigorously measuring such motives and the personality factors noted earlier to elicit the individual's dynamic structure or lattice. Such extensive and intensive measurement does require rather precise calculations and the use of computer methods.

PART II

Treatment

The Varieties of Psychotherapy

The word psychotherapy tends to be used in a very limited way to define those forms of psychological treatment whose techniques and underlying theoretical assumptions can be traced back to the pioneer work of Freud. While little can be done to change this general usage now, we shall take a view which is broader (and more correct semantically) and define psychotherapy as any method of psychological treatment. This brings into discussion techniques as diverse as the use of placebos, hypnosis, behaviour therapy and psychoanalysis.

It is a curious fact that in this country, although the view has been expressed that what we have called fundamental background distortions (p. 46) may well be most appropriately treated by the psychologist or the educator while the more recently developed 'illnesses' come to the psychiatrist, it is the psychiatrists and particularly the psychoanalysts who have adopted a long-term 'historical' approach, whereas the psychologists have, with their 'behaviour therapy', concentrated on rapid symptom relief. At present, therefore, there is little logical demarcation of function and patients are treated in the ways which seem appropriate to their condition by those with particular training and experience in the method involved. In the United States analytic methods of treatment are used by clinical psychologists to a greater extent than in this country while various other techniques may be used by all workers in the field. We propose in this section to describe in outline the different psychotherapies and to discuss their techniques and the theories underlying them. Our discussion is in no way intended to teach psychotherapy of any type but only to present an introduction to the wide range of methods available. This introduction will indicate ways in which information from other branches of psychology can be applied in therapy, the possible present and speculative use of psychological techniques in various aspects of psychotherapy. In particular, psychological tests can be used to select patients for therapy and to assess the progress and results of whatever method is used.

For the purpose of discussion we propose to classify the psychotherapies into those based on the theories of the psychoanalysts, those based on the work of experimental psychologists, and miscellaneous techniques. The 'analytic' and 'behavioural' approaches are based on differing, but not necessarily mutually exclusive, theoretical approaches. A variety of other 'therapies', like hypnosis or the use of drugs in a psychotherapeutic setting, are in our view best regarded for present purposes as techniques which can be used in association with one or more of the basic methods.

Although psychotherapy has developed through treatment of individual patients, the analytic theories have also been applied to the treatment of patients in groups. Originally used as a substitute for individual treatment, the method is thought by some therapists to have certain advantages of its own. Treatment of this kind usually involves small groups, but its underlying assumptions inform most of the large group methods of the 'therapeutic community' type. Despite some isolated attempts the behaviour therapies have not been used much with groups but other experimentalists have studied group behaviour and it should prove possible to apply their findings to the treatment of patients.

In this section on treatment it will be evident that (apart from the case of behaviour therapy) psychology has contributed less than in the more formally studied areas already discussed. Behaviour therapy is said by some to constitute the psychologist's scientific method applied to the field of psychotherapy. Many psychiatrists and psychologists would consider such a view to be premature. Possibly some other aspects of psychotherapy could, with advantage, be directly studied and developed by psychologists. At present, the psychologist or psychiatrist engaging in the field of psychotherapy often tends to do so without the necessary evaluations that would automatically be made in, say, the field of drug therapy. Many problems exist in the design of experiments to assess the effects of psychotherapy even at the basic level of deciding what variables to measure and finding means of measuring them. A few techniques mainly derived from personality assessment are available and there are some studies concerned only with results which get by on very simple assessments. These unfortunately tell us little about the process of change and all too often only inform us hat nothing significant (or measurable) has happened. As all sychotherapy involves a social group of at least two members ocial psychology, too, should be able to make a contribution but s yet has not done so.

Some discussion of social psychology has also been included in his section, particularly in reference to small and large groups. Many group studies are based on therapeutic groups but there are lso many studies of social groups which might well be relevant to herapeutic groups. Furthermore, considering the hospital as a ociety of therapeutic intent leads inevitably to considering social rocesses as being exemplified in the hospital. By using our knowedge of social psychology in the hospital setting, the therapeutic alue of the hospital can be improved.

8

Psychoanalytic Therapy and its Derivatives

The word 'analytic' as applied to psychotherapy has now taken on a fairly broad meaning. Ultimately all therapies of this type derive from the pioneer work of Freud, although many of the concepts and techniques have changed as the subject has developed. There is a confusing collection of names attached to the different schools of 'analytic' theory and practice. These include, for instance, Freudian psychoanalysis itself, individual psychology (Adler), non-directive psychotherapy (Rogers), interpersonal psychiatry (Sullivan) and others. Some of these names have specific connotations, particularly psychoanalysis, which refers to the theoretical system and method of treatment founded by Freud and continued by members of psychoanalytical institutes around the world. To become a psychoanalyst requires membership of an institute and this in turn requires a training which includes a personal training analysis. Other schools also have their training and membership requirements. Psychoanalysis is often treated with deference by the educated public and is often regarded by novelists and biographers as a modern scientific theory. We shall see that it is not properly scientific, nor (like behaviour therapy) can it fairly be called modern. Its roots lie firmly in the nineteenth century.

Furthermore, it often appears to outsiders that training requirements in psychoanalysis are such as to ensure that people recognized as psychotherapists have been thoroughly indoctrinated with the beliefs and theories of their particular school. The system of thought and technique of treatment often appear to have a quasi-religious flavour. This flavour is intensified by the common attitude that the only people who are competent to judge or criticize the system are its qualified practitioners who are, of course, already committed both intellectually and financially. Many people who accept parts, often large parts, of these systems cannot accept the training requirements and the abrogation of their critical faculties which these seem to imply but continue to practise psychotherapy 'on analytic lines'. Normally they style themselves 'eclectic' psychotherapists. This is a reasonable point of view but there is some danger in the term and the approach. This danger is that therapy may be carried out against an inadequate, or even internally inconsistent theoretical background using a poor, often self-taught, technique. It is difficult to assess the extent of such dangers because of the lack of generally accepted evidence about the effects of psychotherapy, beneficial or otherwise. Opponents of analytic techniques claim that they have no beneficial effects at all. Perhaps they should also accept that they can do no harm either. However, patients undergoing psychotherapy can be observed to show a variety of phenomena, pleasant and unpleasant for them, which appear to be related to the treatment. Although the evidence for such phenomena may be stigmatized as anecdotal we consider that it is adequate to justify the conclusion that something does happen during psychotherapy.

We have already defined psychoanalysis as that body of psychological theory and treatment techniques founded by Freud and currently accepted by the various psychoanalytic institutes. The theoretical structure of the system is not so monolithic as is sometimes thought but there are certain assumptions which are fundamental to it. Our discussion will be based in the first instance on Freud's views, as summarized in *An Outline of Psychoanalysis* to which the reader is referred for a fuller but still didactic presentation. More detailed accounts are presented in Freud's extensive writings, while an elementary discussion of recent changes in the theory is available (Brown 1961) and there are some useful books on technique.

Psychoanalytic theory describes a theory or model of the mind and its development and function. The model attempts to be a dynamic one, concerned with the balance and interplay of forces, derived from observations made on psychiatric patients, introspection (in the case of Freud himself) and the analysis of trainees. It has often been pointed out that the subjects used in the formative years of psychoanalysis were nineteenth-century Viennese drawn from a restricted social class. Consequently, it has been argued that psychoanalysis, if it is true at all, is only true for such a population. Modifications are necessary in considering people of other times and places. In its final form two opposed instincts, Eros and Thanatos, are postulated and various forms of behaviour are related to their effects interacting in different ways. However, much of the early work was concerned with the viscissitudes of the sexual drive and this is still considered to be the major factor in the causation of personality difficulties while its direction and variation during development constitute the main factors in personality development. It is this sexual drive which is usually referred to as libido.

The system in which this force operates is divided into three levels, conscious, pre-conscious and unconscious. These levels define those parts of mental content which are in awareness, or can be brought to awareness, or are inaccessible. Functioning within this matrix are three mental 'organs', the id, the ego and the super-ego, while the system as a whole is influenced by the pressure of external reality. The ego is regarded as the active part of the system in the sense that it has a manipulative function, modifying the behaviour of the organism to achieve a compromise solution to the conflicts aroused by the pressure of the other forces. The system is goal-directed, the aim of the ego being assumed to be the achievement of a state of balance and tranquillity. It exercises its functions at all levels, having a large unconscious component in addition to its more commonly recognized conscious and preconscious elements. For example, the ego defence mechanism of repression is unconscious and, therefore, quite different from conscious processes of suppression.

The id is entirely unconscious. It is regarded as the repository of all the basic drives of the organism. These drives are constantly seeking overt expression, but their expression will in many cases cause conflict either with the ego because they are antipathetic to the demands of external reality or with the super-ego. It is, therefore, necessary for their expression to be prevented or, where this is impossible, for them to be transformed in such a way that their modified form will pass the other constraints.

The constraints of external reality are fairly well defined, embodying as they do the limitations imposed on behaviour by the laws of physics and society. Those of the super-ego, however, are more complex. This 'organ' is formed from the ego during early childhood by various means, but mostly by the incorporation and separation into an entity of a body of precepts derived from people who are regarded as having authority. Authority in this context implies the ability to give or withhold satisfaction. Most of these ideas are derived from the parents, particularly the father, but others may arise from parent-like figures, such as school-teachers, and others from siblings or peers. These latter influences arise, of course, much later in life and are not so easily incorporated but nonetheless their influence can often be detected.

The conscious and preconscious parts of the super-ego can be roughly equated with the 'conscience' but the more important part is said to be unconscious. Here are to be found a large number of constraints upon behaviour which are unknown to the individual and which remain unverbalized but which either prevent certain forms of behaviour altogether or arouse guilt and anxiety when they occur. As the determinants of these responses are unconscious the behaviour appears irrational and is not subject to modification in the light of reason.

As an oversimplified example, we may consider the situation of someone who has bought an unsatisfactory article in a shop. At present it is regarded, at least in some parts of society, as socially highly desirable to return the article and insist on its replacement. However, some people, although accepting the principle, are either unable to do this or experience great anxiety at the time. The anxiety may be partly rationalized as a fear that there will be a 'scene' but even if we disregard the possibly neurotic fear of 'scene' the explanation remains unrealistic as such a contretemps is extremely rare. It is possible that a reason for this behaviour is that some of these people have, in their unconscious super-ego, a strong prohibition of aggressive behaviour. This will have resulted in a repression by the ego of any aggressive impulses arising in the id. Where this process occurs there tends to be considerable generalization of the concept of aggression so that any behaviour which expresses a conflict of any type becomes classified as aggressive. Expression of such behaviour will then be forbidden or, where indulged in, even to a slight extent, punished by feelings of guilt and anxiety. Associated with this situation may be a fear, partly justified, of uncontrollable outbursts of rage. Here a situation may arise where the stimulus to aggression is sufficient to overcome the prohibition of the super-ego and because the individual is unable to make a controlled response the flood gates burst and aggressive behaviour occurs in an overwhelming fashion. (Freudian theory has been aptly described as an exercise in hydrodynamics.) This aggression may be outwardly or inwardly directed and in the latter case may lead to self-destruction. This hypothesis then, defines a recognizable type of person, normally mild, even submissive, but liable to sudden outbursts of rage, often for little reason, as the final precipitant may be only the last of a series of insults, followed by periods of remorse and apprehension.

Given a mental structure, psychoanalytic theory describes a process of development in which the individual passes through a series of stages determined partly by the mode of expression of individual urges and partly by its relationship with parental figures. Development may be wholly or partly arrested (fixated) at the different stages or the individual may, under stress, regress to a greater or lesser extent to an earlier stage. The stages are defined by the relative predominance of the erogenous zones, that is, those parts of the body from which libidinal satisfaction can be acquired. These are, in order of appearance, the mouth, the anus and the genitals. Normally the individual passes in succession through phases in which each of these gives libidinal satisfaction, ending at a stage of genital primacy. It is considered that this evolution is completed in the first five years of life and that at the end of it the individual encounters the Oedipus situation. The resolution of this situation results in a generalized suppression of libido and the onset of the latency period which lasts until libido is mobilized again in association with the biological changes of puberty. It might be noted in passing that fixation or regression to a particular stage is thought to be associated with particular kinds of mental illness. The oral stages are linked with the psychoses—the early oral sucking stage with schizophrenia and the subsequent oral biting stage with manic-depressive psychosis. The anal expulsive stage is linked with paranoid (projective) mechanisms and the anal retentive stage with obsessive–compulsive phenomena. Difficulty at the genital to oedipal stage with its use of repression is linked with hysterical mechanisms.

The Oedipus situation and its resolution are of great importance in this hypothetical scheme of mental development. It describes the difficulties of the male child whose sexuality has reached the genital level and who desires incestuous relationships with his mother. This arouses the hostility of the father whose reaction will be (or is feared to be) to punish the child by castration. The female child creates similar anxieties either because of her desire to possess a penis or because she believes she has lost hers as a punishment. For some time the object of analytic treatment was to attain recall of these situations and their appropriate emotions. Recovery was thought to follow adequate catharsis.

Freud, however, continued his investigations beyond this stage. His final formulation is based on the concepts of Eros and Thanatos (the instinctive forces of 'life' and 'death'). This is not wholly accepted even by psychoanalysts. The most important later development of the system is the concept of the transference neurosis and it is the analysis of this phenomenon which is now the major part of therapy. A transference neurosis develops during therapy when the patient views the therapist in the role of a person whose behaviour had emotional significance in the past. The patient reacts to the therapist as if he were that person (usually a parent) while the therapist's function is to observe this reaction, note where it is pathological and attempt to modify it by interpretation to the patient of the nature and meaning of his behaviour. Some of the more recent derivations of psychoanalysis, for instance those proposed by Harry Stack Sullivan and his co-workers, consist essentially of a whole-hearted application of this analysis of the transference. The therapy is considered as an analysis of the 'here and now' situation and all the patient's behaviour is regarded as governed by the transference and subject to interpretative comment.

Such comments are, of course, a divergence from the earlier techniques of psychoanalysis, which relied on the technique of free association to enable the patient to understand his own behaviour and motivations and where the intention was for the therapist to be as inert as possible, acting only as a figure on whom the patient could project his fantasies. The content and nature of interpretation will vary from one therapist to another and will be related to the therapist's attitude towards some of the more recent developments.

In this brief outline of psychoanalytic ideas of personality development and adjustment, reference has been made to mechanisms such as repression and projection. A number of such mechanisms postulated by the psychoanalysts do occur in mental functioning. They are regarded as defence mechanisms which enable the ego (given the psychoanalytic structure of the mind) to function more or less efficiently. They are also, however, when too weak or strong, evidence for maladjustment.

The most well known and probably most important mechanism is that of repression. Repression, an unconscious mechanism (as indeed are all defence mechanisms), prevents material becoming conscious which is unacceptable, for one reason or another, to conscious life. Repression enables us to forget unpleasant and unacceptable experiences. Among other things, it is held to account for our inability to remember both the first years of life and our dreams. Projection occurs when we ascribe to others feelings and attitudes (usually unacceptable) which are really our own: 'I hate X' becomes 'X hates me'. (The opposite of projection is identification where we modify our ideas and behaviour after someone we have taken as an ideal. Such a process is held to be common in a child's development where he uses the parents as such ideal models.) Certain ideas, impulses and so on become channelled into socially acceptable directions by a process known as sublimation. In other words sexual and aggressive motives become the springs of, say, artistic creations or religious ideas. Reaction formation, the name given to the mechanism whereby an unacceptable impulse becomes substituted by its opposite: 'I hate X' becomes 'I like X'. It has been pointed out that such mechanisms as projection and reaction-formation, particularly when combined, can cover all the possibilities of overt behaviour. As such, they are virtually impossible to verify according to ordinary scientific principles.

All these phenomena can occur as normal mental processes as well as in abnormal states but fixation, where behaviour remains at an earlier stage of development or regression where a person's behaviour becomes more characteristic of an earlier stage of development are considered to require unusual items to bring them into action and are usually regarded as pathological.

Adler's ideas are hardly recent, indeed many of them are so widely accepted that their originator is forgotten, but his arguments that compensatory mechanisms to inferiority feelings give rise to an individual life style result in a much more directive therapy. This therapy seeks to explain the life style of the patient, particularly the manipulative aspects of his neurosis, and thereby to bring about changes in his behaviour. Adler argued that it is not only the weak and the timid who feel inferior. As a child everyone suffers from inferiority feelings, if only because of his small size and lack of knowledge compared to adults. The individual can adopt various techniques to deal with his inferiority feelings which may or may not be successful.

A similar didactic approach characterizes the methods adopted by the school of Otto Rank. Here, however, one may suspect that the intensity of the patient's 'resistance' may be related to the implausibility of this group's basic assumption that all neuroses are derived from birth trauma. Melanie Klein formed an important off-shoot from orthodox psychoanalysis. Her postulation of various developmental stages in the first year or so of life tends to undercut some of the theoretical neatness of the original Freudian scheme. Even more so than is usually the case in psychoanalysis, interpretation tends to be unsupported by validation.

Broader approaches, considering the patient's interactions with those around him, are taken by Sullivan, already mentioned, whose therapy is described by Fromm Reichmann. Karen Horney thought, like many, that the Freudian system was male-centred with too little consideration of cultural variations. Instead of regarding females as inadequate males she postulated that, in some cultures at least, it is the male who feels inadequate to the female because he can never take part in the child-bearing.

Jung, one of the first to break with Freud, developed an equally large, if less choate system of his own. He minimized Freud's theory of the personal unconscious and its domination by the residue of the infancy years, especially infantile sexuality. He postulated the greater importance of the collective unconscious derived from a person's phylogenetic rather than ontogenetic past. There are corresponding differences between Jungian-type analytic therapy and Freudian-type psychoanalysis. Jungian therapy stresses the naturally forward-looking, problem-solving nature of the mind rather than the backward-looking, deterministic psyche of the psychoanalysts. Much of Jungian theory forms a palatable alternative to Freudian theory but like the latter, it is essentially a system of beliefs rather than empirically verified facts. Furthermore, although there is much fascinating reading, there is a great deal, particularly in his later works, of a mystical content discordant with many modern attitudes. (Jung is also well known for his 'extraversion–introversion' typology of personality and for his studies in word-association (pp. 50, 62).)

Despite the variety of theoretical backgrounds there are many common features among analytic therapeutic techniques. In this chapter we are concerned with individual treatment and shall discuss the treatment of patients in groups later. Patients undergoing this form of treatment all attend for a series of interviews with their therapist. Normally each interview lasts for about an hour and no other person is present. The interval between sessions varies but is rarely greater than a week except for specific transient reasons. Certain rules for the patient's conduct are laid down. These usually include the requirement that he talk freely, concealing nothing from the therapist, that all expression of emotions shall be verbal as far as possible, that there shall be no contact between patient and therapist between interviews, that the patient shall refrain from disturbing and antisocial behaviour while under treatment and, when treatment is undertaken privately, that he shall pay his monthly accounts on time. Any or all of these rules may be stretched considerably during the treatment of the individual patient, but they represent an ideal which is aimed at. The first two are essential parts of the therapy; the others are more concerned with maintaining conditions under which therapy can continue and with making life tolerable for the therapist.

In return, the therapist undertakes to help the patient to conduct an exploration of his psyche in an attempt to understand the reasons why he behaves and feels as he does and hence to be able to modify his reactions. As the underlying theory holds that the symptoms of psychiatric illness arise from disturbed interpersonal relationships there is also some implication of a hope of symptomatic relief. However, at present, symptomatic relief is not guaranteed and often is not explicitly regarded as one of the goals of therapy. In pursuit of his aims the therapist agrees to accept the patient and his verbalizations and to continue treatment despite the expression of of emotions which, in other circumstances, would end any relationship. He will use his special skills to enable the patient to come to decisions about the future course of his life and will refrain from using those skills and the position which therapy gives him to modify the patient's ideas and feelings in ways which are personally gratifying.

It is not clear in what way psychotherapy works, or indeed if it works at all. Certain elements in the process are given prominence at different times and probably all play a part. Catharsis, or the dramatic re-experience of emotion connected with traumatic events, was early regarded as important and in some treatment methods, for instance the treatment of battle neurosis by abreaction with drugs, is still regarded as crucial. Here, the traumatic experience is 'relived' on several occasions and, as it were, detoxicated. Another factor in the therapy is the gaining of insight into the motivations of behaviour. It was in keeping with a climate of social and scientific optimism to believe that once these hidden motivations were uncovered they could be controlled by the rational intellect and that the patient would, therefore, improve. Although such understanding may be helpful it does not necessarily result in much improvement. The belief that it is an important factor may also be artly responsible for the suggestion that fairly high intelligence is ecessary for psychotherapy to be successful. Some writers have ressed the primary importance of allowing the patient to develop satisfying relationship with the therapist which then gives the atient a background to making more satisfactory ordinary social elationships. Obviously, such a therapeutic relationship has to be urtured by techniques which overcome the difficulties the patient ormally has in dealing with other people. What remains unclear is what is essential in the different techniques that are offered by heir various adherents.

More recently the factor of emotional relearning has been hought to be of great importance and much psychotherapy nowa-ays is conducted on this assumption. Broadly, it is assumed that he patient has always been punished by people who are emotionally mportant to him when he expresses various emotions. In the trans-erence situation which arises during therapy he re-experiences hese emotions, on this occasion directed to the therapist in which-ver role he happens to fulfil at the time. Gradually the patient earns that these emotions can be expressed in the therapeutic ituation without the feared punishment and that the therapist loes not reject him because of his feelings. From this initial emo-ional relearning the patient can go on to develop more reality orientated ways of relating to people, both within and without the herapeutic situation. Although it may be possible for such emo-ional relearning to take place without the verbal expression of eeling such expression is of great help in clarifying the process and helping the therapist to assess progress.

The object of the therapist, therefore, is to manipulate the situa-tion in such a way that the phenomena described above occur. This can be done using a 'non-directive' technique. That is, after the initial examinations and explanations have been completed in early interviews the patient is left to talk about whatever he wishes. It is considered that the whole of his conversation during therapy is re-lated to his problems and to the therapeutic situation. Every part of his conversation and every part of his behaviour is, therefore, rele-vant and liable to interpretative comment. To some extent, classi-cally analytic type therapists can be considered non-directive in that, within certain limits, no constraints are put upon what the patient says or does. On the other hand, it is clear that the beliefs held by the analyst, especially as they influence the comments and interpretation he gives to the patient, lead to a directive method of therapy. With increasing knowledge by the public of psychoanalysis, the patient knows what sort of subject he is expected to mention. Carl Rogers has been a leading exponent of a counselling technique where an attempt is made to make the therapy more truly non-directive. Here, much of what the patient says is simply turned back to him, leading him to clarify his problems himself and eventually develop his own solution.

Nevertheless there are doubts as to how far any technique can be non-directive. Some therapists, for instance, comment favourably upon exchanges of this type:

PATIENT   What shall I talk about?
THERAPIST Anything you like.
PATIENT   Can I talk about the weather?
THERAPIST If you want to pay £X to talk about the weather I don't mind.

The idea that the last comment leaves the patient free to talk about the weather if he wants to can only be maintained by therapists curiously ignorant of the principles of their art and poorly endowed with common sense.

Another pattern which has been observed runs:

THERAPIST Good afternoon.
PATIENT   Good afternoon.

Silence, more or less prolonged.

THERAPIST You seem to be feeling rather hostile today.

Such an observation, based on negligible evidence, will, with luck, arouse sufficient hostility to be self-confirming; if not, it will at least serve to tell the patient what he is expected to talk about.

These examples, however, really indicate poor techniques. Our doubts about the non-directive nature of the therapeutic situation are based more on work which suggests that the patient pays great attention to non-verbal cues from the therapist. Patients learn rapidly that certain aspects of the therapist's behaviour indicate increased or lessened attention and differing attitudes to the problem under consideration. Even leaving considerations of the transference aside it is reasonable to think that the patient will consider it advisable to concentrate upon those matters which the therapist appears to regard as important. The danger is still present in the classical psychoanalytic situation when the therapist sits outside the patient's field of vision, as the amount of small movement which he patient hears may give the necessary cues, while on occasion a light snore has been known to give negative reinforcement.

This subtle direction may occur despite the most careful attention o techniques by a skilled therapist and is probably related to the ommon observation that the patient's verbalizations tend in eneral to support the theoretical system of the therapist.

Despite the doubtful efficacy and scientific standing of these orms of therapy derived from Freud's pioneer work they are not wholly at variance with the approaches derived from the experimental psychological laboratory such as behaviour therapy. Many of the concepts and processes of psychotherapy can be translated into those of learning theory while the importance of early learning o the future development of the organism is emphasized by the work of the ethologists. Their concepts of critical phases in development are, of course, of great importance here and, if substantiated n man, will help to delineate the situations where neurotic behaviour may start. It is not inconceivable that the psychotherapeutic re-evaluation of infantile behaviour may be of help to people with personality difficulties.

Although most therapists claim a high degree of validity for the observations made in their consulting rooms this is rarely accepted by the experimental psychologist with his knowledge of the bias which can be introduced by an observer, even in more 'objective' situations. Szasz considers that such criticism is overdone and claims that much experimental psychology bears little relationship to the function of the mind. Indeed, we must agree that in many papers the need for the concept of mind is explicitly or implicitly denied. Provided the problems of observer bias are considered there is nothing wrong with observation as a scientific technique. After all, one of the oldest and in some ways most refined of sciences, astronomy, is based on observation rather than experiment, while much of the knowledge of the physiology of the human nervous system is based on observation of the changes brought about by disease processes and their correlation with post mortem findings. Our defence of observations as a scientific method must recognize that its findings should be confirmed where possible by other techniques. We have argued elsewhere that theories derived from laboratory experiments must fit the facts of clinical observation.

The clinical psychologist may develop several roles in relation to these forms of therapy. He may, of course, actually be a psychotherapist but this is rare in adult psychiatry in this country although it occurs more frequently in child guidance clinics. It is more likely that he will adopt behavioural techniques as his therapeutic medium. He may, however, help to select patients for therapy, reduce its duration by techniques which will help to delineate rapidly the psychopathology and possibly guide therapy by further similar assessments. Finally he will help to assess the results of treatment, measure the changes which occur as it goes on and formulate the mechanisms which operate and so help to improve the technique of therapy.

There are at present few standardized techniques which the psychologist may use to fulfil these functions, but some attempts have been made, using various personality measures which we have described in the chapter on personality testing (p. 63). One of the difficulties in assessing the effects of therapy of any kind is of finding techniques that are not only sensitive to change but are also valid measures of the patient's condition regardless of what the patient and therapist wish to believe. These difficulties arise both from the poverty of available psychological techniques and the vagueness or unprovable nature of the therapist's aims and concepts. Some of the methods of content analysis and interaction process analysis which are now fairly well developed may be of value, but they are most complex and time-consuming, usually requiring computer assistance.

Behaviour Therapy and Behaviour Modification

The term 'behaviour therapy' is of fairly recent origin and is currently used to include a considerable variety of techniques. These techniques have a common link, which may be rather tenuous, with the theories and results of experimental psychologists concerning learning processes. These approaches also make the fundamental assumption that mental disorder can be adequately treated by a direct attack on its signs and symptoms without the need for postulating an underlying illness. The signs and symptoms are the illness. This viewpoint is in keeping with the general behaviourist position in denying the usefulness of hypothetical variables like the unconscious or the mind. Such an approach might appear strange to the medically qualified and is not necessarily accepted by psychologists. Although the multifactorial nature of the aetiology of many diseases is increasingly recognized doctors are still trained to include as many as possible of the patient's complaints under a single cause and to treat that cause. Even where many factors may be relevant to the manifestation of a disease and to the form which it takes, as in tuberculosis or neurosyphilis, there is still a necessary cause. In these two diseases this cause in an infection with the appropriate organism, which must be present before anything can happen at all. It can be maintained that this approach remains more 'scientific' than the sometimes rather naïve sounding formulations of the behaviour therapists. On the other hand, some psychologists prefer the use of the term behaviour modification to behaviour therapy. It is argued that the term therapy implies not only disease and illness but that the area concerned is a medical preserve. Such psychologists prefer to ally their techniques and aims with those of other non-medicals who set out to change behaviour, such as teachers and educationalists. Oddly, a similar attempt to remove psychiatric disorders from the category of 'medical' illness has been made by Szasz, an eminent psychoanalyst. He claims that the humanitarian gains brought about by this classification as 'patients' have been counterbalanced by increased difficulty in behaviour modification.

Of course, some behavioural techniques have been used in rather simple ways by psychiatrists for many years. Direct removal of hysterical symptoms by hypnosis is associated with the names of Mesmer, Braid, Janet and Charcot and its inadequacies led Freud to start his investigations into psychoanalysis. Many psychiatrists have treated patients with phobic states by gradual exposure to increasing doses of the feared situation without appreciating the part played in their treatment by the mechanisms of reciprocal inhibition described by Wolpe. Aversion methods, too, have a respectable antiquity although the use of whirling chairs and similar methods is not usually dignified by this title. 'Brainwashing' techniques have some affinity with the behaviour therapies but, of course, a different purpose. Human beings have always attempted to control and alter behaviour for therapeutic or other reasons. However, it is only in recent years, with the advent of modern psychology, that psychological methods of altering behaviour have been given something of a scientific footing.

These rule of thumb methods have now been refined by the application of principles derived from the laboratory. Before discussing the therapeutic techniques at present in use we must consider in more detail the experimental background. This involves work done under two headings in standard psychological classification. The first, of course, is learning theory itself, which is fundamental to the process, while the second is motivation. This latter is considered relatively rarely in discussions of behaviour therapy, possibly because learning is considered to occur as a result of positive or negative reinforcements which are defined as stimuli which result in learning. The evident circularity of this definition gives a hint of the often difficult practical problem of selecting appropriate reinforcements and it is our contention that an understanding of motivation is necessary for this. We have discussed motivation separately (Chapter 6) and shall now present an outline of learning theory. An understanding of learning theory is a necessary antecedent to an understanding of its application in behaviour therapy. An important point to make at the outset is that there is no unified learning theory generally accepted in modern psychology. There are a number of learning theories which are usually divided into wo major groups known respectively as classical and instrumental conditioning. In recent years attempts have been made to put mathematical models forward but they are still only models for these theories.

Classical conditioning is particularly associated with the Russian, Pavlov. His famous experiments with dogs typified this technique. In his experiment a dog, restrained in a harness and thus limited in movement, is presented with food. The food is called the unconditioned stimulus (UCS) as it naturally produces in the dog a response (salivation) called the unconditioned response (UCR). Now if a bell is sounded just before the food appears on a number of occasions the sound will eventually produce salivation in the dog even if food does not follow the bell. When this happens the bell is called the conditioned stimulus (CS) and the salivation the conditioned response (CR).

If the bell is repeatedly sounded without food succeeding it the conditioned response of salivation will eventually cease to appear. It is said to have been extinguished because of an absence of reinforcement. Technically this is called experimental extinction. This extinction is held to be caused by a process of internal inhibition (in the nervous system) and is contrasted with what is called external inhibition. With the latter an unusual stimulus occurring before the conditioned stimulus (e.g. a loud noise) may produce extinction. Extinction is rather similar to the effect known as habituation in animals. If an animal is repeatedly exposed to a stimulus to which it normally reacts (possibly an innate response) the reaction will eventually disappear. The tendency for any response to wane (if only temporarily) after repetition is often called inhibition and, as reactive inhibition, is an important concept in many learning theories. Inhibition itself is not learning as it diminishes with time and rest and it has some affinity with fatigue processes. But if it is associated with particular stimuli and responses it is learned and then called conditioned inhibition. The natural recovery from inhibition with time may be important in considering the apparently spontaneous recovery of patients with various behavioural disturbances.

An important feature that appears in classical conditioning is that of generalization. For example, a bell with a different tone to that used in the original conditioning experiment will still evoke the conditioned response, although the greater the disparity in tone, the weaker the response. In fact the original experiment can

I

be complicated by having two bells of different tones. Food follow one but not the other so that the dog only develops a conditioned response to one of the bells. Now if bells intermediate in tone be tween the first two bells are used there is a point at which the dog is put into conflict. Such an experiment illustrates an example of what is called experimental neurosis although the word neurosis has been criticized here. It is a common criticism of applying learn ing theory to psychopathology that what, for example, is called neurosis by the one experimenter is not what is meant by another particularly if the second is also a psychiatrist. From such experi ments of Pavlov this theory of learning has developed to such an extent that it claims to account for all learning, including that of humans.

It has been found that for classical conditioning to occur an essential element is the closeness in time of the presentation of the conditioned and unconditioned stimuli. Classical conditioning may therefore, be called contiguity learning and has been argued to be the real principle operating in what is called instrumental learning But as we shall see the advocates of instrumental learning have also argued that the real principle involved in classical conditioning is the reinforcing agent (such as food).

Rather independently of Pavlov, J. B. Watson in America also evolved a learning theory based on a contiguity principle. Further more, he conducted a classical experiment with Albert, a little boy (eleven months when the experiment began). Every time the little boy reached out for his pet white rat a loud noise was made by striking an iron bar with a hammer. Eventually, he cried whenever the rat appeared, a learnt response which was generalized to some extent to a rabbit, a dog, a fur coat and Watson's hair. Watson speculated that, retrospectively, Albert's fears may, to a psycho analyst, represent a fear arising from forbidden contact with his mother's pubic hair.

The beginnings of instrumental conditioning theory are to be seen in the work of Thorndike who, in his law of effect, stressed the factors of reward and punishment. Behaviour that was rewarded was stamped in, behaviour that was punished was stamped out. Hull went on to develop an imposing edifice of a systematized be haviour theory containing many postulates put in a quasi-scientific manner. The final equation in the system was

$$\text{Behaviour} = \text{Habit strength} \times \text{Drive.}$$

Hull's edifice has crumbled in recent years and B. F. Skinner's sysem has become ascendent. He rejected much of Hull's work on the grounds that his theory required too many unobservable (i.e. non-behavioural) items. In his methods of operant conditioning the organism has to do something—a marked contrast to the passivity of the subject of the classical conditioning experiment. Reinforcing agents are either positive (rewarding) or negative (punishing). Reinforcers of responses are primary, such as biological needs, or secondary where they are associated with a learnt need. In his studies of schedules of reinforcement Skinner has clearly demonstrated that reinforcement can be most effective when applied at intervals, rather than on every occasion. Speech is characteristically regarded, as verbal behaviour, in the same way as non-verbal behaviour. For the behaviourist, thinking tends to be assumed to be speech which is not uttered. Such an assumption helps the behaviourist in his standpoint of only studying measurable behaviour. Skinner has developed studies of speech by simply regarding it as a particular form of behaviour, namely verbal behaviour. According to this form of orientation, the speech (or verbal behaviour) of individuals can be modified and shaped in the same way as can any other behaviour. Its acquisition and development in the child can also be accounted for on reinforcement principles, for the babble produced in the pre-speech stage of infancy contains an immense repertoire of sounds. Selection of those which are appropriate and their refinement to the required standards of accuracy are achieved by differential reinforcement, usually social. Some have argued that the formation of intelligible speech and the loss of 'baby talk' can be delayed by the too ready interpretation and reward of sounds which will later be regarded as inadequate.

Both the classical and instrumental types of learning theory have attempted to explain psychopathology in terms of learning. We have already discussed a Pavlovian type of experimental neurosis. Pavlov also thought there were individual variations in the degree to which an organism showed an excess of either of the two main forms of nervous activity—excitation and inhibition. In humans this has been linked with introversion and extraversion respectively and in neurosis with the consequent polar distinction between hysterics and psychopaths on the one hand and anxiety states, reactive depressions, obsessionals on the other (Eysenck). Eysenck has argued that, as the extravert is characterized by a greater than average tendency to build up reactive inhibition, he will be a relatively poor learner. Alternatively, the introvert will be a relatively good learner. It is claimed that such a distinction helps to account for the aetiology of these two groups of neuroses and their fundamental differences in social conformity, a product of this differential learning. Others maintain that if there is differential learning, it is of a much more selective kind than Eysenck postulates. With regard to psychotic states, Pavlov envisaged a weakened nervous system which did not function in a normal manner, producing so-called paradoxical and ultraparadoxical effects. In such conditions, weak stimuli evoke stronger responses than strong stimuli, and positive stimuli evoke negative responses.

Psychopathological phenomena have been described in terms of Skinner-type ideas. Hysteria, repression and obsessions are seen as avoidance responses to an aversive situation. Schizophrenia might be considered as a learnt avoidance of human contact. Depression might occur where little of a person's behaviour secures reinforcement.

Such is the broad outline of learning theory and its approach to psychopathology. But, as noted, learning theory is really a complex of theories and each of them can be criticized from a theoretical point of view. It follows that particular experimental results might not be correctly accounted for by the theory which the experimenter applies. It is doubtful, for example, how far writers like Skinner can justify their avoidance of non-behavioural items. It is doubtful how far experiments with rats (Hull), dogs (Pavlov) and pigeons (Skinner) can alone lay down a learning paradigm applicable to human beings, especially adults. It is here that the layman and some psychologists would stress the importance of such factors as intelligence, planning ability and insight in learning. If one's criticism became more negative it could be pointed out that the training of behaviour seen in child-rearing, the control of animals as in the circus or in special circumstances such as the sheepdog has been very efficiently carried on without the aid of a learning theory and has not changed since its advent. The learning theory advocates could then, of course, argue that much training is carried out on an *ad hoc*, inefficient basis, as in child-rearing, or more efficiently, as in the circus, by implicit use of what are now known to be learning theory principles. Incidental learning or latent learning appears to occur without an individual being motivated or required to make a response. Furthermore, at least an 'exploration' or 'curiosity' drive must be postulated to account for an individual paying attention to his environment in such circumstances. It is

round such problems that many learning theories run into
erious difficulties. Yet the learning theorist would suggest that
nuch in our ways of attempting to modify behaviour is an anti-
hesis of what common-sense learning theory implies. For example,
o punish a homosexual by putting him in prison with people
xclusively of his own sex is hardly likely to extinguish his homo-
exual response. The learning theorist sees psychotherapy, includ-
ng psychoanalysis, as a process that may work, if it works at all, by
earning processes. For example, Freud's classical account of a
phobia in Hans, a 5-year-old boy, could readily be explained in
erms of learning theory much like Watson's Albert. Of course,
t is also true that the psychoanalyst sees applied learning theory
working only on account of such unconsidered variables as the
development of an emotional relationship between subject and
experimenter.

Another major criticism of learning theory has been its tendency
to attribute all behaviour, especially human, to learning. This
tendency is true not only for normal behaviour but also for abnormal behaviour. In much of mental illness, of course, it has been
accepted that genetic and constitutional factors are often the major
ones. Some modification of this rather unrealistic position of the
learning theorist has occurred in recent years. For example, instead of trying to cure schizophrenia as such, the learning theorist
now tries to modify some of a schizophrenic's more socially unacceptable symptoms. The ethologists have also contributed something of a half-way house in their studies of imprinting. Imprinting
is the name given to a period, usually short, in development which
appears critical for the development of a certain response. The
well known example here is the 'following response' in young ducks
and geese. These birds, during such a critical period, rapidly learn
to follow a large moving object. Usually this is the mother, hence
the value of such an imprinting mechanism. But if the mother is
removed, the birds will imprint to follow a man, if present, or even
an inanimate object such as a tractor. The ethologists have also
transformed instinct theory so that now, discussion concerns innate
releasing mechanisms (IRM's) to specific sign stimuli. Thus the
robin will attack the red breast of an intruder. He will not attack a
live young robin without a red breast but will, in fact, attack a
lifeless bunch of red feathers.

It has been suggested that imprinting, IRM's and sign stimuli
may all be important in human development. The young baby

appears to smile at human faces and, indeed, at all things th
approximate to human faces. Conversely, it has been suggeste
that adults have an IRM to a baby-type face, hence the appeal
the young of many species. Certain periods in development hav
been conjectured to be critical ones, possibly involving imprintir
mechanism. Such possible periods involve abilities such as readir
but also more emotional ones such as the ability to make huma
relationships or even the nature of one's sexual response. Moi
recently as we have seen, Lorenz has accounted for huma
aggression on ethological principles rather than in terms of ind
vidual acquisition as the psychoanalyst or learning theorist woul
maintain. Lorenz sees much of human aggression as being an ex
ample of aggression generated by territorial defence. In specie
who can naturally harm one another (e.g. wolves) there are buil
in protections to such aggression in the ritual patterns of dominanc
and submission. In naturally non-harmful species (such as man
there is no evolutionary need for such rituals. But when the specie
acquires weapons (as man) the absence of protective rituals i
painfully apparent.

It is worth pointing out that learning cannot be directly observe
or measured. Learning is a postulate to account for certain change
in behaviour that occur when an organism is adapting to it
environment. But whatever may be in dispute about theories o
learning, consistent data exist on certain performance changes tha
occur in learning situations. The rate of learning can be illustrate
by a learning curve showing how a person's skill improves with th
amount of practice. Frequently plateaux appear in such curves
perhaps when one stage of learning is completed before the nex
stage begins. For most situations, short periods of practice with
intervening rest periods are more effective in learning than long
continuous spells. An effective feedback of information or knowledge of results is also more effective than an absence of such knowledge. Material that is meaningful is more readily learned than
material without meaning. In the question of whole versus part
learning, a combination of both methods seems most effective.
Where the whole method would involve continuous practice, the
latter counters its advantage over part methods with regard to
meaning. An important effect in learning is that known as retro-
active inhibition which occurs when subsequent learning has a
detrimental influence on what has been learnt earlier. The reverse
possibility is referred to as proactive inhibition.

Whether we call a particular example of learning a habit or a skill depends to some extent on how much value or attention we give it. In performance a skilled operator is striking because of his excellent timing and anticipation. A lack of timing and of smoothness between the phases of a skill are particularly evident in awkwardness and errors of performance. In performances there are points of no return where the behaviour cannot be effectively altered. Thinking processes have been considered skills of a particular kind and in no way different to bodily skills. But what we might call reality, problem-solving, thinking, needs to be distinguished from the autistic kind of thinking that occurs in dreaming and fantasy. We may also note that some thinking processes, when they occur in the normal waking state, are considered pathological. These are processes resulting in delusions, irrelevant associations and so on.

In man, thought processes are very much associated with language, though it remains problematical what precisely are the relationships between thought and language. It is clear that the acquisition of language is a feature of normal childhood development and learning. In the first year of life the child's spontaneous babbling sounds are channelled into the words of the language he hears. The next few years show a steady growth in the numbers of words used, in the parts of speech used and in sentence construction. This growth is peculiarly human in that no other animal has developed language that can be used in a symbolical or abstract way to express what is not present at the time. This suggests that communication methods existing in non-human animals tend to be qualitatively as well as quantitatively different from those in humans.

Language is also an important expression of personality and a lack of speech is always a sign of serious disturbance. A vocabulary test is an efficient indicator of intelligence and subnormality is often shown in the early years by an absence, or relative lack, of normal language development. Schizophrenics often show particular kinds of language disturbance. They make 'new' words (neologisms) and the hallucinations a schizophrenic reports are typically of an auditory nature involving words. As we have noted, intellectual impairment in an organic case may involve language loss as in dysphasia or in the ability to learn the meanings of words. In any personality the manner of speech and the use of techniques such as word association again indicate the close relationship of language and personality.

Language is only one form of communication, but a highly developed and important form in human beings. As in all communication it is information that is being transmitted. In recent years there has been a steady growth in the attempt to apply information theory to the study of behaviour, particularly language. Information theory, a mathematical system for the analysis of information and its transmission, uses a binary system of notation (either/or) and it is interesting and convenient that such a system is used by digital computers. Similarly, neural activity is of an either/or pattern. Hence computer analysis and information theory approaches to behaviour including language tend to be currently fashionable.

Another aspect of learning is seen in the data of memory. There are memory images in various sensory modalities, but in humans they are usually predominantly visual. But some people's memory images are predominantly in another modality while many others find they rarely experience memory images at all. In the early days of psychology, study of such data was frequent and a controversy of the time revolved round the possibility of imageless thought. Occasionally individuals (usually children) have memory images which are virtually a photographic reproduction of the original. Such imagery is called eidetic and may be demonstrated in people who can, when blindfold, play a number of chess games simultaneously. Other individuals report they tend to have images where numbers or dates are diagrammatically arranged in a certain order. Such images are called number forms or date forms.

We have noted how, in perceptual processes, an important feature is the attitude or set of the perceiver and how he tends to impose his own meaning on data (Chapter 3). Such features are important in learning and are particularly evident in remembering. The distortion of data to terms which are meaningful to the rememberer is easily demonstrated in experiments. But such distortions play an important part in real life situations, and need to be particularly kept in mind when dealing with the evidence of witnesses.

We can now go on to describe the main forms of behaviour therapy.

Aversion treatment

We can regard the aversion treatments as the first attempts to treat psychiatric patients on lines suggested by experimental findings even though the initial techniques were somewhat unrefined. It is interesting that the first group of patients subjected to this rather unpleasant procedure should be alcoholics but one possible reason is the general acceptance among psychiatrists that alcoholism, although it may be only symptomatic of an underlying conflict, is so destructive that the patient must be stopped from drinking before any other treatment, e.g. psychotherapy, can be effective. The traditional procedure is to produce aversion to the patient's favourite tipple by associating it with drug-induced vomiting using either emetine or apomorphine. It is of some importance that there should be a reasonable approximation in time between the ingestion of alcohol and the vomiting, and this is ensured by trial and error in determining the time which the drugs take to act. Of course, many things may vary this time and, therefore, the approximation may not be very close. Experimental findings in conditioning studies imply that the time interval for conditioning is critical (less than a second) and that, therefore, the method cannot work. Such few studies of the results of treatment as have been carried out are not entirely convincing, but they relate normally to the effectiveness of the method in preventing drinking over a period and not to its effectiveness as a conditioning procedure. We think the observational evidence that at the end of a period of apomorphine aversion the patient is nauseated by his drink is satisfactory but agree that the conditioning model may not be the appropriate one to use, at least in a simple form. The term 'second signalling system' is used in Pavlovian terminology to define the elaboration of verbalized concepts and their effects on behaviour and this system has been invoked to account for the formation of a response in drug-induced aversion treatments.

More recently electric shock has been used to induce aversion. Here the timing of the aversion stimulus can be more closely controlled and the therapeutic set up can then be based on a classical conditioning model. The UCS is the electric shock and the UCR is the anxiety response. Any form of undesirable behaviour is made the CS and the anxiety response becomes the CR. These techniques have been used particularly in the realm of sexual deviation and have less often been applied to the treatment of the alcoholics. Clearly it is difficult in some forms of sexual deviation, for example, homosexuality, to use the actual behaviour as the CS. Various approaches to the behaviour are, therefore, used. For instance, if we retain homosexuality as our example, the CS is developed using words, concepts and fantasies which have homosexual associations, and appropriate pictures. Once conditioning is established it is hoped that the aversive effects will become attached to the actual behaviour by generalization. Often the aversion technique is associated with a technique which utilizes the positively reinforcing effects of anxiety relief. Thus a method of dealing with transvestism is to administer electric shocks while the patient is dressed in the clothes of the opposite sex, usually female, and to continue these until he has got the clothes off. The cessation of noxious stimuli is then the UCS and the reduction of 'anxiety' the UCR which becomes the CR to the CS of 'getting out of female clothing'.

As an illustration one may consider the case of a 35-year-old man, married with one child, having a history of transvestism which since marriage involved him wearing his wife's clothes. Apart from this his relationship with his wife, who was sympathetic, was good. The patient selected a series of pictures of female garments which was mounted in a tachistoscopic presentation. The therapist could give a shock to the back of one hand with each presentation at the optimum level of roughly half a second. The series of pictures was then interspersed with ones of a nude female, when no shock was given. At this point, the patient was given control of the tachistoscope. After a number of sessions, a partial reinforcement schedule was introduced, giving a shock on only a proportion of the clothing pictures. Even so, very quick rejections of 'pathological' stimuli occurred. After three months with a reducing frequency of therapeutic sessions, the patient and his wife confirmed an extinction of the undesired behaviour. As is frequently the case in behaviour therapy, prospects of success are also related to the presence of normal sexual behaviour and adequate motivation to deal with the undesired behaviour.

Another example of the use of aversive shocks is the treatment of writer's cramp. Here, two behaviours need to be averted, excessive tremor of the hand and an excessively tight grip on the pen. Electrical circuits can be constructed to administer shocks when the patient develops a tremor while following a predetermined course with a stylus and when the stylus is gripped too tightly. Repeated practice with such a device may lead to improvement. A third behaviour, pressing the pen too hard on the paper, may be contributory but, in a case we have seen, was an essential part of the patient's job and, therefore, could not be modified.

It will be seen that the possibilities of aversion treatment of undesirable behaviours are limited only by the ingenuity of the therapist. Because of this it has been suggested that the compulsory treatment of deviant social behaviour by behavioural methods, usually aversive, may be more effective than the methods currently in use. This attitude disregards the problems of motivation in the acquisition of new behaviour. In patients who are anxious to be treated, the development of what they regard as 'normal' behaviour is a positively reinforcing agent. This would not necessarily be the case among those compulsorily treated. Furthermore, it is necessary to decide what is desirable behaviour and who is to set up social norms. It has been said that many of the problems tackled by the behaviour therapist are not, properly speaking, psychiatric ones. It is true that behaviour therapy is most readily applied to mono-symptomatic or otherwise circumscribed difficulties and at present cannot cover the bulk of psychiatric disorders. This difficulty is held to be only one of application and the real criticism is that such circumscribed disorders are considered by some people to be relatively peripheral to psychiatric illness.

The conditioning approach to bed-wetting perhaps illustrates this difficulty. For years a bell and blanket system has been used. The patient, if he wets while asleep, completes a circuit which rings a bell, waking him up. Repeated, this process conditions him to wake up in time to control himself. Many workers have found this method to be highly effective, but perhaps only if limited to those patients whose enuresis is not only one symptom in a marked personality disorder.

Operant conditioning methods

We have noted in our discussion of aversion techniques that the reduction of anxiety can itself act as a positively reinforcing agent. Such anxiety reduction can, therefore, be used to aid the substitution of approved behaviour for that which is being discouraged by the aversion method. Many other stimuli can be used in this way to produce modification of behaviour using an operant conditioning model. Again, the method is potentially very versatile and examples of this can be found in the collections of published papers on these techniques. One of the most valuable points about the method is that it seems to be particularly applicable to psychotic behaviour. As an example of this and to illustrate the method, we shall outline an experiment carried out by Ayllon and Haughton. They observed that 50% of a ward largely made up of long-term schizophrenics had a history of refusal to eat, despite the use of spoon feeding, tube feeding, intravenous feeding and electro-shock. The experiment commenced by stopping all feeding aids and the patients were left alone at meal times when they had to go into the dining-room to eat. The next stage introduced was that patients could not eat unless they entered the dining-room within half an hour of being called. After half an hour, the doors were locked and any patient who had not arrived missed the meal. This procedure eventually established successful self-feeding in the dining-room social situation.

When the eating was so far under control, the patients had to drop a coin in a slot to get into the dining-room. At the same time access to the dining-room was restricted to five minutes from being called. The writers show that by such shaping procedures psychotic behaviour can be controlled by operant conditioning techniques. Speech and language disorders, common in schizophrenics, can also be tackled by applying operant methods to the verbally deviant behaviour. For example, with a schizophrenic whose speech is socially unacceptable because of neologisms such speech is ignored by the therapist, who only responds to normal speech utterances. Such a process punishes the verbally deviant behaviour, extinguishes it and rewards the acceptable speech.

It will be seen that one of the important factors in this form of treatment is the selection of an appropriate positively reinforcing 'stimulus' or 'reward'. When operant conditioning techniques have been applied to normal subjects, for instance, with teaching machines, it has been found that successful completion of a task is sufficiently reinforcing for the procedure to be effective. Similarly, when desirable behaviours are induced in neurotic patients the formation of these behaviours may itself be an adequate reinforcement. However, the motivation of the psychotic patient is a much greater problem. It may be that such patients will respond to many of the normal social reinforcements and some work, as noted, suggests that conditioned behaviour will occur in schizophrenics, when reinforced only by approving verbalizations on the part of the therapist. Some protagonists of this view have argued that the chronic mental patient persists in deviant behaviour because such behaviour is differentially reinforced by the hospital environment. Certainly, many of the phenomena of institutionalization can be accounted for in this way. Alternatively, we may be faced with a situation where the patient does not seem to be motivated by the same goals as those which are generally accepted, or to use the learning theory jargon which we have been employing, stimuli which are usually positively reinforcing are not found to be so in these patients. Our problem will then be first to find adequate reinforcers and later to link them with the normally effective ones so that the patients' behaviour again becomes socially acceptable.

It will be seen from this discussion that the result of operant conditioning procedures is to strengthen an emergent behaviour. Most neurotic illnesses are characterized as much by the presence of a behaviour which must be eliminated as by the absence of desirable behaviours so that operant methods will rarely be the first line of approach. They will have their use in strengthening desired behaviour simultaneously with the removal of the disturbed behaviour as we have mentioned in our discussion of aversion treatments. They may also be used to strengthen a behaviour which will inhibit a neurotic response. Wolpe's suggestion that anxiety may be inhibited by aggressive behaviour is put into practice by the operant reinforcement of the aggressive response using social stimuli as reinforcers, albeit in a rather haphazard way.

In some cases a deviant, non-psychotic behaviour can be modified by operant methods. An example of this is given by Goldiamond who treats stuttering by first distorting the speech in another direction by using delayed auditory feedback to produce prolonged speech, then shaping this speech by operant methods to produce a normal reading rate without stutter.

Extinction methods

We have already mentioned Wolpe's technique of inhibiting an undesirable anxiety response by the deliberate production of aggressive responses. This is one example of the treatment of such symptoms by methods which result in their extinction. Oddly enough, the phenomenon is well known to psychotherapists of a more analytic persuasion, who often have to deal with undesirable aggressive behaviour which their patients have developed mainly because of its anxiety-reducing properties. We have not yet seen a report of such an unfortunate consequence of treatment by the behavioural method. This particular example of extinction methods involves the use of the phenomenon known as reciprocal inhibition but there are other techniques available which we shall also consider in this section.

Reciprocal inhibition occurs when two stimuli which produce incompatible responses are presented simultaneously. Thus, aggressive behaviour, eating and sexual activity will all inhibit anxiety responses and all can be used in the treatment of neurotic anxiety. Wolpe has described the technique in detail and we have outlined it above. In our example the patient is taught to produce aggressive behaviour by direct instigation and support by the therapist. In fact, the aim is to produce assertive behaviour, that is, aggressive behaviour which is socially acceptable and realistically directed. Sexual behaviour is even more difficult to use in this way and so far seems to have been used mainly in the treatment of anxiety associated with disorders of sexual activity, particularly impotence. Eating, like aggression, is commonly chosen spontaneously by patients as an anxiety relieving activity and it is a common fact of clinical observation that some patients are concerned about the weight gained consequent upon this. Equally commonly, a patient's anxiety is sufficiently severe to inhibit his eating behaviour and weight loss ensues.

The last phenomenon suggests a point which is rarely considered in discussions of extinction methods. There is nothing in learning theory which requires the changes to occur in the direction desired by the therapist so, if the anxiety response happens to be predominant we shall not get extinction but generalization and the patient will get worse. So far, although many therapists are 'amateurs' and this fact is often used by protagonists of the method to explain its failures, patients do not seem to have got worse as a result of misapplication of the procedures. Perhaps some should have done so. Extinction of an anxiety response also occurs if it is elicited but not reinforced by either the occurrence of a real danger or by avoidance behaviour. In theory, if a patient suffering from a specific phobia, for example, of closed spaces, is enclosed for a sufficiently extended period with no other anxiety-producing stimuli intervening and no prospect of getting out, the anxiety response will extinguish. This set-up is difficult to obtain in practice so the problem is usually approached more gradually. The less severe the response, the more quickly it will extinguish as it is easier to arrange an appropriate situation. Further, it appears that when the anxiety response to a stimulus is extinguished the more severe responses to related but more potent stimuli become attenuated. Phobic states where the anxiety response is elicited to varying extents by a limited and interrelated set of stimuli can be approached in this way.

The first step in this method of treatment (often called desensitization) is to arrange the stimuli in a hierarchy in terms of the intensity of the anxiety response they induce. Then the patient is, if possible, exposed to the lowest of these stimuli and at the same time the anxiety response is inhibited by suggestions of relaxation. When the response fails to occur the next stimulus in the hierarchy is presented and the process repeated. Of course, not all stimuli can be presented physically and when this problem arises the patient is asked to imagine the stimulus. Where possible imagery and relaxation are both increased by the induction of a state of light hypnosis. The procedure of ascending the hierarchy, extinguishing the anxiety response to stimuli of increasing potency, is still followed.

For example, a married woman, Mrs A., aged 29, had a phobia of bees and wasps which seriously affected her whole life. She was unable to go outside, except on rare occasions, to shop, to take her children out or to go out with her husband. The phobia was less marked in winter but never entirely dissipated. She remembered having a fear of bees and wasps as a young child but the problem had become more and more acute in adult life. She was of average intelligence and did not show a generalized personality disturbance. An attempt was made to draw up a hierarchical list of stimuli producing her specific fear. This ranged from real (but dead) bees and wasps at varying distances from the subject to different pictures and drawings of them. This hierarchy was then used in systematic desensitization. The patient was seen for 30–45-minute sessions, at first twice a week and then, with increasing success, once a week gradually reducing to one a month. For the first sessions, a relaxation technique was applied before any of the stimuli were introduced and also when apprehension developed on their being introduced. As the patient made progress throughout the hierarchy, she was also encouraged to start making forays, even if slight, into the outside world. At times, several sessions were required with a particular stimulus but a session was always concluded with an 'easy' stimulus. By the end of the summer the patient was leading a reasonably normal life. The next spring provided a minor recurrence of her problem but a few further sessions proved effective.

We have suggested here that the stimuli which provoke the anxiety response should be related, that is, that the clinical condition should be a specific phobia. Convinced behaviour therapists argue that all forms of anxiety state can be broken down into a number of specific phobias with parallel hierarchies which can be tackled separately. Similarly, it can be argued that an illness like obsessional neurosis represents a conditioned avoidance pheno- menon where compulsive behaviour is repeatedly reinforced be- cause it results in a diminution of anxiety. Unfortunately most of the reported results of behaviour therapy suffer from that tendency to anecdote which the behaviourists stigmatize so strongly when demonstrated by psychoanalysts, while the few controlled investiga- tions suggest that the method has a relatively limited usefulness. There are, however, some weaknesses in these trials apart from the factor of inadequate training of the therapist which is always in- voked by partisans to explain away the failure of their methods in the hands of others. The sphere of effectiveness of these methods has, therefore, yet to be defined.

Various other methods of extinction have been described, but are not yet in common use. Most have some relationship to the two techniques we have described above, but one type uses a different principle, that of reactive inhibition. Again, the method is quite versatile and we shall describe only one application. Here the therapist is concerned with the elimination of an undesirable piece of behaviour, for instance, a tic. It is assumed that this tic persists because, when it occurs spontaneously, it is in some way reinforced. However, repeated performance of the act without reinforcement will lead to an increase of that somewhat mythical quantity, reac- tive inhibition, which will result in increasing difficulty in carrying out the act. The patient is, therefore, made to perform the act deliberately and repeatedly for extended periods of time. This is known as massed practice. After such a therapeutic session where the tic has been repeated without reinforcement the frequency of spontaneous occurrence is much reduced. Extended treatment of this type should lead eventually to elimination of the undesirable behaviour. This method has not by itself been shown to be generally effective. It is thought that massed practice is most effective when used in conjunction with a negative reinforcer such as electric shock.

Behaviour therapy is really only at the beginning of what might be a fruitful development. It appears to have potentialities and must appeal to the ingeniously minded therapist. While it is of great interest and importance to evolve new techniques and appli- cations it will be a pity if the fascination of this work should outweigh the necessity for the rather tedious and sober assessment of the actual results. We have noted already that there is a tendency to assume that results from single cases are universally valid. There is no doubt that in the assessment of psychological methods of treatment great caution is needed. The techniques involved are often quite simple and so far are based on simple psychological concepts and the field is one where psychiatrist and psychologist can profitably work together. Some workers in both spheres tend to resent the influence of the other but to judge from much of the presently published work the psychiatrist's lamentable lack of scientific method unhappily balanced by the psychologist's indifference to factors outside the experiment such as the continuing care of the patient.

In both behaviour therapy and psychotherapy controlled studies of groups of subjects are required to establish which therapy is the most effective with different disorders. Over both types of therapy looms the disturbing feature often referred to as spontaneous remission. Not only have the two major psychological forms of treatment to be evaluated against each other, but they have to be shown to be better than the natural, but mysterious, processes which result in a large proportion of psychiatric illness dissipating after an interval of time.

Having outlined learning theories and particularized their application in therapy, it must also be stressed that any valid learning theory should have an important place in education and training. It should have an effect on not only the education of normal children and training schemes in industry but also in more specialized areas such as the handicapped and the mentally subnormal. Indeed, the rate of learning, or its occurrence at all, is thought to be greatly influenced by properly breaking down the material to be learnt and the introduction of reinforcing agents. Automatic ways of doing this are often referred to as programmed learning techniques. The teaching machine is one example, which would appear to have a great potential in many fields.

K

Some Other Psychotherapies

In most discussions of psychotherapy supportive methods are men
tioned, usually briefly, in the introduction. We have elected t
consider them later because we feel that their application shoul
depend on a knowledge of the underlying psychological processe:
Furthermore, we consider that treatment techniques which are s
widely used merit a more extended consideration than they ar
sometimes given.

It is a regrettable consequence of the psychiatrist's preoccupatio
with the possibly complex meanings of their patients' utterance
that they have great difficulty in communicating with each othe
and in using words in a simple way. Thus the term 'psychotherapy
unadorned has come to imply the protracted treatment of on
patient by one therapist using a Freudian model, probably modi
fied to some extent. This has resulted recently in the use of the tern
behaviour therapy for another form of psychological treatment
For a considerable time the addition of the word supportive ha
been made in a rather belittling way. Psychotherapists tend t
assume that supportive therapy is in some way inferior, does no
help to cure the patient and can at best only be a stop-gap pro
cedure. All psychotherapy which does not seek to achieve insigh
and behaviour change as predicated by the model in use is casti
gated in this way. This attitude would be more comprehensible i
there were consistent evidence to support the efficacy of any kind o
therapy as against any other. Supportive psychotherapy, so-called
is a method of treatment which is widely used, often with littl
understanding of its mechanism, and whose techniques and result
require further investigation. We propose in this chapter to con
sider some of the techniques which are commonly recognized a
supportive and to examine briefly the ways some of these technique
have been extended in attempts to achieve similar results to thos
claimed for the 'deeper' therapies. It will be seen that the idea

developed often approximate to those of the more formal schools of psychotherapy or are extensions of them. Unless the therapist is an adherent of a particular method he is unlikely to accept the claim that any one of these approaches represents an adequate comprehensive theory of human behaviour or even of abnormal human behaviour. Our own opinion is that in the present state of knowledge the best course for the 'eclectic' therapist is to be aware of the variety of ideas which have been applied so that he can select that model which will be most useful to him as a framework to understand his patient. The selection of ideas and approaches presented here cannot claim to be comprehensive but we hope that it will serve as an introduction to a vast area of thought. Little of this thought has been substantiated by observation or experiment other than in the most general way and this chapter is, therefore, almost entirely descriptive.

Environmental manipulation

This term includes methods of treatment varying from the provision of money or social services to intricate social casework. Many patients' symptoms are directly related to obvious environmental stresses, for instance the difficulties experienced by an unintelligent woman of unstable personality in dealing with a large family on a low income. Here certain features of the situation may be susceptible to modification depending on the expertise of the therapist and his working colleagues. It may be, for instance, that the family are not receiving all the financial assistance to which they are entitled. Some problems may be alleviated if children under school age can attend a day nursery. Occasionally it proves possible to improve living accommodation. All these methods of improving the social environment may result in the relief of symptoms. A factor in their effectiveness may well be that the symptoms are not in fact 'neurotic' This situation will arise when the symptoms, for example those of anxiety, are related to stresses which the observer regards as both realistic and adequate to provoke the response. (One of the fairly widely acceptable definitions of neurosis is that it is a response which is, in an observer's opinion, inappropriate to the stimulus.)

Although the technique is widely accepted and is the basis of much social work, it has certain disadvantages both practical and theoretical. If we take a learning theory point of view it becomes apparent that manipulation of the environment may serve as a reinforcement of the neurotic symptomatology. In other words, the symptoms have been rewarded and are, therefore, liable to recur. Strictly, of course, the time relationships of such reinforcement will not accord well with learning theory as it stands at present. We have already pointed out that learning theories at present, based as they are on experimental evidence in animals, perhaps do not take sufficient account of the complexities of human behaviour, particularly where they avoid the effects of internal states of the organism. However, the danger is present and is a commonplace of clinical practice. For example, it is found that suicidal attempts are sometimes made by people to communicate distress or dissatisfaction with their environment. In dealing with these problems it is common to attempt to relieve environmental pressures to some extent. In the example given it is also important to supply the patient with a more effective and less dangerous means of communication. If this is not done there is a likelihood that suicidal attempts will recur. Where the change in the environment produces material gain, the dangers are obvious. Indeed they are often over-emphasized and made the excuse for a failure to rectify circum-stances which require change on humanitarian grounds, regardless of the medical condition of the patient. Changes in the inter-personal environment, however, can present the same problem. If, for example, the suicidal attempt cited above occurred in relation to a spouse's misdemeanours, obsequious repentance by the spouse will be bad for both partners.

Although we have noted these difficulties, much treatment is based on attempts to manipulate the environment, especially the interpersonal environment, often in complex ways. Some social caseworkers do this, working on the implicit assumption that dis-turbed behaviour in one member of a group may be symptomatic of some form of social pathology within that group. Such cases demonstrate that, not only do the fields of psychiatry and psy-chology overlap, but either may also overlap into the fields of sociology and anthropology. It is fruitless for the behavioural scientist or therapist to attempt to work in artificially watertight compartments.

We shall consider group pathologies later, but in this section we are still concerned with the individual who, in this model, is reacting in an abnormal way to stress. Bateson's double-bind hypothesis of the genesis of schizophrenia is a theory of this type. Such an approach, stressed by Laing among others, sees schizophrenia as a mode of reaction between the patient and a parent, usually the mother. Other workers have also described schizophrenia as a family illness. The whole family is considered psychopathological but only one member, the schizophrenic, is chosen to manifest the overt pathology.

Games theory has recently been applied to many aspects of behaviour and its application to psychopathology is one example. Berne, using an approach based on transactional analysis, has defined neurotic and other behaviours in terms of 'games' where the patient and the people in his immediate environment follow a series of moves which result in a 'pay-off' for the patient. In addition to treatment based on analysis and explanation of the process Berne suggests that in certain situations the other participants 'refuse to play' or change the rules in one way or another. Here again, by such an analysis, we have a sophisticated manipulation of the inter-personal environment but this time the process is much less 'supportive' and intended to give the patient more insight into his own behaviour patterns. The implied relationship with the mathematical theory of games of Van Neumann and Morgenstern is explicitly denied by Berne in his introduction. Other authors may not be so explicit and the reader of accounts should always assess whether mathematical or transactional game analysis is in progress.

Explanation, reassurance and suggestion

These three varieties of support are usually used together. Little work has been done in estimating the efficacy of these methods in relieving distress and in alleviating symptoms, nor on the mechanism of such effects, if they do indeed occur. The common-sense view is essentially denial that the symptoms which are treated in this way are neurotic in the sense in which we have defined the term. It is argued, for instance, that anxiety symptoms associated with abdominal discomfort and fear of cancer are due to this fear. From the standpoint of the medically naïve patient his fears are justified by his symptoms and are, therefore, not unrealistic or neurotic. The therapist then examines the patient, 'excludes' the feared disease, reassures the patient about this, explains the genesis of the symptoms and suggests that now the matter has been cleared up the symptoms will resolve. From the analytical point of view the situation can be represented as a conformity by the patient to the views of a respected and perhaps rather feared father figure who encourages the patient to take a dependant attitude. Experimental psychologists have not commented on the procedure, possibly because of difficulties in communicating with their subjects. The method is probably overvalued by general physicians and surgeons who do not see its failures and undervalued by psychiatrists who only see the failures.

These techniques may be used separately and are part of the physician's routine, often to such an extent that he is largely unaware of their use. There are many anecdotes illustrating the value or sometimes the ways in which the physician's speech or behaviour can have harmful effects for his patients. A common tale of this type is the account of the patient suffering from an incurable condition who is brought to an uneasy awareness of the situation because the doctor passes the bed without speaking or with only formal courtesy.

A hazard of investigations into the effects of various forms of treatment is the bias introduced into patient's response by the way they are interviewed. The cheerful optimistic doctor may obtain answers favourable to the treatment, the pessimist the reverse, while careful neutral questioning will reveal different opinions again. None of these answers need reflect the patient's state very accurately. They may only show a desire to give the appropriate response, or indicate underlying personality characteristics rather than present changes in the illness.

This aspect of the doctor's behaviour at interview can be of great importance. Many patients suffering from chronic psychiatric illness are maintained on a basis of recurrent treatment consisting of reassurance by direct and indirect suggestion. Direct suggestion is given both verbally and non-verbally at their interviews at a surgery or an out-patient clinic, while indirect suggestion is provided by means of medication. This is true not only of so-called placebos but also of drugs which have physical effects on the central nervous system. Balint has provided an interesting discussion of this subject within a psychoanalytical framework saying that in many cases the effective ingredient is 'doctor' which can be administered in many ways at varying intervals. The potency of this ingredient will depend on the values of many variables, of which the personalities of doctor and patient, their relationship and their cultural attitudes are probably the most important. There are usually components of reassurance and suggestion in such effects.

Some quite elaborate psychotherapeutic formulations can also e included in this section although such inclusion may give a egree of offence to their originators. For instance, Phillips pro-oses a didactic type of therapy based on what an analyst might vell call the interpretation of the 'here and now' situation which onsists mainly of the explanation of the patient's behaviour in ymptom-producing situations in terms of an analysis of the atient's self-assertions and the conflicts which arise from them. This emphasis on the self concept is also found in Kelly's formula-ion and is one of the factors underlying the use of the repertory rid (p. 63) in his work. More recently Laing and Philipson have tressed the importance of the patient's concept of what the 'other' hinks of him and the complexity which results from several levels of his, for instance even simply: 'He thinks that I think that he thinks I'm a fool'.

We have mentioned these ideas and approaches only briefly. Their theoretical derivations vary widely, from the experimental aboratory full circle to existential philosophy and the interested reader or psychotherapist seeking to extend the range of conceptual tools available to him can only be recommended to read widely but critically. It remains a failure both of therapists and of academic psychologists that the only assessments which are made of this sort of technique are those of the intellectual critic. Experiment and systematic observation are, it seems, too negative or too difficult. Some sympathy may be available for the therapist in this situation as it does seem that present-day experimental techniques tend to be too biased and oversimplified and it may be that inappropriate variables are measured. It is also true that there is little incentive for the researcher to spend his time demolishing concepts which have no other virtue than that someone has thought of them, they are superficially attractive and have gained a degree of support. Further, he is unlikely to be believed.

Acceptance

One of the ways in which the drug 'doctor' can be used is to give status to the patient by acceptance. Recently the social role of the doctor has come under discussion, in particular in this context his function as the arbiter between society and the patient as to whether or not the patient is 'ill'. Illness in our society conveys a peculiar status, in many ways advantageous to the patient. It has been

questioned whether the undoubted humanitarian gains of including psychiatric patients in this area do not outweigh the therapeutic
harm. Unless society's attitude changes that discussion is of only
academic relevance, as those psychiatrists who attempt to prevent
patients using their illness to escape reality know only too well. As
many patients do not get better it is often useful to maintain them
at some sort of functional level by classifying them as 'ill'. This
implies that they are entitled to be seen by a doctor at intervals
(often quite long intervals will suffice), that they are entitled to take
some form of medication because, at present, the bottle of tablets is
the membership card of the society of the sick and that they are to
be given certain privileges. Among these privileges are the right to
complain and to suffer, bravely or otherwise, to be excused some
sins of commission and many of omission and to be complimented
extravagantly for small achievements. Extra attention may be
provided and is usually welcome.

Presented in this way the gains from illness appear great but
must, of course, be set against the losses. In some patients the losses
are not large and here it is easy to see that there will be difficulty in
producing health again. Where this situation obtains and in many
which are marginal little psychological insight is required to discern
the relevant factors in the balance. Rejection of the patient may
then occur, not only by those immediately around him, but also by
his physician. Although there might theoretically be therapeutic
advantages from this in that the illness is much less rewarding,
sometimes even punished, so that the patient should decide (unconsciously, of course!) to recover, it does not often work out in
this way in practice. Usually the patient has become ill partly in
response to long-continued ideas of rejection and the response to
the rejection during illness may well be to become sicker.

Acceptance of the patient may, in this situation, prevent deterioration and even, provided he is not expected to recover completely,
produce a considerable improvement both in his own state at least
as evidenced by the number and intensity of complaints and in his
level of function.

Hypnosis

Although hypnosis is not a specific therapy of any type but rather a
technique which can be used to further the course of many therapies, it is commonly regarded by the unsophisticated as a form of

magic which will remove neurotic symptoms. In so far as this is true, hypnosis is a powerful form of direct suggestion and is occasionally used in this way, for instance, in the treatment of warts. Some patients gain considerable relief from long-standing neurotic symptoms by this means, but may become very dependent on their hypnotist. Again, the phenomenon is accounted for in analytic theory as a consequence of the transference phenomenon. There have been experimental investigations of the hypnotic state and it has been used as an adjunct to treatment by progressive desensitization but the subject has only become sufficiently respectable to be subjected to rigorous investigation for a relatively short time.

It seems clear that two types of phenomenon are considered as hypnotic. The first of these is the state induced by continual repetitive or rhythmic stimuli. This state is probably identical with physiological sleep and is also the state which has been called animal hypnosis. The second group of phenomena is that which is generally accepted as hypnosis proper. Here the physiological state is not that of sleep, despite the use of the term in many of the methods of inducing hypnosis. Although hypnosis has been defined as a state of increased suggestibility induced by suggestion, this does not help to elucidate the findings. Barber, for example, has carried out experiments from which he claims that all the phenomena thought to be peculiar to hypnosis can be produced by suggestions to normally conscious subjects. This view would not be accepted by many and also arouses the criticism that all the subjects involved were to some extent hypnotized. In many ways the hypnotic state can be regarded as a heightening of concentration with a great narrowing of the field of awareness. The subject pays attention only to those aspects of the external environment to which he is directed, while his response to internal signals may also be greatly modified by instructions from the hypnotist. Remarkable bodily changes can be produced by this means in suitable subjects, as can more psychological manifestations often associated with hysteria. Charcot was able to demonstrate the imposition and removal of hysterical symptoms by hypnosis many years ago and it has long been possible to treat such symptoms directly in this way. Despite this, the method is rarely used, even on the relatively few cases of *grande hystérie* which are seen nowadays. This is a consequence of the general feeling amongst psychiatrists that such symptom removal is not permanent and either the original symptom returns or another takes its place.

It is this experience of the phenomena of symptom substitution coupled with their medical training which prompts them to seek an underlying cause for symptoms, which makes many psychiatrists sceptical of the behavioural approach. Unfortunately all schools of thought tend to assume the universality of their theory, so the possibility that many phobias and antisocial behaviours may best be understood and modified in the light of the findings of experimental psychology is upsetting to the analytically inclined, while the inadequacy of learning theory to account for the phenomena of hysteria is not accepted by its proponents.

Hypnosis clearly raises more problems, particularly for those interested in theory construction, than it solves. Even the possibility of using it to obtain evidence for a theory of mental functioning is unpromising because of the danger of contamination of the data by the influence of the hypnotist. Despite this it can be a valuable adjunct to psychotherapy. The psychologist may help to use it more effectively by his assessment of the type of therapy needed, help in the selection of patients and work in elucidating its mechanisms. Although treatment using hypnosis in a medical setting is largely carried out by doctors it is not commonly regarded as a medical procedure and could well be done by the clinical psychologist. Indeed, one of the most scientific accounts of the subject is by a psychologist (Barber). A combined approach to the problem could well continue the present revival of the fortunes and acceptability of the subject even if this occurs at the cost of the therapeutic benefits of its magical associations.

Thought reform

Psychotherapists, particularly those of an analytic persuasion, are often horrified at any suggestion of a relationship between their techniques and those of the practitioners of thought reform or 'brainwashing'. The term tends to be applied to techniques outside the field of psychiatry which have as their aim the rapid modification of fundamental attitudes, which threaten to be effective, and which are directed to ends of which we disapprove. Commonly the methods depend in part on the production of an altered physiological state with its concomitant modification of the psychological description of the system. The physiological methods all involve the induction of lowered efficiency, usually by deprivation but sometimes also by damage and intoxication. (Intoxication in this con-

.ext includes that consequent upon infected wounds etc. as well as
.he administration of drugs of various types.) We are concerned
here mainly with the psychological aspects of the process and shall
mention physiological techniques only in so far as they can be
regarded as the quickest way to bring about desired psychological
states. Although the terminology now refers to a current ideological
conflict the techniques have a respectable antiquity and we shall
not confine our examples to the twentieth century.

Thought reform technique can, for the purpose of description,
be divided into two main types, individual and group and into two
main phases, preparation and reconstruction. Both types and
phases may be mixed in varying proportions. The theoretical background tends at present to be Pavlovian, but Freudian interpreta-
tions have also been put forward to account for the changes which
occur. On the whole, the methods seem to be largely empirical and
to make use of phenomena derived from many areas of psychology
some of which are very poorly understood. Much of the theory
seems to be a later addition.

We have called the first phase of a thought reform procedure
preparation. In some contexts this might be called destructive and
in all cases the aim is to abrogate the reformee's intellectual critical
judgement and to increase his suggestibility. The eventual aim is a
change in thinking based on an emotional change and a change in
certain individual premises with consequent modification of the
self concept (p. 87) rather than some form of intellectual conviction which is susceptible to removal by argument. In general, the
beliefs which the thought reformer seeks to instil are moral, often
with religious overtones, so the first stage involves an attack on the
reformee's judgement of such issues, a process aided by an attack
on his capacity for judgement in other spheres.

Certain techniques for bringing this about depend largely upon
compulsion but have been used by those already committed as a
means of intensifying their commitments and can also be used on
some susceptible members of society who will undergo them volun-
tarily. These techniques are those which depend on deprivation or
some form of punishing situation or on drugs. Deprivation and
punishment may be classified as physical or psychological depending on which system of description is most apt, but their results are
best described psychologically. The effects which are sought from
these three methods are alterations in the state of consciousness
and perceptual capacity. Even where the technique of choice is

regarded by the outside observer as punishment the aim is not negative reinforcement of a preceding behaviour but rather a modification of psychological state by excessive stimulation.

The process of deprivation, intoxication or prolonged excessive stimulation produces disorientation accompanied by increasing self-awareness and self-examination. Thought processes become increasingly disorganized and illogical. These phenomena occur to varying extents whether the technique is that of starvation, beating, intoxication, sleep deprivation or social and sensory isolation. The extent to which they occur and the forms which they take will depend on the personality of the subject and his previous experience and knowledge. For instance, the similarity of the hallucinatory experiences undergone by users of LSD 25 may be related as much to their knowledge of what to expect as to the commonalty of their collective unconscious. In the same way the results of sensory deprivation experiments tend to vary more between experimenters than between subjects in the same experiment (as do the unconsciouses of analysands of analysts of different schools). In all cases doubt arises in consequence of the increasing inconsistency of mental processes, the loss of sense of time and the instability of the perceptual ground.

Where the subject is compulsorily detained there is, of course, already a degree of anxiety present in the uncertainty of the situation. This is increased both by physical methods and by the demands of the interrogator for confession. Confessions which do not meet with the interrogator's requirements may be punished. Similarly in a group situation there are normally a few members of the group who know the party line and guide the newcomers in their thinking. Psychotherapeutic situations present similar aspects. Behaviour therapists quite openly punish undesirable behaviours while those of an analytic persuasion follow more subtle techniques relying to a large extent on the arousal of guilt. Evangelists, too, usually attempt to arouse guilt, mostly by their oratory which has been preceded by a great deal of rhythmic stimulation and procedures effective in involving the individual in the group so that his responses become more stereotyped. There is a proposition in cybernetics which postulates that a complex system taken through a standardized series of states tends towards a standard state.

Under certain circumstances the subject may become so overwhelmed by stimuli that the state known as transmarginal inhibition is produced. The individual becomes passive and very receptive to direct suggestion. Some theorists hold that it is necessary to induce this state to achieve an effective conversion but it is not certain that this is so.

Once anxiety and guilt, perhaps aided by physical deprivation, are sufficient to reduce the subject's critical faculties and to undermine his previous convictions it is possible to begin the second stage which we have called reconstruction. This is mainly directed to rewarding correct thinking and feeling. Certain clues as to what is correct may be supplied by the reformer/therapist but the goals to be reached are rarely described explicitly or in any detail. It appears to be generally felt that the subject's conversion will be more firmly fixed if he has to struggle to reach the light. Heretical thought may still be punished. The subject's responses are, therefore, moulded by techniques very similar to those of operant conditioning (p. 126) to those responses appropriate to a given system.

It is noteworthy that the system to which the subject is to be converted tends to have certain general characteristics. First it serves to provide an explanation for the anxieties and guilts which have been aroused in the first stage of the thought reform process, second it offers a means by which they can be expiated and holds out the promise of relief and forgiveness. It is irrelevant (theoretically) whether the forgiveness arises from God, the state, or the self when it realizes that its previous troubles arose inevitably from its parents' behaviour. In addition to this immediate help the system will offer comprehensive guidance on living and the assurance that future difficulties can be resolved by its methods and beliefs.

This last involves the use of an important sequel to any thought reform technique: the follow-up. It is in this follow-up stage that didactic instruction in the minutiae of the system of belief will be given. Support in the new system of thought will be given by other believers and where possible small groups will be formed to maintain the faith. A little persecution by society at large has been found by some thought reformers to be of great value here, reinforcing the intra-group relationships. This is particularly true, of course, where society at large is opposed to the tenets of the new belief or where there are conflicting systems of thought. Simpler methods involving fairly casual supervision may be adequate where a society is organized around the system to which the subject has been converted.

The long-term effectiveness of thought reform procedures has not been fully established. We incline to the view that for the majority of subjects the follow-up is critical. Some historical evidence seems to support this view. Obviously, although the Inquisition was apparently successful in persuading heretics to change their ways they had little faith in the lasting effects of this change as they despatched their penitents to a higher sphere very rapidly. Methodism, however, as a Christian sect founded on conversion, had a most effective follow-up system and is still a considerable force. Some more recent conversions by Communists have been followed by the return of the converts to their original society. It seems that in most cases the older established system of belief reasserts itself, aided by a certain amount of re-education (or thought reform) even though in present circumstances those connected with 'security' are unlikely to regard such persons as 'reliable'.

Vocational guidance and work placement

Possibly this aspect of treatment can be classified as environmental manipulation and such a description is certainly merited when neurotic symptoms related to basic insecurities are precipitated by a work situation which arouses these insecurities. For instance there is the well known, but not formally classified, clinical entity of 'promotion neurosis'. However, now that the emphasis in the treatment of chronic psychotic patients, particularly schizophrenics, has been placed on community care, with the patient at work as much as possible, and where patients who have been in hospital for many years are being rehabilitated and re-employed, the problem of appropriate placement of the patient assumes great importance. It may well remain true that the only really adequate test of a patient's capacity for a certain employment is to try it, but where continuing placement of patients in local industry is required it is important that the failure rate be kept as low as possible. The clinical psychologist should be able to help in this, both by selection procedures and by assistance in devising training or retraining methods. In this field the use of programmed learning methods and teaching machines will certainly become more important.

Selection procedures can be considered from two points of view: first, the more difficult and liable to error, advising the patient what type of job he should attempt; second, selecting individuals for specific jobs. Provided that the requirements of the work are well understood it is often possible to devise specific tests, but even where they are not some general factors can often be found. For instance it is found that speed of working is a common limiting factor for chronic schizophrenics and laboratory tests which correlate with this can be carried out. Such tests can be of reaction time, simple repetitive motor tasks, or tests involving attention and concentration. The latter tasks may be straightforward ones where, for example, every odd number in a series of random digits has to be crossed out.

Data on a patient's ability, attainments, interests and personality can be obtained from psychological tests. We have already dealt with these areas (Chapters 1 & 4). Assessment for occupational purposes entails matching job requirements with the right person. Such data can be used by a psychologist in terms of what is known about various job requirements from occupational psychology. Ministry of Labour Industrial Rehabilitation Units and Remploy also undertake to assess and place appropriate patients. Such rehabilitation involves a combination of test procedures with an appraisal of actual working efficiency.

11

Physical Therapies

We have to some extent considered the relevance of physical factors to mental functions in our discussion of the organic states (Chapter 2) and brain-washing techniques (Chapter 10). Here we are concerned more with the effects of drugs and other physical methods used with the intention of relieving mental symptoms. This use may result either in the direct alleviation of the symptom or in a facilitation of the effect of a psychological treatment. Our consideration is intended only to provide an elementary survey and introduction to the psychological results of physical intervention for this area of psychiatric treatment has become so extensive that is has acquired a literature of its own.

Although we have avoided extensive discussion of the mind–body problem we think it desirable at the start of this chapter to reiterate our own position. A full discussion of the mind–body problem is beyond the scope of the present book. However, the reader should be wary of accepting the uncritical belief that mind (and hence experiencing and behaviour) is simply an aspect of physiological structures as they are at present understood. At its simplest (and perhaps most naïve) such a view is the epiphenomenal one that experience is nothing more than a by-product of brain activity. Such views are impossible to maintain, at our present level of knowledge, with even a slight amount of critical evaluation. Yet it is true that mind–body dualism is built into our language to a remarkable extent so that attempts to use a monistic system usually result in pedantic tedium. Despite this we consider that a monistic approach involving the identity hypothesis is the most appropriate for this type of discussion. In essence this assumes that the system under observation is constant, but that the attitude of the observer and the system of description he uses may vary. There are then two different descriptive and explanatory languages used in the study of the organism, that of 'physics' or physical science and that of psychology. The relationships between these are those of translation rather than of cause and effect. Which language is to be used in any given situation will depend on various factors including personal preference, applicability, effectiveness and economy. Ideally the two languages should not be mixed but avoidance of this can be most difficult. Even if we struggle for linguistic purity in this discussion in everyday circumstances we shall be discovered using such pidgin expressions as psychosomatic.

If problems of cause and effect are thus evaded some will find difficulty in conceptualizing the effects of physical agencies used to modify psychological states. We consider that such effects are inevitable if the system is changed. Indeed we regard mental change as a concomitant of any physical change and suggest that the monistic approach may help us to escape from an attitude to psychology which is now perhaps too brain centred. It remains true that within the system which is man the brain is predominantly the area where small physical changes, when translated, become large psychological changes, but it is also true that physical changes elsewhere, e.g. the loss of a limb, will alter the psychological description of the system. Similarly, brain changes alone may not account for the observed disturbance in female psychology around the time of menstruation. Changes in the physical system using hormones or diuretics may modify the psychological description adequately. These physical changes do not take place entirely in the brain. Of course, in both these examples there are brain changes, both of input and activity (oestrogens increase brain excitability) but this may not be the whole story.

In essence our standpoint on the effects of physical methods of treatment is this: a modification of the physical state of the system which is the individual is made by a physical procedure. As the psychological state is a description of the same system this state, too, will be changed if the system is altered.

The psychological effects of drugs

We have already remarked that our consideration of these effects can only be a summary one. Our intention is to indicate the effects of drugs on some aspects of normal and abnormal psychological states. For detailed information the reader needs to refer to works on pharmacology and therapeutics on the one hand and to studies of the effect of drugs on psychological functions on the other.

L

The effects of drugs on psychological functions are still considered in fairly elementary ways. A long-standing dichotomy is that between stimulation and sedation and for many years drugs used in psychiatry have relied on one or other of these effects.

Eysenck has suggested that the stimulant drugs increase cortical excitation and hence behavioural inhibition. In other words they shift the individual (temporarily) towards the introversion pole of extraversion–introversion. Conditionability should be increased and Eysenck has suggested that the psychopath might acquire the social conditioning he lacks through training regimes being carried out at such times. Sedative drugs on the other hand are held to increase cortical inhibition and hence behavioural excitation. Consequently, the individual's behaviour becomes more extraverted. Criticisms of this hypothesis follow the same lines as general criticisms of Eysenck's view on introversion–extraversion (Chapter 10). These are that Eysenck sees more generality in drug action, conditionability and introversion–extraversion than others think is permissible. But it must be admitted that there is a general lack of precision in defining the changes in behaviour and experience a particular drug is supposed to produce.

Sometimes the two types of drug are given together in combinations which are thought widely to be effective despite their inherent illogicality. The proliferation of drugs used in the treatment of various psychiatric illnesses has been associated with an expanding nomenclature of alleged effects. Thus we now have sedatives, hypnotics, tranquillizers, neuroleptics, thymoleptics and so on. It remains uncertain whether these labels differentiate qualitative or quantitative actions, at least from the psychological viewpoint, even though the pharmacology may vary. It has even been argued that some antidepressants are merely sedative in their action.

Sedative drugs in general produce an impairment of metal function with a greater liability to error in intellectual tasks, a certain amount of affective release consequent upon the reduction in inhibition followed as the dose is increased by a reduction in affective response as the inhibition spreads. Related to the initial cortical inhibiting effects of this group of drugs is the increased difficulty found in establishing conditioned responses when they are administered. Larger doses lead eventually to unconsciousness. Within the general range of action there is a wide variation of individual effects and it is generally accepted that different groups of drug

:xert different main effects. Broadly these groups are shown
below:

Group of Drugs	Examples	Main Use
Hypnotics	Sodium amylobarbitone Dichloralphenazone	Sleeping tablets
Sedatives (or tranquillizers)	Meprobamate Chlordiazepoxide Sodium amylobarbitone (in small doses)	Neurotic anxiety
Tranquillizers (or neuroleptics)	Chlorpromazine Haloperidol	Agitated psychotic behaviour

It will be noted that we have given an example of a drug that can
be used either as a sedative or as an hypnotic according to its dosage.
This is true for the others as well, but is of less practical significance,
because the margin between the two doses is large. Chlordiaze-
poxide, for instance, will produce an adequate effect on neurotic
symptoms in a much smaller dose than that necessary to produce
sleep.

The so-called major tranquillizers or neuroleptics, although used
in small doses in neurotic states, have their main use in the treatment
of the psychoses. It seems that they are effective in reducing psychomotor agitation and other psychotic behaviours. Some effect is also
found on the hallucinations and thought disturbances of psychotic
patients. Attempts have been made to relate individual drugs to
effects on 'target symptoms' but the results are not entirely convincing.

Although we cannot regard the hypothesis of specific anti-
psychotic action of these drugs as established it is of interest that
one of their effects is to abolish drug-induced hallucinosis. We shall
discuss the possible relationship of such hallucinosis to schizophrenia later in this chapter. At present we suggest only that this
may indicate that the action of this group of drugs at least may be
more complex than simple sedation. (We are, of course, referring
here to 'psychological effect' and not to pharmacology.) Perhaps
our difficulties in describing the effects are a consequence of difficulties in evolving a terminology.

A similar problem is found in the consideration of drugs used for
their antidepressant action. Continental psychiatrists have used
terms like thymoleptic or mood-elevating and thymerethic or

drive-stimulating in an attempt to separate various actions of anti
depressant drugs. Terms of this type are less commonly used by
British psychiatrists and the drugs tend to be classified broadly as
antidepressants. Some attention is paid to the importance of
different clinical states (Chapter 4). It does seem to be the case
however, that the effects of the commonly used drugs on mood are
different from those of drugs of, for instance, the amphetamine
group, which are almost entirely stimulant in their action. The
effects of such stimulation are shown in increased activity, flow of
talk, elevation of mood and increased conditionability. Some antidepressants show similar effects, but these are regarded as incidental
to an effect regarded as a normalization of mood. This normalization is in fact not very well defined and tends to be assessed on rating
scales and evaluated by clinicians. An effect can certainly be
measured but may well be only a facet of general improvement.
Certainly assessments of a patient's general state tend to be more
reliable than assessments of individual symptoms. If this is so, the
so-called antidepressant effect is only an inference from the clinical
hypothesis that mood change is primary in depressive illness. Despite the work that has been done on rating scales our techniques in
this area remain predominantly descriptive.

The same is true of our knowledge of the other main group of
psychoactive drugs, the hallucinogens. Drugs of this type have
aroused great interest both among the philosophically minded,
who are prone to think they give an insight into transcendental
reality, and amongst those who search for a physical cause for
mental illness, because they regard hallucinosis as a model psychosis. These drugs, of which mescalin and lysergic acid diethylamide
are examples, have as a main effect the production of states of
hallucination. The hallucinations are mainly visual. Some of them
may be truly hallucinatory but others are more of the nature of
illusions, at least in the sense that they are transformations of an
external stimulus, for instance the perception of parts of the body
as having an infantile form. Some of the experiences might even be
classified as affective in that simple patterns may be perceived as
parts of a complex whole and to take on a greater meaning.
Occasionally delusional ideas occur and may be expressed.

Some of these symptoms undoubtedly occur in schizophrenia
but we remain unconvinced that the analogy is sufficiently close to
be of great value. A similar psychosis can occur as a result of
amphetamine intoxication, but here may be inadvertent. Hallu-

nosis also occurs in other organic psychotic states, but there is
usually more impairment of consciouness than occurs with the use
f hallucinogenic drugs.

As with other techniques that have attempted to simulate psy-
hotic states (e.g. sensory deprivation), early publicized studies,
ften poorly controlled, tended to confuse perceptual distortion
vith hallucinations. They also tended to ignore the often more
mportant factors of experimental set and expectancy. Better con-
rolled experiments have suggested that the drug-induced psychosis
if it occurs) is more analogous to toxic psychoses in general than to
chizophrenia. Furthermore, the effect of individual variations in
ersonality and predisposition is undoubtedly important.

Much is often made of the biochemical similarities between some
allucinogens and both normally and abnormally occurring con-
tituents of the nervous system. Yet such similarities tend to be
uggestive rather than conclusive. For example, there is a chemical
imilarity between mescaline and adrenochrome (a breakdown
roduct of adrenaline). Serotonin (5-hydroxytryptamine) is
hought to be antagonistic to adrenochrome and in schizophrenia
t has been suggested that there is a brain deficiency of serotonin.
ertain broad resemblances exist between these chemicals and
hose used therapeutically such as the phenothiazines. These simi-
arities underly much interesting research.

The content of the drug-induced experience is sometimes con-
idered as part of a psychotherapeutic process. In this situation the
allucinogen is used in much the same way as sedatives and stimu-
ants have been used to ease the expression of ideas and feelings held
o be unconscious by reducing inhibition or by increasing the
pressure' of these aspects of the individual. Where an hallucinogen
s used it is thought that the content of the experience of the patient
vill be related to the psychopathology. Early work at least tended
o use a Jungian framework to organize the data.

In the work of this type, as in similar analytically based work
with hypnosis, the therapist has to beware of the influence of
uggestion. Many subjects describe similar experiences. While this
may well reflect common features between minds it may also
demonstrate a widespread familiarity with at least some of the
popular literature. It is within our experience that some naïve
subjects can be given quite large doses of an hallucinogen with
little effect. In another area an eminent committee has considered
it to be a remarkable feature of cannabis that those who partake of

it are little affected at first but become increasingly susceptible later. There may indeed be oddities in the mode of action of cannabis when inhaled but it is just as likely, when the present situation where groups of adolescents are indulging for 'kicks' in an extralegal activity is taken into account, that suggestion and the need to conform to the group culture are important factors in forming the experience.

Sometimes the recall of experience induced by drugs is associated with the release of affect. Strictly it is only when this occurs that the procedure should be described as abreaction. Repeated abreaction of traumatic experience is again a fairly well established method of treatment. By its means the anxiety associated with the recall or threatened recall of a traumatic experience is extinguished in the same sort of way as in behavioural treatments (Chapter 9).

Problems of dependence and addiction may arise in association with the use of these drugs, therapeutically or otherwise. The usual medical definition of addiction or drug dependence involves a mechanism of physiological change making the individual need the drug. To some extent this is outside our terms of reference, but as we maintain that the organism is one we also maintain that the psychological aspects of addiction are very relevant. There is evidence that personality factors are important in the genesis of addiction, while the nature of the drug plays a considerable part. It is noteworthy that drugs to which patients become addicted produce a rapid transient effect and that this effect in general decreases the individual's appreciation of reality. Their attractions are, therefore, only too clear. Either the patient's personality or the actual unpleasantness of reality may make a drug-aided flight desirable. It is possible that the need which some people find to increase the dose taken arises as a conditioned response to the relief of anxiety. This may be particularly true where the relief is incomplete so that the symptoms continue to generalize at the same time as the patient finds that some relief is possible.

Apart from drugs other methods of physical treatment have been in use to varying extents in psychiatry. In many cases their evaluation has been inadequate. For instance, insulin coma therapy was regarded as the treatment of choice for schizophrenia for many years but in the whole of that time no adequate assessments of its efficacy or indications were made. A single controlled trial, coming at a time when the major tranquillizers were introduced, was enough to cause it to fall into disuse even though, despite its hazards, it might have had a certain value in certain patients.

Similarly the use of brain surgery in psychiatric disturbances has been greatly reduced following a period of uncritical enthusiasm. It seems clear that selective destruction of parts of the brain can produce a variety of psychological effects. Some of them, for instance the reduction in aggressive behaviour following anterior cingulectomy, are still relatively experimental, whereas others like the reduction of tensions following the various types of prefrontal leucotomy are well established. Unfortunately these effects can be overdone and a state of disinhibition and sometimes of fatuity can be produced. Full descriptions of the symptomatology of frontal lobe states will be found in psychiatric textbooks.

When prefrontal leucotomy was a more popular technique, a number of studies were made of its effect on intellectual performance. The latter tended to show some impairment for a month or two after the operation but then performance tended to revert to normal. One exception to this was performance on Porteus Maze type tests where a characteristic pattern of impulsivity and impaired planning ability tended to persist. This result tended to match with the general increase in disinhibition noted of the leucotomized subject. But long-term follow-up of leucotomized subjects has also tended to suggest that a more general reduction in intellectual efficiency may only appear several years after the operation. It is of interest that this is an area in which therapeutic use of psychological/physiological knowledge followed the observation of patients suffering from trauma.

More recently refined methods of selective destruction of brain tissue have been developed. In these techniques multiple electrodes have been inserted into the brain substance, abnormal electrical activity correlated with abnormal psychological symptoms (particularly obsessional symptoms) and the relevant area temporarily or permanently inactivated. It may be that in time much more detailed knowledge of the function of different parts of the human brain will be achieved. Research on animals has given us some valuable clues, but the findings cannot be reliably transferred from one species to another.

The oldest method of studying brain function is by ablating or destroying some region of the brain. At least in dogs, it would appear from decorticated animals that both classical (Pavlovian) and avoidance conditioning can take place in the absence of the neocortex. It therefore follows, and is supported by experiments, that lesser ablations do not remove an animal's learning capacity. But lesions in sensory areas tend to reduce the animal's capacity to acquire *differential* conditioned responses. It would seem that the frontal cortex is important in the *retention* of avoidance responses.

Conditioning has also been studied using the stimulation of the brain by electric currents. A frequent phenomenon of cortical lesions is the production of amnesia for a particular habit but with the subject able to relearn the habit. There is evidence from animal experiments that this post-operative relearning can take place at subcortical levels. Indeed, Lashley thought that his results from studies on maze learning indicated that the cortex was relatively non-specific and equipotential in learning. The only effect of a lesion on learning was a general one where the loss in learning ability was proportional to the mass of the lesion. However, subsequent work has suggested there is some specificity of function and particularly important is the varying effect of lesions on sensory and motor capacities.

It is doubtful how far work on one species can be applied to another species. The foregoing only indicates that this is a large area of study involving many varying techniques and many species.

With humans, knowledge is limited and an important factor in this limitation is the absence of the experimentation possible in work with non-humans. Another problem is the apparent occurrence of individual differences in response. Something of this occurs in non-humans where there is some evidence to suggest that bright rats are less affected by a brain lesion of a certain size than dull rats. Variations in recovery may reflect a subsequent lack of motivation or retraining. Nevertheless there is again evidence that recovery of function often takes place even after severe lesions. Some of this recovery can be attributed to something like Lashley's equipotentiability or simply vicariousness of function. Age has an important bearing on recovery. Brain injury early in life appears to have a greater effect on intelligence than injury in adult life. One reason for this is that brain injury tends to impair learning ability more than what has already been learnt.

In a general way, injury to the dominant hemisphere tends to affect verbal abilities and skills. Injuries to the non-dominant hemisphere tend to affect visual–spatial abilities (Chapter 3). The question to what extent various psychological functions are located in a precise manner in the brain has long been hotly debated. At one end are non-localizers such as Lashley, opposed to other workers who postulate a specificity so marked that they believe a kind of brain map of psychological functioning can be made. Even here, elementary problems tend to have been avoided for many years. For example, it is only fairly recently that subjects with an obvious specific complaint (such as aphasia) have been shown to possess also a less obvious, but significant degree of generalized intellectual impairment.

At present, it would appear that some functions have little or no localization. Others show some specificity but, with the exception of primary motor and sensory functions, the localization is not very precise. Receptive disorders such as the agnosias and sensory aphasias occur usually with lesions in the posterior part of the cortex. Where the receptive disorder is visual–spatial (e.g. reading) it tends to be in the posterior parietal lobe. Difficulty with the understanding of words tends to relate to lesions in the temporoparietal area. Expressive disorders (e.g. the apraxias and motor aphasias) tend to be related to lesions in the frontal lobes although nominal aphasia is frequently located in lesions in the parietal and temporal lobes.

Electrical stimulation, particularly the work of Penfield, has shown some interesting results. Stimulation of the temporal cortex produces a sequence of memory images in some subjects but not all.

As noted in discussing the prefrontal leucotomy, damage or removal here results in difficulties of attention and planning. Results tend to recall, in a broad manner, the impairment in delayed response capacity produced by frontal lobe damage in experiments with non-humans.

The last physical treatment we shall consider is convulsive therapy. In this treatment an epileptic fit is induced in the patient. The induction may be by many methods but at present the passage of an electric current through the brain is the most common. Similarly the motor manifestations of the fit may be modified by drugs. Whatever technique is used the electrical activity of the brain follows the pattern of a *grand mal* epileptic fit. Where no anaesthetic is given the patient is rendered unconscious by the treatment. Following cessation of the fit the patient recovers consciousness fairly rapidly, but there is a period of confusion and some retrograde amnesia.

A fairly frequent complaint made of ECT by patients is of a

resultant memory difficulty. Although this appears to clear up, studies of leucotomy (above) might suggest that a longer-term follow-up should be made of memory capacity in patients who have had repeated courses of ECT. Apart from this it has been suggested that unilateral ECT to the non-dominant hemisphere is just as effective without producing the troublesome, if temporary, memory loss. It has also been suggested that ECT to the dominant hemisphere affects verbal memory (the sort usually 'tested' by the clinician). Tests of visual–spatial memory appear to show that it is affected by ECT applied to the non-dominant hemisphere.

ECT is regarded as specifically indicated for psychotic depression but is used in a much more widespread way. It seems probable that it is of value in many abnormal mental states in their acute phase, particularly where the abnormality is severe. There are many theories as to its mode of action, both physical and psychological. None of them can be regarded as substantiated. It is still uncertain, for example, what is the incidence and course of severe depression in epileptics. Among the psychological theories are the suggestions that the convulsion serves a symbolic role, as orgasm, as punishment, or as death and rebirth. Other psychological theories stress cognitive and psychomotor changes. For example, that depressive memories are temporarily forgotten and give the individual a chance to normalize his behaviour. A suggestion has been made that the treatment is disruption of behaviour and that the recent (abnormal) behaviour has to compete with the longer established (normal) behaviour for reinstatement. This is perhaps more plausible. The physical theories are couched in terms with more 'scientific' appeal but are equally unsupported by evidence.

At present the indications for the use of physical methods of treatment derive almost entirely from clinical psychiatry, as do the assessments of their results. Psychology's main contribution has been in the design and construction of rating scales for the investigation of drugs. It may be inevitable that physical methods of treatment will develop clear physical indications but at this stage in their development there is scope for a considerable expansion of psychological work.

As noted earlier, the effect of drugs on behaviour is still often recorded at a purely clinical or even anecdotal level. This is often compounded by the further fault of proving that drug B is more effective than drug A whereas a more relevant finding might be that neither are any better, or only marginally so, than some earlier preparation. Whether or not it becomes possible to provide an acceptable link between a physical cause of some psychiatric illness and a physical antidote or treatment, some acceptable methods need to be developed for measuring the psychological aspects of these. Although these psychological aspects would involve some attention to cognitive functioning (ability, memory, learning) the more important are, as would be expected, those of personality, emotion and motivation (Chapters 4, 5 and 6). The problem is not so much a specific one of devising suitable measures for a particular illness or drug but more the need for the establishment of an acceptable theoretical and measuring framework. This may involve assessments of personality, emotion and motivation as discussed in earlier chapters but a wholly physiological system of measurement is theoretically possible.

12

Small Groups

Although we can propose no rigid definition of a small group as opposed to a large group it can be accepted that a small group is one of such a size that all its members can meet face to face and can achieve a fairly detailed understanding of each other's behaviour. In therapeutic situations such groups may contain up to a dozen patients. Certain smaller groups, particularly family groups, are also relevant to clinical psychiatry, and some psychiatrists have evolved a theoretical system and method of treatment involving such groups. It is, of course, possible to view the normal dyadic psychotherapeutic situation as a special case of a group, but the usual concepts of group psychotherapy imply the presence of six to ten individuals. We shall discuss here some of the clinical features of groups and some of the methods which have been used to study them. Unfortunately there has been as yet no adequate, experimental examination of the processes in therapeutic groups nor is the clinical psychologist often called upon to help in selection procedures or to advise on therapeutic techniques. There is, however, a great deal of work, mostly in the borderland between sociology and psychology, which is relevant to the study of both the small groups discussed here and the larger ones discussed in the next chapter.

Whatever view is taken of theoretical systems like the Freudian one, it is usually accepted that the learning which takes place in the family group is of great importance in the development of the individual. Nevertheless, it is justifiable to point out that there may only be a limited causal connection between childhood experiences and adult behaviour. Both may be manifestations of the same genetic or constitutional factors. Yet the family, at all ages, is the small group *par excellence* to which an individual belongs. It is common sense, though perhaps emotionally provoking, to consider all human interactions as being illuminated by examining the role of any individual in his family group.

Many psychotherapeutic concepts are explicitly derived from intrafamilial relationships and it is considered that the individual's reactions to other people throughout life may be conditioned by his perception in them of attributes derived from early experience. Apart from this aspect of familial influence there are the problems arising from day-to-day conflicts and interpersonal difficulties.

It is customary to describe two types of family group, the nuclear family and the extended family. The nuclear family consists of parents and children, while the extended family includes grandparents and often other relatives, uncles, cousins and so on. Nowadays in many parts of this country the nuclear family is the more common group, whereas at other times and in other cultures the extended family is predominant. Both systems of organization present their problems, some of which we shall outline as an introduction to the consideration of other groups. Problems in the nuclear family group may be a consequence of the limitations imposed by its size in a purely practical way. There may be difficulty in obtaining help in the task of caring for sick or otherwise dependent members or because of the small number of people with whom close relationships can be formed. In this second class of problem, with which we are concerned here, it may prove possible for unsatisfactory relationships within the family to be compensated by external ones or the individual may be caught in a complex and contradictory situation.

In the extended family there are, of course, more people to deal with, giving both more opportunities of conflict and better chances of refuge. Because of the continued closer contact between members of the family greater friction may arise over the problems of changing roles as its members age. The extent to which this occurs will be determined not only by the individual personalities concerned but also by the social mores in which the family group is embedded.

It is not essential that the members of an extended family live under one roof, although where this is not the case some inquiry will be needed to determine the geographical extent of the family group. Willett noted that in the working-class area he studied it was common for a married couple to live near the wife's parents, so that while the husband became relatively detached from his family the wife's relationships, and particularly the matriarchal hand, remained firm. Mobility, both social and geographical, is probably one of the major determinants of the separation of nuclear family groups, accounting for the predominance of this type of group in the middle-class families compared with the greater extension found (in this country at least) in upper and lower classes. Ownership of land may contribute to extension or to dispersal of a family group, depending often on the customs of inheritance of a culture. Consideration of the nature of the family group involved may well clarify some problems arising in clinical practice.

Once the extent of the group has been established it is possible to proceed with its analysis. At present there are two principal aspects of the group which can be subjected to analysis, namely, its communication systems and the roles enacted by its members. These approaches are complementary and consideration of one will often

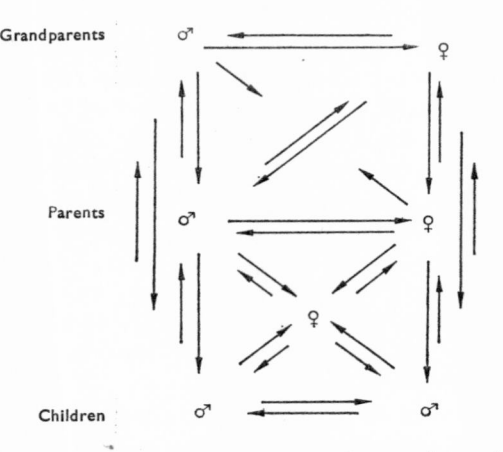

Fig. 8. The communication structure of an age/masculine dominated extended family group (some vectors omitted).

throw considerable light on the nature of the other. In the family group we are describing, the possibilities are fairly limited but, as we show in our discussion of therapeutic groups, they can be generalized.

Within the group there are usually two systems of communication—verbal and non-verbal. An adequate examination of the group should involve both communication systems. Each system has its formal structural characteristics which define the channels of information flow, their capacity and the direction of travel of information. Consideration of these parameters alone will give us a fair amount of information about the nature of the groups and a suggestion of the roles adopted by its members. For instance, if we represent communication channels as vectors with the length of the

ector corresponding to the amount of communication (consider-
ig only verbal communication and ignoring information content)
e may find the structure in an extended group to be as shown in
ig. 8.

We have not shown all the possible vectors in this group but the
attern is clear and implies an hierarchical family structure in which
eniority is the first determinant of status and masculinity the
econd. This type of pattern is quite common and contrasts with
he idealized pattern of the 'democratic' nuclear family (Fig. 9).

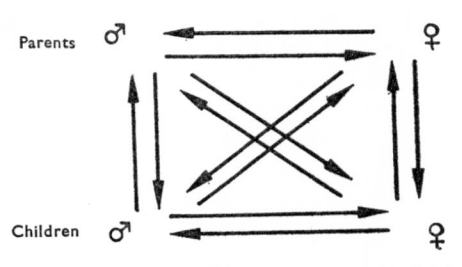

FIG. 9. The communication structure of a 'democratic' family group.

Such a pattern must be rare in nature and some hierarchical
elements can often be found. Where an approximation to this
pattern is achieved, however, members of the group may suffer
considerable uncertainty about the role they are expected to
adopt. This uncertainty is in contrast to the hierarchical group
where the role is only too clear and the difficulty is in its acceptance
or performance.

Clearly the communication and role structure of the group are
related and should be mutually appropriate. We have already
indicated the two major role relationships, i.e. mutual equality as
contrasted with an authoritarian dominant–submissive relationship. These relationships are modified by feeling states and personal concepts of the individuals in the group. Thus, in a
consideration of a family group the father may be viewed as an
authoritarian figure who may in addition be fiercely punitive or
alternatively a supporting and encouraging individual. On the
other hand the mother, although she may maintain an authoritarian status, may also be regarded as accepting or rejecting.
Similarly, siblings who may be more or less equal in the hierarchy
can be mutually affectionate or hostile or may take opposing views.

Further, the roles of each member of the group may be viewe
differently by other members and may also differ according
which of the parameters of the structure are under consideratio
Again, as an example, siblings may have a relationship of mutu
equality between themselves while in their parents' eyes they a
graded as dominant or submissive according to their ages and se
At the same time, age and sex may also determine the amount
affection lavished upon them, sometimes in reverse order to th
first hierarchy.

We have here taken certain broad concepts and applied them t
the family structure in a rather abstract way. Normally, of cours
the roles within a family are defined by common words—mothe
father, child, son, daughter, brother, sister, grandmother, etc. I
psychiatric discussion this term of relationship is often modified b
an adjective with affective (and unfortunately sometimes moralistic
overtones, like rejecting, passive, demanding, etc. The adjective i
usually clear in its meaning and, in discussion of a family, the nou
often refers appropriately to a specific person. However, this is no
always so and particularly when these concepts are again general
ized, it is important to be clear what is meant by the noun. I
seems to us that in almost all of these discussions the terminology i
applied as derived from an age/masculinity dominated hierarchica
structure. This is hardly surprising as this descriptive system
derives eventually from Freud who was a product of such a struc
ture. Possibly some recent emphasis on rejecting mothers is a con
sequence of role conflict where the culture appears to be changing
to an age/female dominant authoritarian structure as is said to b
occurring in parts of the western hemisphere.

Role conflict is one source of discord in family relationships. I
may express itself in the behaviour of the whole group or in the
behaviour of individual members while its expression may be
verbal or non-verbal. So far we have not considered the none-
verbal communication structure of the family group. It is more
difficult to elucidate than the verbal structure, particularly when
they are not congruent. Nonetheless, where role conflicts are under
investigation an analysis of the formal structure and content of both
verbal and non-verbal systems is essential. Non-verbal structures
can be illustrated by vectors in the same way as verbal ones but the
major problem is in measuring them. Observer error can be surprisingly large when dealing with recordable verbal communications and this is greatly increased when the significance of things like

posture and gesture are being considered. Recently the situation has improved in some centres with the provision of cameras to provide a record of the situation but even then it is necessary to establish standards between observers as to what has information content and is, therefore, communication and what has not. The simple course of asking the subject is not aways available because he may be unaware of or unwilling to admit the communicative nature of his actions, while once this is pointed out to him the situation is drastically modified.

Research is at present in progress, particularly in the United States, in an attempt to devise a method of analysis of bodily movements associated with speech. The verbal communication powers of the researchers are unfortunately poor and severely infected with with jargon but it does seem that some progress is being made. Movements of body parts have been observed to occur in association with specific references in speech and the direction of movement is related to the subject of the reference. Thus, a movement of a body part away from the speaker is associated with words like 'he', 'those' or 'some' and towards the speaker with words like 'I,' 'here' or 'now'. Many other more complex movements have been observed. Another study is more directly associated with psychiatric interviewing noting, among other things, that the psychiatrist tends to have two main total body postures, leaning forward to give advice or to urge the patient to give more information and leaning back for passive listening. Other, more diffuse, postural communications are described in Argyll's book on social psychology. As yet though there is no formalized investigation of non-verbal behaviour which seems to oppose the verbal communication.

Another factor to be considered in the assessment of role conflict is the efficiency of transmission of information. In our discussion so far we have assumed that the communication is transmitted without interference or 'noise' and that it is not processed in any way on reception. This is rarely the case. There is now a mathematical theory of communication which is extending rapidly and is used in physical systems to describe and analyse problems of this type. Many psychological experiments have made use of the theory to analyse the findings of suitably designed experiments but as yet the method has not been extensively used in the clinical field. Our use of terms (like 'noise') derived from this discipline, therefore, represents at present a hope that they will prove applicable rather than a rigid interpretation.

M

Role conflict will arise when there are differences between the role assigned to the individual in the formal structure and his own interpretation of his role or the interpretation of the role which is made by other members of the group. Such conflicts may be most complex and difficult to analyse so we shall give here only two examples of a possible role conflict situation. In both cases we shall consider an age/masculine dominant nuclear family structure as the cultural stereotype and consider the position in that group of a father whose personality attributes are submissive and who may, therefore, be considered to see himself in the role of a son, or possibly even a daughter. In the first instance we shall assume that this pattern is not accepted by the family group and in the second that it is. Where the family do not accept the situation a variety of difficulties may arise, depending largely on the extent to which the individual members are aware of the position. If even the deviant father is unaware of the role conflict he will attempt, with little success, to fulfil the role which is expected of him. His failure will give rise to anxieties within himself and within the other family members. When he is aware of his own inclination and attempts to enact his chosen role the problems will be a consequence of his family's attempts to divert him from it. They may continue to behave in accordance with the usual expectations, for instance the children may misbehave without correction from other adults in the family because everybody expects the father to correct them, or the whole family may combine to force him to fulfil a more 'normal' role. Even more complex situations will arise when individual members of the family interpret differently from each other their own roles and those of others within the family group.

Occasionally the whole family may accept the situation. In fact it may fit in with their own role concepts. A situation may then arise which, although a little unusual, is not unknown in clinical practice, where the wife goes out to work while the husband stays at home and looks after the house. As this type of behaviour is not acceptable to our hypothetical community the family must find an adequate reason for it. A good reason is the illness of the husband and father and it is where this phenomenon manifests itself in psychiatric symtomatology that this type of family disorder is seen clinically. In other circumstances, for instance, chronic disablement, the acceptance of an unusual role may be a satisfactory method of adjustment for the patient and his family.

When the communication structures of these situations are

analysed we find that they vary considerably. They tend to be simplest in those conditions which are most obviously deviant. Thus, when the family all accept an abnormal role for one of its members the communication structure will be unusual in some respects—for instance, the frequency and direction of communications—but in general, the verbal and non-verbal networks coincide and the content of a communication is usually simple and is understood. On the other hand where no member, not even the sufferer, is fully aware of the conflict situation, the verbal and non-verbal networks may well differ in formal structure and in content to a considerable degree and in complicated ways.

Disruptive family patterns such as this are important in a number of related theories attributing schizophrenia to family interaction processes. The schizophrenogenic mother as described by Fromm Reichman and others was one of the earlier concepts in this field. This concept suggested the development of schizophrenia to be associated with the child rearing practice adopted by mothers of a certain personality make-up. Interest is now centred on the whole family as a unit for study rather than on particular individuals. The Bateson double-bind hypothesis postulates a special learning situation from which the child (being a child and dependent) cannot escape. This situation involves the repeated experience of incongruent instructions where punishment might be expected whatever the choice. Schizophrenic behaviour is thought to result from such a pathological communication situation. Lidz thought a blurring of age and generation boundaries to be an important feature in the families of schizophrenics. Parents behaved inappropriately for their age and sex, not only with each other, but also with the child. The child consequently learns inappropriate behaviour and his identity development is faulty. The entire family is seen as pathological. The Lidz formulation is, in many ways, an application of classical psychoanalytic ideas to the family group. Wynne's suggestions in this field stem more from normal social psychology and stress that thought disorder in schizophrenia derives from disturbed interaction patterns in the family. Wynne's emphasis is on the family system rather than on dyadic and triadic relationships within it. Patterns of interaction within these families are amorphous and meaning is blurred and irrelevant.

Laing has been an ardent British exponent of the disturbed family as a key factor in schizophrenia. It is clear that such

approaches suggest that the schizophrenic patient is only one aspec
of a general family psychopathology. His madness, in fact, enable
the other family members to appear normal and they may resis
any normalization of his condition. Interesting as such approache
are, proof of their validity is still required. It is obvious that the
interaction processes within a family will be disturbed if one of it
members becomes schizophrenic. It is still unsubstantiated that the
family disturbance generally comes first and on those occasion
when it does, may only reflect the presence of other schizophrenic
personalities in the family. Such a standpoint would be the more
orthodox one in attributing schizophrenia to genetic and constitutional factors. Unfortunately the orthodox views are also unsupported by convincing evidence.

The family group has been studied with regard to other disturbances of behaviour. The psychopath or delinquent may come
from a family where the social roles are generally of a kind liable to
be in conflict with those of society. The role of the mother has
tended to be emphasized but in recent years, particularly with
regard to delinquency, the role of the father has been held to be
important. It is postulated, for instance, that the father may have
been absent for some reason or lacking in effectiveness.

We shall now extend our consideration to the small therapeutic
group. Typically this consists of one therapist and six to twelve
patients of assorted ages, sex and diagnosis. Many variations can
obtain; groups may have additional non-patient members, contain patients of only one sex or diagnosis and so on. There is a great
variation in the practice of group therapy. The therapist may
adopt a Freudian attitude and be passive or very active and
directive as when group therapy is regarded as a course of lecture
discussions. Although when it was first introduced group psychotherapy was seen as an economically feasible substitute for individual psychotherapy, it has gradually developed into a technique
in its own right with emphasis on the analysis of the behaviour
of the whole group rather than on the behaviour of individuals
treated as though they were in some way distinct from the group.
In our discussion we shall again apply the concepts of communication and role which we discussed in relation to family groups and
also refer briefly to some of the emotional and motivational factors
which we discussed more fully in earlier chapters.

Much group psychotherapy has been developed by psychoanalytically trained or orientated workers. As their theoretical

framework is couched in terms of the family group, many of the descriptions of group interaction tend to use similar terminology in a more metaphorical way. Provided that the derivation of stereotypes for such a discussion is agreed, usually on our hypothetical assumption of an age/masculine dominant hierarchical structure, descriptions in 'family' terms provide a simple shorthand and are more readable than the alternative, more jargon-ridden approach. Despite this we shall, with apologies, tend to jargon.

At the time of its formation the generalized therapeutic group contains two classes of individual: patients and therapists. For simplicity in discussion we shall assume first that there is only one therapist and that the patients are, psychiatrically speaking, naïve. The therapist will have a more or less distinct idea what his role is in the group and a similarly clear or unclear idea of the verbal and non-verbal communication structure which will occur and which he will endeavour to establish. Similarly, the patients will have varying ideas and expectations about the group. Their ideas may conflict with those of the therapist and where this is the case, the first changes to occur in the group will be directed to resolving the conflict. With its resolution the group may obtain cohesion which it did not possess before.

As in our discussion of family groups, the structure may be more or less hierarchical. Usually patients anticipate an hierarchical structure of two levels, the therapist directing the patients who are equal among themselves. In didactic groups, which may include groups where an attempt is made to use principles of learning theory, this may well be true and, as the therapist has the same concept of his role, the group functions smoothly, at least in its initial stages. Most group therapies, however, are based on some form of analytic principle, using the term in its general and not necessarily its Freudian sense. This means that the behaviour of the group as a whole is to be studied and interpreted and the atmosphere which is usually sought is one of a common research endeavour to elucidate the intricacies of the situation. Even though this is explained at the outset patients do not necessarily accept it, so the first event which occurs in such a group is that the therapist attempts to abdicate. This move arouses considerable feeling among the patients in the group which provides material for discussion and also, if successful, precipitates a revealing struggle for leadership. We should point out here that in our opinion this abdication can never be entirely successful, even with the most non-directive of therapists.

It must be rare, for instance, for a group assembled without the therapist to continue its discussion without pause or modification when he enters. Indeed, the inexperienced therapist is often at a loss to overcome the hush which occurs when he joins a group. Further, when the struggle for leadership takes place, the therapist is usually at hand with interpretative comments which will modify it to a great extent and in many groups he will become the *eminence grise*. Sometimes, of course, the group will not permit the therapist to abdicate formal leadership and its structure will remain authoritarian. A good deal of investigation of these group processes is yet to be done even at the verbal level while examination of non-verbal processes in therapeutic groups is very much in its infancy.

In practice the process does not occur in an overt manner. The group tends to remain silent, awaiting a lead from the therapist. When nothing is forthcoming a request for guidance usually occurs. In an analytic type of group the therapist refers his question back to the group. A member of the group may then attempt to take over the leadership. One way in which this is done is for that person to state aloud the assumption that the group is for treatment and then to ask directly for the symptoms of individual members. If he is a little diffident he may recount his own symptoms first. Where this patient is more aggressive his manner may come to resemble a stereotype of prosecuting counsel.

At this stage the therapist may elect not to interpret the behaviour as it may be of more value to await responses. These can be cohesive within the group, accepting or rejecting the dominant member, or indeed both, in that the group members may give appropriate replies but in a resentful manner. Alternatively another individual may challenge for the leadership, perhaps by using a modicum of extra knowledge, thus:

1st patient	Well, what are we supposed to discuss?
Therapist	You can discuss whatever you wish, as what is relevant will eventually emerge.
1st patient	I suppose we all have something wrong with us. I'm here because I have headache all the time. Perhaps it would help if the first thing we did was to get to know what is the matter with everybody.
2nd patient	I'm not so sure that it's the shaking and so on that I get that's at the root of it. It seems more that other people upset me and I wonder why I'm so sensitive.

And then the battle is on, but discreetly. The therapist may be sought as an ally, probably by the second patient if he continues: 'Before I came the doctor said I should have to sort myself out'. This ploy may well be successful as it probably represents the direction in which the therapist wants the group to move. However, it may still be too early to interpret, while support at this stage may result in the therapist acquiring the leadership in such a way that he will never lose it again.

The methods of observation available are those of the therapist/observer, observation using one-way screens or television, possibly supplemented by recording devices, and observation of changes in the patients made outside the group situation, either directly or using questionnaire and other techniques. All have their place in building up a picture of group processes. We have discussed communication structures earlier and here will only add that these fluctuate according to the leadership of the group and the roles which its members play. One of the fundamental assumptions of group psychotherapy is that the patients in the group will enact the role which they normally prefer, but that in the group setting the behaviour patterns will become obvious and subject to modification by interpretation and by group process. This was shown in a surprisingly simple way in the case of a young man who complained that he was unpopular with his fellows. Several sessions of individual psychotherapy failed to elicit any reason for this apparent insecurity, so he was placed in a group. In this situation the true difficulty rapidly became apparent. He was indeed unpopular for he had a most unfortunate personality with large components of conceit and aggressiveness. The rest of the group pointed this out and he was able to modify his behaviour appropriately. Of course, such simplicity as this is rare and it may take a considerable time for an individual's preferred role to become apparent. Further, discrepancies between various roles will be observed. For instance, it may happen that in some situations a patient may play or wish to play a dependent role while all the rest of the time he may show dominance. Where the dominant behaviour is a major part of his self concept, the submissive roles will give rise to difficulties both in understanding what they are, and in coping with them. Both these problems can be dealt with in the group situation.

Emotional disturbance is often associated with these conflict situations and, of course, with the fluctuating roles played by group members. We have described a struggle for leadership which may be renewed at different times in the group's history. This struggle will often be associated with feelings of hostility between the contenders for the leadership. Such feelings will be pointed out by the therapist and examined by the group. In the course of such a conflict the contenders will form alliances with other group members. Such alliances may be reinforced by a positive affective bond which could be called liking or love, depending on its strength. These emotional relationships, too, will be conditioned by the patient's individual self concepts and by his perception of the roles of the other members of the group. As with individual psychotherapy on analytic lines, a fundamental assumption of this approach is that the patient's disorder is in the area of interpersonal relationships.

The therapist/observer studying group processes as they occur is in a very difficult position from the point of view of recording data. Unfortunately many claim that the introduction of additional methods of collecting and recording data distort the situation to such an extent that the observations are valueless. This is a rather extreme view and, if accepted, would invalidate much work. Our feeling is that the interference with the situation is probably not excessive and that, provided the necessary reservations are borne in mind, meaningful conclusions can be drawn.

Powdermaker and Frank used the observer within the group in their examination of group processes by a method which they describe as 'situation analysis'. They describe the interactions taking place in groups in situations where hostility is aroused, where a patient attempts to monopolize the situation and others. Their work considers the problems of observer reliability and the problems of assessment of progress and demonstrates that these problems can be examined in a meaningful way. A situation analysis considers in detail the setting and effects of events which appear particularly significant in the progress of a group. Much of the discussion is based on analytic theory but there is also an appreciation of the relationship of this to considerations of status and leadership within the group. In this, as in most such discussions, some of the theoretical formulations of Adler with respect to the motivational aspects of power are implicit. It seems to be Adler's misfortune that his important theoretical contributions are so widely accepted that he is rarely given credit for them.

We have described group therapy in its normal, analytically orientated form. Every possible variation has probably by now been tried and has some value. Even leaderless groups have been described wherein patients examine and learn about themselves. The interesting feature about the latter report is that at least one-third of the patients were psychotic but that such groups compared favourably at follow-up with traditionally therapist-led groups. The researchers point out that a leaderless group has no problems of therapist dependancy, is less likely to become symptom orientated and is more likely to tackle its problems. The need for personal contact with staff members can be satisfied in other activities.

Other groups also function for a therapeutic purpose. Alcoholics Anonymous is an organization very dependent for its efficiency on the help the group can bring to an individual. Such a group organization with an aim of immediate therapeutic help has been adopted in other fields such as suicide. Psychodrama is a method of group therapy first devised by Moreno. Here a group of people act, in a therapeutic situation, the roles and situations known to produce conflict in them. Attempts have also been made to examine group processes using outside observers viewing the situation through one way screens or television transmissions. Such techniques have usually included recordings of the proceedings on tape but the subsequent records need adequate analysis. Analysis of the tape transcriptions by techniques with a verbal anxiety scale as done by Gleseret or the interaction chronograph of Bales have been reported. In most of these investigations the mass of data makes analysis extremely difficult.

Bales, in what he calls Interaction Process Analysis, uses twelve categories in observing and recording behaviour, each category being part of an interaction system. This analysis is directed more to the types and methods of interpersonal behaviour than to the content of speech. Individuals can be compared with each other and pooled interaction profiles can be used to compare different groups.

Kraupl Taylor has attempted an examination of group attitudes by obtaining indices of individual preferences amongst the members. His techniques are derived from the sociometric methods introduced by Moreno. Moreno analysed group interaction patterns by eliciting who related to who in any group. For example, studies of combat groups in wartime would show that in successful groups the nominal leader was also the effective leader. Less successful groups would show a more fragmentary social group pattern. Such sociometric analysis and its consequent sociograms of group

interaction have been much used in the analysis of group effectiveness. The mathematical techniques which Kraupl Taylor uses are,
at least to most psychiatrists, complex and sophisticated but in
essence his argument is that if patients are asked to indicate the
intensity of their love–hate feelings for other members of the group
and what they think the other members feel towards them (the
guessed self appeal) it will be possible to relate the scores to three
social–psychological dimensions. These dimensions are the public
dimension of events in the group, the dyadic dimension of events in
person-to-person interactions and the autistic dimension of intra-
psychic events. Scores can be obtained for these variables but it is
not yet clear whether they vary as a therapeutic group ages. Such
variation is to be expected if they are to be related to changes in the
group.

We have already discussed the place of social factors in motivation. We have noted the relevance of the family group as a criterion
for studying a person's social interactions. It is clear that when
meeting another person we immediately start to make decisions
about them. Such decisions will determine our precise way of be-
having with them and include factors such as age, sex, personality
and social status. Such interactions may be studied by recording
how long A speaks to B and B to A and what deference, physical
proximity or eye contact is shown. Is there cooperation or competition? Are emotions expressed? What determines the growth of a
relationship? It has been found that physical proximity is a
necessity for the development of a relationship. Only then can the
necessary similar interests and attitudes be manifested and interwoven.

Groups of two (dyads) are the simplest form of social interaction
and have an important place in the family structure in the roles of
the husband–wife (father–mother). Studies of spouses tend to show
that they are like each other in respect of age, intelligence, social
class and personality factors. Similarity, despite common belief, is
more often the rule than spouses who complement each other.
Perhaps differences lead to conflict. In a group of three each of the
original members of the dyad now has to relate with another person. Various kinds of competition and pairing will occur. It has
been pointed out that such a triad occurs in the father–mother–child
group and that so-called Oedipal conflicts may be explained on this
basis rather than in sexual terms. If group size increases from three
to ten or more, less individual participation is ensured. Only by

forming rules and dividing the tasks of the group members is its stability maintained. In such groups a hierarchy of status is always evident. At a simple level such varying degrees of dominance can be seen on the pecking order of chickens.

Obviously, in human society an individual may have varying social roles as he belongs to more than one group. At home he is a father and dominant, but at his work he may be relatively low in the hierarchy and submissive. A dramatic change in social role is experienced when a person becomes a hospital patient. A patient, unfortunately, tends to be at the bottom end of the pecking order, thus perhaps severely lowering his self-esteem. In fact it is revealing to consider a hospital and its staff as comprising a small society containing many social groups, each with its own pattern of motives. Such groups frequently possess an organization in which the patient all too often becomes only of secondary concern. The hospital organization, in a social group sense, may exist for the benefit of its staff rather than its patients (Chapter 13).

Interaction between people involves the use of the social conventions of the culture of the people concerned. We may note in passing that cultures may vary a great deal in their social conventions. Such cultural variations may be quite dramatic and obvious or less marked and unregarded as such. If such differences are not allowed for, a person of culture A tends to judge another person in terms of his own culture A, instead of the other person's culture B. Whatever the social convention a person has for governing his interpersonal behaviour, it has to be learned. As such, the social skills involved may be considered in the way any other skill can be studied. The play, *Pygmalion*, explicitly deals with such an approach and it may well be useful to consider many personality disorders as arising from an insufficient or inefficient repertoire of social skills. In psychotherapy, individual or group, behaviourist or analytic, what is important may be the acquisition by a patient of a more efficient and acceptable repertoire of social skills.

To regard at least some personality disorders as being primarily a disturbance of social or group behaviour is quite different from the Freudian emphasis on the sexual instinct and its vicissitudes. Whether the social disturbance is regarded as primary or secondary, it seems reasonable to expect that an increase in social competence can only be beneficial to a mentally ill person. Many schizophrenics rarely engage in social behaviour. Manics and depressives bring to group interactions the limitations of their prevailing mood, the one being disruptive, the other contributing little in a nihilistic way. Neurotic behaviour is almost synonymous with social incompetence arising from the constraints the neurosis puts on normal interaction. Psychopathy on the other hand, is a disorder where the only disturbance to be observed might be in the psychopath's social (or more properly antisocial) behaviour.

Although we have largely discussed small group behaviour from a psychiatric illness point of view, we have tried to show how our understanding of social behaviour in mental illness is enhanced by a knowledge of the social psychology of normal groups. The therapeutic interview, of course, is only one example of the interview which is used in many contexts for many reasons. The personnel officer, bank manager, salesman and so on are all skilled in their own way in conducting social interactions in a small group situation. It is often said we live in the age of the committee and accordingly the success of our society depends on how efficiently such committees function. The committee, too, is a small social group, as are such different assemblies as the family, the jury and one's immediate work colleagues. All are subject to much the same governing principles and of necessity to the same weaknesses and dilemmas. In recent years T (training) groups have become fashionable. To some extent they are similar to psychotherapeutic groups and they aim to teach people how to deal with social situations more effectively. Such training is thought to be useful to people whose work involves dealing with other people. One of its main features is to teach people to give and receive information concerning their impact on others.

It is almost self-evident that all social groups establish accepted standards of behaviour and to be accepted as a group member each individual must conform to these standards. What is more surprising is the extent to which an individual's judgement and attitudes can be influenced by other people. In laboratory experiments, for example, as carried out by Asch, a subject faced by a group making decisions apparently at variance with the 'facts' would tend also to distort his decision in a similarly erroneous way. Some such subjects did so in order not to disagree with the majority, but others apparently accepted the group's decision. Obviously such phenomena are not only relevant to group behaviour but also to perceptual data.

Festinger has coined the term 'cognitive dissonance' for the effect produced when simultaneous cognitions do not fit together or are dissonant. Such dissonance leads to efforts to make the cognitions fit better, by reducing the dissonance. This reduction may be made by dismissing the dissonant person or item as unimportant; by changing one's own opinion or attempting to change the other's; or by seeking support elsewhere. Conforming to the group is one method by which a person may reduce dissonance. It has been claimed that non-conformers, compared with conformers, are more intellectually effective, more realistic and objective about their parents, more permissive in child-rearing methods and less authoritarian.

It is in the social group that the question of leadership arises, to some extent, leadership might be linked with dominance, and in the family group the parents have a leadership role compared with children. Conflict may arise where the parents compete with each other for the role of overall leader. As we have seen, the social group of the family may be disturbed where the chosen leader, say the father, can not or will not accept his role.

Leadership has been studied since the last century by psychologists and sociologists. At first attempts were made to identify the personality traits typical of leaders. On the whole this approach has not been successful although it might be suggested that leaders tend to be more intelligent, have greater social status and are 'responsible' and achieving. But an alternative view, namely that everyone is a potential leader given the appropriate situation, is also probably invalid and may only reflect a cultural ideal of social equality. The classic work of Lewis, Lippitt and White, showing that democratically organized groups were more successful than autocratic or *laisser faire* ones, may again only reflect the social views held in certain societies. A recurrent problem in studying leadership is the varying definition of leadership. For example a distinction needs to be made between participatory and supervisory leadership. It is probably true in any event that an emphasis on leadership in group studies has led to an unwarranted neglect of the behaviour of the other group members. Perhaps this undue emphasis on leadership rather than peer relationships is a reflection of somewhat pathological dependency needs in our society.

Social groups have also been studied with regard to problem solving. Obviously a group may have advantages over any one individual, having more members to call on. But in fact a number of studies suggest that group problem solving may be inefficient. It not only takes longer than an individual would, but the results may be in error. Such errors can arise through faulty communication and through the emotional attitudes set up by the group. Various communication networks have been studied and it seems that the wheel-type network is the most efficient. In such a network nobody can communicate with anyone else except through a central subject.

Problems of leadership and communication in small groups can be seen in various studies of group dynamics. The classic experiments in this field concern small groups where authoritarian, democratic and *laisser faire* types of leadership are compared. Such studies stress the advantages of democratic leadership in that it produces greater output, less conflict and more originality. Nevertheless, although a democratic group may work efficiently, any group brings a pressure to bear on individual judgement. Rather than feel excluded from the group an individual might conform to a group decision against his own feelings. Experiments have shown, in fact, that group pressure can result in an individual altering his previously accurate judgement to agree with an erroneous group decision.

It will be apparent that we have here only been able to give an outline of some of the phenomena of small groups and the methods which have been employed to study them. Group psychotherapy is now widely practised in many different forms, yet there is no adequate theoretical structure for it, neither is there any adequate examination of its results or the indications for treatment. Investigation of these problems will be slow and difficult because of the problems of experimental method, the time involved and the masses of data to be handled. In this field of research as much as any other, the cooperation of psychiatrist, psychologist and probably the mathematician and his computer are essential.

Large Groups

As in the last chapter, our concept of large groups is not identical with that of the sociologist. We are concerned with communities larger than that of the usual therapeutic group where the inter-action between members can be closely studied but still small enough for all the members to meet, at least occasionally and in theory. It is also worth noting that much in the study of group behaviour can be resolved into questions concerning small groups as large groups almost inevitably break down into smaller assemblies. Our limits can be defined in terms of hospital structure and are conveniently set as the ward unit at the lower end and the hospital as a whole at the upper. Psychiatry is, of course, concerned with the larger community and, in its pursuit of respectability and that even more chimerical phenomenon mental health, will be interested in the methods of influencing public opinion and modifying community behaviour which we shall discuss more briefly.

More than 30 years ago the now classic Hawthorne studies showed that workers' productivity might be more affected by the interest taken in them by experimenters than by the variation in the physical condition of their working environment. We might also note Patterson's demonstration of the importance of status factors and communication channels in maintaining morale and func-tional efficiency. Despite this it was not until 1954 that sociological studies really began to affect psychiatric methods. The seminal books is of course *The Mental Hospital* (Stanton and Schwartz, 1954). Although there had been previous attempts to examine hospital cultures, this work had much more influence, perhaps because it appeared at a time when faith in a well established physical treat-ment (insulin coma therapy) had been struck a damaging blow and was soon to be demolished entirely.

At this point it is useful to describe briefly the development of studies of large groups. Gustave Le Bon in 1896 focused attention on the relationship of the individual to a large group. In the crowd he thought characteristics were displayed which were more than the sum, or average, of the component members. It was an entity in itself, with a feeling of power, and the individual members of the group were liable to imitative behaviour due to a condition of heightened suggestibility. Later writers have agreed with Le Bon in stressing the emotionality and suggestibility of a crowd. Furthermore, the tendency to behave at a more primitive level than many of its component individuals has frequently led to comparing crowd behaviour to psychopathic behaviour. On the other hand it has been stressed that crowd behaviour may only enable an individual to behave in a way he would normally (by virtue of inner or outer constraints) be unable to. There are many people, for example, who would probably never, under any conditions, become members of a lynching mob. But obviously there is an interaction between the large group and the individual and this results in a difficulty in predicting to what extent any individual can remain uninfluenced by the group.

In the past, such group phenomena have been strikingly seen in what have been called 'mental epidemics'. Examples of these are the various medieval crusades and pilgrimages, particularly the children's crusade. In more recent times are the more political crowds with pathological behaviour such as the Nazis or the Chinese Red Guards. Cantril, Gaudet and Hartzog in 1940 made an analysis of the panic following the famous Orson Wells broadcast in 1938 of an invasion from Mars. It was estimated that out of six million people hearing the broadcast, at least a million were frightened and disturbed. Many left the city in panic conditions.

As we are all members of large groups (temporary or permanent), it is important to stress that the behaviour of any individual member may appear relatively irrational and disturbed. It is no use expecting the behaviour of people in large groups (as in institutions such as factories and hospitals) to be consistently rational and to accord with the formally laid down rules of that institution. Such expectancies clearly pay insufficient attention to the non-rational aspects of motivation and personality. At a more complex level we shall see that individuals resist attempts by the larger formal group to pigeon-hole them into conveniently restricted roles. Striking examples of this are the worker in the factory and the patient in a hospital. In both cases attempts to limit the role of the individual for the convenience of hierarchy of the larger group lead to disas-

trous consequences. In the first instance the obvious disturbances
of strikes and under-productivity occur. In the second case there
are the less obvious but none the less severe disturbances of being
forced into a narrow 'patient' role rather than being treated as an
individual, if sick, personality.

Both in factories and hospitals the human factor of the group tends
to be ignored until its presence becomes inexorably expressed.
Attention is directed to manipulating physical conditions as if the
human group is a simple stimulus response mechanism. The classic
example of this is the Hawthorne investigations. Productivity was
increased by improving the lighting or by giving longer or more
frequent rest pauses. But productivity still went on increasing with
a return (or even worsening) of the original conditions. It was felt
that the physical conditions did not really matter unless they were
clearly bad. What really mattered was the nature of the social
grouping and the motives the individuals experienced. Furthermore, the real social grouping took little regard of the formal
hierarchical, occupational grouping. Since the Hawthorne studies
(carried out in the time of the American depression) these broad
conclusions have had to be demonstrated over and over again, as
their results were not known to industrial organizations generally.
Even today it is common to hear of wild-cat strikes or strikes over
apparent trivia (such as the provision of toilet-rolls), where the real
causes, albeit unknown, are to be found in the social groupings of
the factory and its cumulative response to emotional rather than
physically visible variables.

What is true of the large group in the factory is certainly also
true of the large group of the hospital. But the patient cannot strike,
although he can delay in getting well or, conversely, be driven into
a premature escape from hospital. Furthermore, if a hospital tends
to have an authoritarian, hierarchical staff structure (and most do)
ineffective social groups can be expected to exist among its staff. It
is clear that in such cases the patient is probably the recipient of the
consequences, ranging from inattention to punitive measures as an
expression of group aggression.

The Mental Hospital presents the results of a three-year study of an
expensive, psychoanalytically orientated, small private hospital
where each patient had daily psychotherapy. Despite the analytic
orientation, some aspects of the hosptial seemed contradictory,
especially to England and perhaps even more to Scotland where
Dingleton Hospital has been fully open since 1949. Locked wards

N

and physical methods of restraint were still in use at Chestnut
Lodge. Stanton and Schwartz spent long periods on the wards of
this hospital, noting the happenings and the interactions and
demonstrating how events in one part of the hospital had reper-
cussions in other parts. They demonstrate how lack of communication between the patient's psychotherapist and ward (or administrative) doctor can react to the patient's disadvantage. There is the
poignant story of a depressive who for quite realistic reasons required to make a will. Each time she communicated this to her
therapist she received ECT as it was thought she was showing
suicidal tendencies. In the end she had to secretly leave the hospital,
make her will legally and again return secretly to the hospital. It is
often forgotten that a psychiatric patient is not just a psychiatric
illness but is also a human personality with its attendant non-
pathological commitments and responsibilities. It is also clear that
enormous difficulties arise when disagreements between the staff
over treatment are not discussed and resolved. From this alone
comes a specific point in management in that when a patient becomes a 'special case' in any way it is of value to search for such a
concrete disagreement and, if one is found, to resolve it. More
importantly the book demonstrates the influence of all members of
the institution, patients and staff, upon each other and the importance these influences can have on aiding or hindering the aims of
the institution.

Other studies followed this, particularly Caudill's examination
of the way patients instruct each other in the way they should
behave, Belknap's demonstration of the continuing influence of
the 'back-ward' culture and Goffman's analysis of the pressures to
conform which exist in institutions. In Britain a series of articles
appeared in the *Lancet* and were published as a booklet which
described the need to rehabilitate the hospitals as a first step in
rehabilitating their patients. Later, Barton expanded Martin's
concept of institutionalization and provided a full clinical description of the results of this process. It is still debated, however, to
what extent (and in how many cases) the behaviour of chronic
schizophrenics is a result of the dehumanizing processes of institutionalization rather than of a disease process.

Attempts were made in various ways to deal with the problem of
institutionalization. Many were to some extent authoritarian and
based on a belief in the curative value of work. It became clear that
many patients who were resident in hospital and who appeared

pathetic and incurable could be activated and eventually discharged while others, although suffering from various more dramatic symptoms, could be usefully employed. Patients' responses suggested that, on the whole, they behaved as they were expected to and that if the tone of the institution implied that they were degraded and dangerous, then they became so. If it was assumed that they were reasonable and responsible, their behaviour improved considerably. On this sort of assumption, mental hospitals gradually modified their practice, providing adequate and appropriate occupation for their patients and opening the doors of their wards. This process is slowly continuing and eventually psychiatric hospitals will approach the standards reached by Connolly at Hanwell and Tuke at York in the nineteenth century. The progress will be aided by the advent of newer drugs although their capacity to substitute invisible for visible restraints will have to be carefully watched. We hope that this time the achievement of humane methods of treatment will be accompanied by sufficient investigation of their effects to justify their retention if the social climate outside the hospitals changes. In this respect it is important to remember that procedures adopted on humanitarian grounds do not necessarily produce therapeutic improvement.

Although not providing such evidence the growth of the therapeutic community approach does give a descriptive framework to the changes which are taking place. The term therapeutic community is at present a catch phrase used by the more or less enlightened to support the claim for any administrative scheme they have in mind. Our view accords with that of Clark who would restrict the term to small communities of the type pioneered by Jones and uses the broader expression 'therapeutic community approach' for the gentler modifications of the institution practised elsewhere. We propose to discuss the full-blown therapeutic community as the prototype on which modifications are made to suit individual circumstances.

The archetypal therapeutic community is an organization where the abilities of all its members are directed to the furtherance of the common aim, the treatment of the patients. It has still not reached the stage where rigid procedures can be laid down but the outlines are fairly clear and generally accepted, at least in theory. At present the basic theories are derived from psychoanalysis via relationship theory and emphasis is placed on mutual exploration and interpretation of behaviour. It is assumed that this insight and emotional relearning will result in personality change and readjustment.

An essential part of the therapeutic community is the extensive multidirectional and completely open communication system. This system is predominantly verbal and where possible non-verbal communications are translated into verbal ones. Guidance in such translation and maintenance of the open system of communication are the main functions of the staff of such a community, at least in its early stages. Frequently, interpretative clarification of the verbal communications is required and may be made by any member of the community. The communications of both patients and staff may be remarked upon at any time.

In such a community, of course, the usual status and authority structure will be disrupted. Indeed, it may be partly a measure of its success when such disruption occurs. There will, of course, be an authority structure in the system but it will be inconstant, dependant on authority derived from experience and knowledge rather than predetermined status and, therefore, different authority figures will emerge in different situations. The overall authority is the community *in toto*.

Despite this theoretical position it seems probable that in the most effective therapeutic communities the hierarchy is much the same as in the traditional mental hospital. The difference, and it is a fundamental one, is that in the therapeutic community the staff therapist's position is earned anew with each new patient and must be maintained by the continued demonstration of ability. It is possible that where therapeutic communities are ineffective or disreputable this is a consequence as much of deficiencies in the staff as in methods. Because of this, work in such a community can be onerous and stressful and where such methods are to be introduced great care must be taken to deal with the fears of staff about the changes in their roles. Practically, this may be even more difficult where a modified form of therapeutic community (Clark's therapeutic community approach) is envisaged. The opening up of communication channels and the flattening of the authority pyramid can be very threatening to those who previously had a secure status in a rigidly hierarchical structure. Their actions will be subjected to comment from below which they will interpret (sometimes rightly) as an expression of hostility, while they will be made insecure by the diminution in the amount of direction from above. In the early stages those who previously had no open upward communication channels will also experience considerable difficulties. They will be unsure of the purposes of the community and will tend to use the new channels in a stereotyped way, usually to express a great variety of complaints, realistic and otherwise. It will be a considerable time before they realize that the changes have not been made in order to close their normal communications.

The therapist who instigates these changes must be prepared to deal with these anxieties and distortions of the situation and must constantly endeavour to guide the community towards the structure he seeks. If he does this successfully it is clear that he does not in fact relinquish his authority, no matter what he says. In order to bring about changes of this type he must have some knowledge of the structure and function of organizations of the size he is dealing with and of techniques for changing them. This will be true regardless of the type of community he is trying to develop for although we have described a 'therapeutic community' in terms of current image there are probably other types. It is a pity the term itself has been pre-empted to describe the one form. While there may well be many psychiatric patients who can respond to this type others may require something different.

It is possible to consider therapeutic communities in terms of the amount of regression which is induced in the patient. We have described a community in which the patients are regarded broadly as adolescents in that they are encouraged to question attitudes and behaviour in an attempt to form their own. Behaviour of this type is, of course, part of the process by which the adolescent frees himself from parental control. The staff in such a society endeavour to maintain this atmosphere. To some extent they act as tutors who are only minimally removed in status from their pupils and who are, if necessary, prepared to learn from them. This community can be contrasted with that established in a general hospital which is primarily orientated to the treatment of physical illness. Here the patient is encouraged, almost forced, to regress to early childhood. The apparent independence induced by early ambulation techniques on surgical wards does not alter this. Patients are still expected to do what they are told when they are told and to show due respect to the parental nurses and doctors. Psychiatrists are well aware of the disruption and hostilities produced in such an environment by a non-conformist, often an old person who has not enough control of his own bladder and bowels to make them perform according to the system and who is in any case resentful of the

attempt to reduce him to a state which, perhaps, he fears he is
approaching again anyway. For those who can conform, however,
regression to this extent may have positive value in physical illness.
Certainly it seems to occur spontaneously to some extent in minor
illness where most people seem either to regress to the stage of the
demanding infant or beyond that to a stage of isolation and with-
drawal. There may, therefore, be a variety of therapeutic communities between and beyond these two types which may be of
value to different patients. This possibility has not been examined.
Indeed the effectiveness of the extant varieties has not really been
subjected to critical assessment.

In the present state of knowledge, therefore, it is highly desirable
that any modification of a community should be preceded by a
study of its characteristics and accompanied by investigation of the
changes which occur and their effects. We must accept that this is a
counsel of perfection and that in this, as in much of our work, we will
often proceed by unchecked intuition, probably often fruitlessly.
Investigation of systems of this type is methodologically difficult
and examination of the findings in detail impossibly complex for
most workers. However, in almost all cases it should prove possible
to formulate and check one or two hypotheses and we feel that any
effort in this direction is highly desirable.

The original community is the hospital or a subsection of it.
Many of its features are those of other groups of similar size; some
are common to all groups. First there is the formal status hierarchy
as laid down by the rules of the institution. In the psychiatric unit
this is normally headed by the doctor, followed by the nursing staff
in order of rank, with the patients at the bottom. The effective
authority may be different; for instance, it is not uncommon for
junior doctors to find themselves effectively subordinate to the
ward sister. In some cases the ward sister, too, may be effectively
subordinate to a wholly untrained nursing auxilliary who has been
on the ward for many years and who may be in the position of
custodian of the group mores.

This latter post, honorary and often unrecognized, can be of the
greatest importance to those who would change the community.
Anyone who attempts changes must hope that his achievements
will continue after he has left but many are frustrated. Often this is
because he has not recognized where the sources of the group culture lie. Even where he does he may not be able to modify them, for
instance when the running of the ward is effectively determined by

a coterie of long-stay patients or staff who may have things well organized from their own point of view. This enduring nucleus is worthy of study in any community.

Thus, within one community there may be at least three hierarchical structures, all different, and each with an appropriate communication network. Each may also have a different dominant mode of communication. That of the formal authority structure will normally be verbal and direct whereas that of the effective authority structure although largely verbal will be allusive in its positive aspects and non-verbal, although not necessarily non-vocal, in its negative aspects. 'Doctor says' can be said in a great variety of ways. Continuity of the group culture will be maintained by its custodians mainly by non-verbal means. These are often very effective. Any attempt to translate the communications into verbal ones may be stoutly resisted while attempts by the staff to modify attitudes by non-verbal methods are usually easily foiled. Failure is often inevitable because continous pressure is impractical, sanctions are inadequate and the motivational system of the patients is unknown, so that positive reinforcement of a desirable behaviour is not possible. Unfortunately, it seems that those psychiatrists who have seized and modified the theory of games have not recognized the need to bring with them a theory of utility and adapt that adequately. This is perhaps not entirely fair because some of their writings suggest that what they have done is, in fact, to evolve a theory of utility but to call it a theory of games.

Although this suggests that the organization of psychiatric units involves work with a different type of system from that studied by industrial and social psychologists the difference should not be overemphasized. Rather the problem, like many in psychiatry, is largely one of definition and of difficulty in choosing appropriate variables to measure or measurements of those variables. Psychiatrists can be overawed by these variables and their complexity, but it may prove possible to obtain valuable preliminary results by simple means even though these will need elaboration later. Thus it rapidly becomes apparent in industrial systems that although money provides an effective, controllable and understandable motivational system other factors are of great importance. In many cases their importance appears to exceed that of money. It is an odd finding to the unsophisticated that men will strike for an increase in pay which is so small that it will take them many weeks to make up for the money they lose while on strike. During the course of the struggle large numbers of men may be put out of work as a consequence of it and will suffer more than the ostensible opponent, the management. Obviously the situation is more complex than it appears.

In many ways the behaviour patterns of such a system resemble those of a neurotic, while analysis of its detail reveals further similarities (always provided that we are not behaviour theorists to an extreme extent). Analysis of an industrial organization which is showing behaviour distortion may demonstrate a variety of covert stresses. These may be intensified by distortions of the group structure. Again, therefore, the consideration of the group will involve examination of its hierarchies, its communications and the emotional states and responses of its members. Much of what we have said about these factors and their operation in small groups will also apply to the community as a whole. We have already discussed in this chapter the possibility that there may be more than one communication system and hierarchical structure within the group and that difficulties will arise when the official and unofficial systems are in conflict.

Consideration of this type of problem must include a consideration of the individuals in the system as, although certain group behaviours are predictable, there are always a few people whose positions or personalities are such that they will produce stress. Some of these stresses are apparent immediately; in other situations their effects may only appear after a considerable time. At times the removal of such people or the weakening of their position may have unfortunate long-term consequences. In considering these possibilities it is simpler to use a commercial rather than a therapeutic model as an illustration because the goals and criteria of success and failure are clearer. We shall take it as axiomatic that the goal of a commercial group is to grow—to make increasingly large amounts of money (we are, of course, also assuming a fairly primitive capitalist environment). During their early stages such systems frequently reflect the drive of their founder and the hierarchical structure has only two levels, the boss and the rest. Communication channels in such a system may be surprisingly open and the boss will often get unexpurgated feedback from his workers. When such a system grows intermediate authority levels are created and it is often at this stage that stress becomes apparent. All will be well if the boss can delegate authority effectively or if those in the intermediate levels of the organization accept their given role as downward communication channels with perhaps a subsidiary function of absorbing ascending complaints. The wrong sort of personality in this system will be speedily ejected or alternatively may acquire support and form a faction whose operations will probably be detrimental to the overall efficiency of the system in a fairly short time. Unfortunately in this type of context the wrong sort of personality is often associated with characteristics akin to those of the originator of the system which could, if properly harnessed, be of great value for its future development. If such talents are not recruited the organization will remain essentially a one-man band and sooner or later the supply of individual leaders will dry up. Where the system is a small one this will lead to rapid collapse but in a large organization there is tremendous momentum and the system can survive a long time under the control of mediocre abilities. Often it will survive several bad misjudgements but even without them its stereotyped approach will result in gradual dissolution or, nowadays, in its disappearance by takeover at some stage.

The necessity to obtain the services of talented men who may have difficulties in their interpersonal relationships and to ensure that they do not drive each other out or engage in guerilla warfare has resulted in the development of an interesting phenomenon, the T-group. We are now back to our therapeutic community and its staff meetings where work problems and interpersonal difficulties are, or should be, hammered out. Although concerned with the function of large groups the T-group itself is, in our terminology, a small group concerned with the personal differences we have considered in a discussion of individuals. Further it seems, as we have previously discussed, that a T-group is not greatly different from a psychotherapeutic group. It might be conducted by a scientific psychologist rather than an unscientific psychiatrist, and with subjects other than patients, but the rationale and techniques are very similar.

Any large group is very liable to be influenced or motivated by non-rational influences. Two such areas are those of propaganda and prejudice. Propaganda implies an attempt to control the attitudes of a group, often for ulterior purposes. It is sometimes distinguished (rather precariously) from education on the grounds that the latter is concerned with truth. In an industrial organization, propaganda can be disseminated by subversive influences working to weaken, for one reason or another, the factory system or by the management to justify a variety of behaviours. Such deliberate manipulation does not often occur in hospitals but the accepted roles and rituals of hospital staff are often perpetuated at the expense of the patient by the dissemination of obsolescent ideas with very little to control them. Typical examples are the ward round of the medical staff and the attention of the nursing staff to physical tasks like bed-making or ward cleaning.

Prejudice involves a pre-judgement, usually of a negative kind. It is a learnt response and in one common form of antipathy to other 'races' it arises from a complex of causes—economic, scapegoating and compensation for inferiority among others. However, there is no doubt that some personality types tend to show prejudice more than others. In particular, prejudice has been linked with the so-called authoritarian personality—the supreme conformist who sees the world as threatening and needs to have fixed rules to follow. On the surface, such personalities may appear self-confident and adjusted but they are fundamentally anxious with strong feelings of aggression which are repressed.

In the hospital we can expect to find the authoritarian personality at least as frequently as we do outside. He resists change and therapeutic innovation and may prefer to see psychiatric patients firmly in their place behind locked doors and in their shabby hospital clothes. Too great a turnover and discharge of patients will threaten him as it will weaken the distinction between the hospital and the outer community. Any mixing of the sexes in his wards will exacerbate the authoritarian's strong fear of sexual license if restrictions are relaxed. But prejudice may operate at all levels in the hospital community. In particular, in the psychiatric hospital, attitudes to patients may be unfortunate ones and only reflect the still existing problem in the community at large of educating the public at large. As with all prejudice, it can be lessened by education, especially when this occurs in the more formative years.

There is no substitute, in the study of large groups as in all the other aspects of this subject, for continuing controlled observation and experiment in techniques and critical assessment of results. At present many factors and changes involving group formations occur with little attempt at proper assessment. As time goes on such *ad hoc* procedures will be considered, quite properly, as pre-scientific and irresponsible.

Appendix 1

Statistical Methods and Experimental Design

Psychological data are very dependent on statistical treatment for their evaluation and interpretation. Modern approaches to psychology and psychiatry involve extensive use of statistics and a knowledge of experimental design. Some people experience an emotional block when confronted with the introduction of statistics. They should remember that, on the whole, the mathematics they will be required to use are not complex. Indeed, certain basic elements in statistics and experimental design are hardly mathematical at all. A summary account of the major statistical terms and methods is given here as an introduction to the subject, but these can really only be learnt by working examples and for actual working methods the reader is referred to statistical texts. A certain amount of the later part of this appendix lists the main statistical methods used in psychology and their formulae. It is doubtful if such a list has much meaning in itself but it can be used as a reference; for example, in explaining why a particular measure has been used in some reported research. We have attempted to clarify their use to some extent by describing some imaginary applications (p. 202). Some readers may prefer to jump to this section and return to the more academic parts of this appendix.

The use of statistical methods of analysis is inseparable from the consideration of the design of an experiment to obtain maximum information from these methods. Most readers will be more familiar with elementary experimentation in the physical sciences. There the variable factors in the experiment are few and can be measured or controlled. It therefore becomes possible to formulate precise laws as to the behaviour of systems under defined conditions and when experiments are carried out to test them, to obtain results of great consistency. Boyle's Law is a good example of this situation: the volume of a given mass of gas is found to vary directly with the pressure if other factors (particularly temperature) are held constant. In more complex physical systems and in most psychological systems such conditions do not obtain. The number of relevant variables may be too great to control, their measurement may be imprecise or impossible, while it may well be that significant effects are only produced by the interaction of two or more variables. In other circumstances it may be that an experiment as such cannot be planned and the method of approach is basically observational. Analysis of the results of the observations may then depend on statistical correlational techniques. Although the statistical theory of these approaches always implies the use of the null hypothesis (p. 191) the aims of the researcher are usually somewhat different. Broadly, it may be stated that the worker searching for correlation among observations is still to some extent in search of a hypothesis while the experimenter seeking changes in specific variables has usually arranged his ideas in a form where more or less specific evidence to support them can be sought.

In all the applications which we shall discuss we are concerned with the use of statistical methods for detecting and isolating relationships or differences and considering whether such findings can be regarded as significant or whether they could have arisen as a result of chance. We shall not discuss descriptive statistics as, though many of them will be encountered in bureaucratic situations, they are of little relevance to our purpose here. They tend to give rise to even more arguments about their interpretation and may well be based on even more suspect data.

It is often claimed that the results of statistical experiments are only as good as the quality of the data subjected to analysis. To a considerable extent this is true, but it should not be accepted unquestioned as a criticism of an experiment. Obviously the experimenter should take pains to gather his data as accurately as possible, but it can be argued that if absolute accuracy can be obtained it will rarely be necessary to use statistics. The object of the mathematics is to permit an assessment of experimental findings in the face of random influences affecting any or all aspects of the experiment. They will not help where there is systematic bias.

Simple probability can be understood by anyone, but even here there are misconceptions, not only by the simple. Errors by the more sophisticated also arise, often because of a failure to appreciate the details of the circumstances which they claim to be analysing. Thus, a standard illustration of probabilities is taken from throwing of a dice. It is apparent that the probability of throwing a 6 is 1 chance in 6, or 1/6 or 0·167. If the dice had 6's on all faces the probability would, of course, be 1 (assuming it does not come to rest on an edge or a corner) and this is the maximum value attained by a probability. The chance of throwing two 6's in successive throws is 1/36 because the probability of two independent events occurring together is the product of their individual probabilities. If, however, on the first throw we permit ourselves a choice of two numbers to win, the probability becomes 1/3, because of the addition property of probabilities. When there is more than one way in which a result (in this case to 'win') can be obtained, the probability of obtaining the result is the sum of the probabilities of the individual ways, provided that they are mutually exclusive. It always remains that the chance of a stated number on a particular throw is constant, and is unaffected by the previous throw. Therefore, the probability of throwing a 6 on *this* throw is unaffected by the fact that the preceding throw did or did not result in a 6, or indeed, if such were the case, that there had been sixes on the previous ten throws or even no sixes in the previous hundred throws. Some writers on probability use this fact to provide a little genteel amusement at the gambler who will bet on the probability of a result because it has not occurred for some time. Yet they may be showing a failure to appreciate the situation for the gambler may continue to bet for some time because, although the probability of a win on any one stated throw is 1/6, over a series, the probability of 6's is still one in every six throws. He may then be right in his argument that if there is no 6 in the first ten throws there is still the same probability that there will be three 6's in the first twenty throws and the gamble is worth while.

We may still find that the gambler has backed the second ten throws for a win and still failed to win. It is unlikely that he will philosophically accept that his intuitive assessment of the odds is wrong and that he should treat each throw as an independent event. He may rather express suspicion of the die. Should this rarity of 6's continue the statistician may well agree with him. Even in our hypothetical situation we can imagine certain difficulties in questioning this and it will be of value to know to what extent this irregular occurrence of certain numbers is itself due to chance. The statistician can help here by providing a method of assessing the probability that a certain distribution of scores will occur.

The statistician's first aim will be to set up a *null hypothesis*. In this particular case the null hypothesis will be that over an extended number of throws there will be no difference between the number of times each face is uppermost. This concept of the null hypothesis is fundamental to statistical experimental method. Every experiment consists basically of an attempt to demonstrate the falsity of the null hypothesis, preferably in a way which has been predicted. It is logically impossible to *prove* the null hypothesis because it states that the observed occurrences are related only by chance, all that is done is to state that it is probably untrue and to place a value on this probability. This value is usually predetermined before the experiment and is known as the level of significance. In psychological and psychiatric work such levels are usually pre-set at 0·05 and 0·01 probabilities, that is, that the probability against the finding being due to chance is 20 to 1 or 100 to 1. If higher levels are attained they will be announced with triumph. The statement sometimes encountered in a paper that a finding *almost* attained significance is not really meaningful. It means only that the null hypothesis has not been rejected at a satisfactory high level of probability and that more work is required to establish whether or not it can be. Alternatively, the level required may be lowered, a course rarely recommended but not necessarily disreputable provided that all the circumstances are carefully considered. Odds of 10 to 1 against might be considered quite long in some circles!

After setting up the null hypothesis for the dice problem the statistician might then see if it can be falsified by calculating a statistic known as X^2 (chi squared). For this he will compare his observed frequencies with the frequencies expected by calculation. He will form a table which might be Table n (the figures are, of course, carefully fiddled).

Number on face of die	1	2	3	4	5	6
Predicted frequency of occurrence	100	100	100	100	100	100
Observed frequency of occurrence	175	75	125	150	50	25

X^2 is then computed using formula 1:

$$X^2 = \sum \frac{(Oi - Ei)^2}{Ei} \quad \text{(Formula 1)}$$

Where Σ means 'sum of',
Oi = observed frequency of each occurrence,
Ei = expected frequency of each occurrence.
$X^2 = 56·25 + 6·25 + 6·25 + 25 + 25 + 56·25 = 175·00$

This can be checked for significance in tables of X^2 and is, of ourse, very significant indeed. To make the check it is necessary to now the number of *degrees of freedom* present in the table. In this ase there are 5, because once the frequency in five of the cells is nown, and the total of trials is known, that in the sixth is fixed.)egrees of freedom for experimental data can always be computed n this principle but there are a variety of routine ways of obtaining hem presented in statistical texts which are generally much simpler. This also obtains for the computation of X^2 in certain ways, for nstance when the data can be arranged in a 2 × 2 table. Such ables occur commonly in psychiatric and psychological work.

In these circumstances it will often be found that there are no *a priori* expected frequencies as in our first example and the expected requency in each cell of the table has to be computed from the ample data in accordance with the *a priori* probabilities based on he null hypothesis. Thus in an investigation of pain in psychiatric)atients the following results were obtained:

Diagnosis	Anxiety	Hysteria	Depression	Other	Total
Pain	19	21	48	18	106
No pain	19	7	37	31	94
Total	38	28	85	49	200

The expected frequency in each cell can be computed from its relationship to the distribution in the whole sample. Thus, in the top left-hand cell $\dfrac{E}{38} = \dfrac{106}{200}$ so that E = 20·14. Similarly all the other E's can be computed and the value of X^2 calculated. In small samples, particularly where the *expected* frequency in a cell is less than 5, Yates's *correction for continuity* should be applied because the mathematical theory of X^2 distribution is based on the assumption of large expected frequencies. This is done by subtracting ½ from the positive difference (O − E) and adding ½ to the negative differences.

The chi-squared test has been extended in many ways and has become very versatile but even in its simple form it is very useful. Its great advantage is that it can be used with data which are only nominally scaled, i.e. classified into yes or no, present or absent, x, y or z groups. The question of the standard of measurement attained has been considered extensively by mathematically minded psychologists. It is customary to place it at one of four levels. The first we have mentioned as nominal scaling, where things are counted and classified. For example, people might be divided into males and females and the respective numbers counted. Second is ordered measurement where the data can be placed in order, e.g. of magnitude, although the size of the intervals is inconsistent. We might now, for example, rank our males and females in terms of height. Third is interval scaling, where the intervals are constant. We would here measure the differences in height between the smallest and tallest. Fourth is ratio scaling where there is a true rather than an arbitrary zero and ratios are

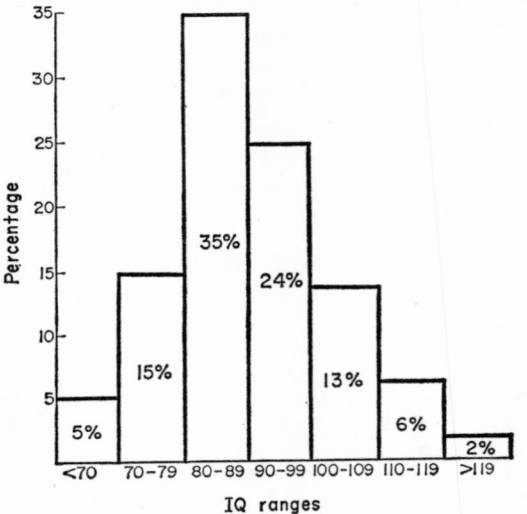

Fig. 10. A histogram depicting percentages of a sample of hospital patients with IQ's in various ranges.

directly meaningful. In our measures of height we would now use a scale, for example, of feet and inches. It should be noted that whatever method of measurement is being used it is advisable in the beginning to examine the distribution of classes or scores. Such an initial survey is usually carried out by means of a frequency diagram of histogram (Fig. 10).

Statistical tests of the significance of differences or associations have been devised for data measured in all of these ways. Table 1 presents a list of some of the more commonly used ones and the standard of measurement they require. Details of computation can be obtained from standard statistical texts.

TABLE 1. TABLE OF USAGE OF STATISTICAL MEASURES

Level of Measurement	Statistical Test					Measure of Correlation
	One-sample Case	Two-sample Case		K-sample Case		
		Related Samples	Independent Samples	Related Samples	Independent Samples	
Nominal	1. Binomial test 2. χ^2	1. McNemar test for significance of changes	1. Fisher exact probability test	1. Cochran Q-test	1. χ^2	1. Contingency of coefficient
Ordinal	1. Kolmogorov–Smirnov one-sample test 2. One-sample runs test	1. Sign test 2. Wilcoxon matched pairs signed-ranks test	1. Median test 2. Mann–Whitney U-test 3. Kolmogorov–Smirnov two-sample test	1. Friedman two-way analysis of variance	1. Extension of median test 2. Kruskal–Wallis one-way analysis of variance	1. Spearman rank correlation coefficient (ρ) 2. Kendall rank correlation coefficient (τ)
Interval		1. Walsh test 2. Randomization test for matched pairs	1. Randomization test for two independent samples	1. Analysis of variance		1. Product movement correlation coefficient
Ratio		1. Critical ratio 2. t-test				

This table, which is after Siegel, lists cumulatively downwards the tests applicable. The parametric tests are those given for ratio measurement but in practice these can frequently be used with interval measurements.

So far we have discussed the detection of significant difference only in the nominally classified data. The use of non-parametri statistics other than chi-squared (e.g. Mann–Whitney U) is sti not particularly widespread and much data in psychology an behaviour are thought to be appropriately dealt with by usin techniques related to the normal curve of distribution. This curv has a typically bell-shaped form as shown in Fig. 11. It can be seer

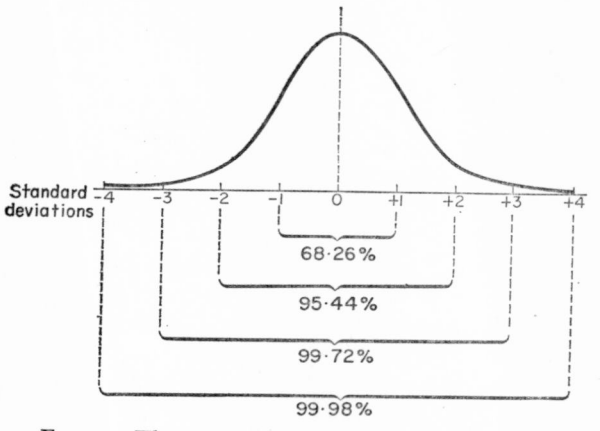

FIG. 11. The normal curve of distribution, showing the percentage of cases within each standard deviation.

that with a normally distributed variable most individuals bunch in the middle of the range. As the extremes are approached, the numbers occurring become proportionately less. Many biological variables (particularly polygenic ones) such as height and intelligence are normally (or near normally) distributed.

A first step is to obtain one or more measures of central tendency. Measures of central tendency give some information on what particular score or value characterizes the group of scores as a whole. One value which characterizes the group's scores is the mean M (or average) which, of course, is the sum of the individual scores (Σx, Σ standing for sum, and x for the individual score) divided by the number of individuals in the group of sample (N)

$$\text{then } M = \frac{\Sigma x}{N}. \quad \text{(Formula 2)}$$

Other measures of central tendency are the mode (the most commonly occurring score) and the median (the half-way score, or fiftieth percentile if the individual scores are ranged in size). The percentage of scores in a distribution that are equal to, or less than, a particular value is the percentile score of that particular value. If the individual scores are ranged in size they can be split at any desired point. The most commonly used points are the quartiles (25th, 50th, 75th percentile) and deciles (10th, 20th, 30th ... 90th percentiles). The use of modes, medians and percentiles depends on what shape or form the distribution of those scores in the general population is believed to follow. They are particularly useful where no hypothesis is made about the shape and distribution or where it is believed to be asymmetrical and/or non-normal, and it is on measures of this type that many of the non-parametric statistics mentioned above are based.

The diagram of the normal distribution curve introduces the concept of the standard deviation. This is a precise measure of the variability of a frequency distribution. Obviously any measure of central tendency (whether mean, mode or median) needs to be supplemented by information concerning the range or scatter of individual scores. The standard deviation gives information about the range of scores with regard to normal distribution. The calculation for the standard deviation

$$(\text{S.D. or } \sigma) = \frac{\Sigma\,(x\text{--M})^2}{N}. \quad \text{(Formula 3)}$$

Different samples, each having similar means, modes and medians, still have quite different ranges of individualscores.

In a normal distribution six times the standard deviation is roughly equivalent to the total range and also has properties (as shown in the diagram) with regard to proportions of the general population being within so many SD's plus or minus the mean. It can be seen that scores within a range of two standard deviations from the mean account for 95% of the total scores. That is, the chance of any one individual's score being outside this range is only 5% or 1 in 10. This estimate of probability might be written in the form P (probability) < 0.05. Less than 1% of scores occur outside the range of three standard deviations from the mean, 1 in 100 or $P < 0.01$.

Variance is another way of expressing data concerning the range of individual scores and is mathematically the square of the standard deviation. Expressed algebraically:

$$\text{Variance} = \sigma^2 = \frac{\Sigma (x-M)^2}{N}. \quad \text{(Formula 4)}$$

Analysis of variance is the term given to a group of techniques in common use in statistics. If, for example, a number of groups of subjects are being studied in respect of some characteristic, the variance of scores can be studied in different ways. Variance can be calculated from the individual scores within the groups and also from the means of the groups. Analysis of variance depends on the hypothesis that all the groups are random samples from the same population. The test of this hypothesis consists in determining whether the ratio (F) of the two estimates of the variance we have calculated corresponds to a value selected as being significant. More complex possibilities exist in the analysis of variance, but this simplest possibility depicts the basic mode of approach.

However, we are often concerned with studying only two groups and wish to know if they are statistically different or similar. The actual difference of the means of the two groups can be examined by the critical ratio method. This ratio is the difference between the means divided by the standard error of the difference σd.

$$\text{Critical Ratio (C.R.)} = \frac{Mx - My}{\sqrt{\dfrac{\Sigma x^2}{Nx} + \dfrac{\Sigma z^2}{Ny}}}. \quad \text{(Formula 5)}$$

When the sizes of sample are less than 50, a modified calculation, the t-test, is used because in such small samples biases arise in the computation of the standard deviation:

$$t = \frac{(Mx - My)}{\sigma d \sqrt{\dfrac{1}{Nx} + \dfrac{1}{Ny}}}. \quad \text{(Formula 6)}$$

Similarly, the statistical significance of a single mean differing from an arbitrary value, in fact normally from zero on the null hypothesis, is indicated by its standard error.

$$\text{S.E.} = \frac{\sigma}{\sqrt{N}} \quad \text{or} \quad t = \frac{M_1 \ \sqrt{N}}{\Sigma}. \quad \text{(Formulae 7 and 8)}$$

The standard score is used as a way of convering scores into a series where all the successive scores in a given range are really equidistant from one another. Such standard scores may be directly compared with another set of scores similarly treated. To convert an individual score to a standard score, the deviation of the individual score from the mean is divided by the standard deviation.

Correlation coefficients determine the extent to which two variables are associated. Two variables can either be positively or negatively related and the product moment correlation coefficient

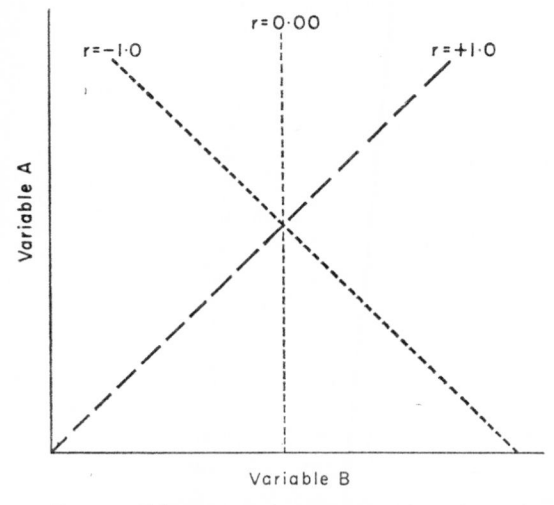

FIG. 12. Diagrammatic representation of correlations. A perfect positive agreement between measures of A and B results in r = + 1·0; a perfect negative agreement between measures of A and B results in r = − 1·0. In the example r = 0·0, the same measure of variable B coincides with all possible measures of variable A.

varies from + 1·00 to − 1·00. Correlations can be represented diagramatically as in Fig. 12. The formula for the coefficient's calculations is:

$$rxy = \frac{\Sigma \ (x - Mx) \quad (y - My)}{N \ \sigma \ x \ \sigma \ y}. \quad \text{(Formula 9)}$$

In this formula, x and y are the two variables being correlated. As before, Σ stands for the total sum, in this case, the sum of the product of each individual's score difference from the mean of each variable $(x - Mx$ and $y - My)$. This total is divided by the product of the number in the sample (N) times the standard deviation of each variable $(\sigma\, x\, \sigma\, y)$. Now if there was a third variable z, we could go on to calculate correlate coefficients of x and z, y and z as well as that between x and y. Correlation coefficients can be calculated, in fact, between every pair of variables that have been measured.

Where a number of variables are each intercorrelated, a correlation matrix can be drawn up to depict the results. A large number of variables and a consequently large correlation matrix can be reduced to a more limited number of mathematical factors using a mathematical technique known as factor analysis. Each variable or test will have a loading on each factor and from an examination of which variables have the greatest loadings on any one factor, that factor can be identified and interpreted. With the increasing availability of computers, factor-analysis using the 'principal components' method of Hotelling is becoming the most popular technique. This method is more sophisticated than, though not essentially different in aim from, the original tetrad equation method of Spearman.

The mere establishment of a statistically significant result may often be inadequate in statistical studies. Values statistically significant (at an agreed level) with one size of sample, will not be significant with a smaller sample. Psychological judgements still have to be made with regard to findings dependent on such factors. For example, a correlation coefficient of $r = 0.081$ will have a $P < 0.01$ if the sample used is large, such as $N = 1000$, but clearly the degree of association between the two variables is psychologically negligible. Even with a correlation coefficient as high as 0.700 the common variance of the two variables is only $0.700^2 \times 100 = 49\%$.

Reliability, in a statistical sense, is an estimate of how consistent a particular measure is. It might be estimated by the test–retest method—giving the same test to the same subject on two occasions and calculating the correlation. If reliability or consistency is desired, the correlation coefficient should be reasonably high. Other methods of calculating reliability are by using either alternative forms of the test in question or the split half method. The latter usually involves correlating the scores on even items of the test with the scores on odd items. The measurement of validity rather than reliability requires some means of estimating that the measure in question really measures what it is alleged to measure. Clearly, some external check rather than a subjective decision is required. But statistically, as for reliability, a correlation will have to be calculated between the measure in question and some other variable or variables. If two variables can be ranked in order of size or merit, Spearman's ρ or Kendall's τ may be used as a calculation of correlation. Where one variable can be measured on a continuum, but the other variable only divided into categories (e.g. diagnosis) a biserial correlation (bis r) may be calculated.

Statistical treatment is very much bound up with experimental design. The ideal experiment, especially with living creatures, is impossible to design. But obviously the assessment of individuals and of treatment needs to be controlled in some way. For example, a group of patients treated with a drug may improve for a number of reasons other than the drug itself. Any clinical trial runs up against the problem of individual differences of many kinds—variations in illness, sampling errors and psychological effects in subjects and observers. These and other difficulties are combated by the use of methods such as the double-blind experiment. Here, both patients and therapists are unaware of which treatment is being given. This can be combined with a cross-over design where half the patients receive the real drug for a given period of time followed by a placebo for a similar period of time. The other half of the patients receive the drug and placebo in reverse order. But even with the best design there are many features to be considered and only experience and attention to details can give a realistic interpretation of results.

In any comparison of groups of subjects it is essential that the groups should not differ (statistically) in their composition. Except where the variable is the one under investigation the groups should be matched or be equivalent with regard to certain basic variables such as sex, age, intelligence and social class. Even so, it always remains possible that a statistically significant difference between compared groups may turn out to be an effect of a lack of equality on some variable other than that being investigated. Alternatively, it can happen that rigorous matching on a particular variable might be arguable as the particular variable may turn out to be associated with the variable under investigation. Further, such matching procedures introduce elements of planning and selection into the choice of subjects. As the theory on which the tests of significance are based assumes that measurements are made on a random sample of the population to be studied the results may be made invalid as a consequence of such selection unless the test of significance to be employed is chosen carefully.

An interesting alternative to cumbersome procedures such as the double-blind method is the use of an independent assessor. A lack of therapeutic involvement reduces bias and increases objectivity. There may still be difficulties arising from therapist–patient interactions obscuring the actual causes of changes in patients, but the method avoids the problems consequent upon the introduction of correlations in groups where random influences are supposed to prevail.

There can be little doubt that where applicable, the parametric analysis of variance is the most elegant and informative technique for analysing complex data. The contributions of various factors and their interactions can be assessed, while the size of the residual variance, which is used as the yardstick to assess the importance of the other factors contributions to the total, may give a clue as to whether possibly significant factors have been left unconsidered.

Application of statistical methods

Our discussion of these statistical methods has of necessity been very condensed and the reader is advised to seek further information from the standard works given in the reading list. In the following section we present some imaginary investigations which may serve as a guide to the appropriate use of various statistical techniques. It will be appreciated that these are also relatively simple and are not intended to cover every contingency. Prospective experimenters are advised to take thought and not to regard our descriptions as blueprints.

Our first example will discuss problems in comparative assessments. This type of experiment will be used in circumstances where it is thought that different groups of subjects will show differences in the variable under investigation. These groups may be, for instance, patients of differing clinical types or patients who are in some way treated differently or in a clinical trial of a drug or a psychological method of treatment. In our discussion of the design of such an experiment we shall consider some possible ways of controlling or diminishing the effects of variables which may affect the results and with the statistics appropriate to the varying standards of measurement of the dependent variable which can be achieved. Other important factors, for instance the problems of definition of the various groups or of pre-experimental variation in the dependent variable, are not considered as our object is only to illustrate the use of the statistical formulae we have described above.

Fundamental to the design of any statistical experiment is the concept of random variation. This is particularly relevant in our discussion to the question of the effects of extraneous factors. When the experimental groups are formed it is desirable that they should be selected from the total population in some way that permits such factors to vary randomly. Thus subjects may be allocated to a group by means of a code related to a table of random numbers or, when a sample is taken from a larger population, by picking people at fixed intervals, e.g. every fifth person from an alphabetical list (the implied assumption that the initial letter of one's name is itself random is rarely stated). Sometimes attempts are made to control various factors as though an experiment in physics is to be performed. Among the commonest factors to be controlled in this way are age and sex. Although it is attractive to control these variables by matching in advance, its effect in forestalling criticism may be counterbalanced by bias in other directions. This difficulty can be illustrated in the problem of seeking tests or behaviours which differentiate between patients suffering from schizophrenia and endogenous depression or organic illness. As on the whole schizophrenia is a disease of the relatively young as compared with most patients suffering from the other conditions, any adequate matching of the sample for age will result in at least one of the diagnostic groups being atypical.

Despite these reservations matched samples, carefully used, will improve the sensitivity of an experiment, particularly if the statistical tests used are appropriate. Fisher points out that in an adequate experiment of this type each individual in one group is matched with an individual in another group, differences between the scores of the two individuals on the dependent variable are measured and the appropriate statistic is the assessment of whether the mean of these differences is significantly greater than zero. Which of the various tests of this type is to be used will depend on the standard of measurement achieved.

In experiments of this type the level of measurement attained will vary greatly. Most investigators will try for as high a level as possible, as this will permit more sensitive statistical tests to be used. The search for sensitivity may lead to loss of reliability or validity and thus be self-defeating. There may be advantages at times in restricting the measurement to simple scales. In some cases this is necessary because of the nature of the material, as for instance, many clinical symptoms can really only be noted as

P

present or absent on the basis of an examination whereas when observation over a period is used the introduction of the time dimension permits a greater range of scoring. Even in this situation many of the scores will be arbitrary and experimenters of obsessional temperament will be reluctant to apply parametric techniques to measures which are at the best ordinal.

If we take a concrete example we may consider one or two groups of people, chosen from the general population, who are to be subjected to two different stresses to determine whether there is any difficulty in the amount of disturbance caused. For instance it might be argued that a sudden loud noise is more or less startling than a sudden flash of bright light. The null hypothesis (p. 191) to be tested is then that 'there is no difference between the startle effect of a loud noise or a bright flash of light'.

An experiment will be set up to expose the subjects to one or both of these stimuli. Ideally some sort of preliminary assessment to try to obtain a comparable stimulus value in terms of subjective experience will be made. Such a cross-modal comparison is possible but at times difficult. Otherwise values will be chosen arbitrarily or perhaps computed according to some psychophysiological formula (e.g. p. 27). Subjects will then be exposed to stimuli in some predetermined way and their startle responses will be assessed. For the sake of illustration we shall propose three methods of assessment. First it will be necessary to define what one means by a startle response. In our examples the definition is implicit in the method of measurement but it is worth describing it in some detail. The fashionable jargon term for this process is that it is the formulation of an *operational definition*.

At the simplest level of measurement of startle we may depend solely on the verbal report of the patient who may be asked to classify his experience as 'not startled', 'slightly startled' and 'very startled'. The definition of response is, therefore, in terms of verbal behaviour. A measure of this type is best regarded as nominal scaling and in our experiment the number of subjects who reported each response would be placed in a contingency table. Thus for 50 responses to each stimulus we have:

Stimulus	Not Startled	Slightly Startled	Very Startled	Total
Sound	a	b	$50 - a - b$	50
Light	c	d	$50 - c - d$	50
Total	a & c	b & d	$100 - a - b - c - d$	100

'rom this table a value of X-squared can be computed (p. 192). It vill have two degrees of freedom (p. 193) and the significance of the value attained can be read off from tables.

The meaning of any significant result will be inferred from the original distribution of scores. To point out the obvious:

$$
\begin{array}{llll}
\text{if} & 50-a-b & > & 50-c-d \\
\text{and} & a & < & c \\
\text{and} & b & < & d \\
\text{and} & X^2 & &
\end{array}
$$

attains the required level of significance then it is reasonable to conclude that under the conditions of our experiment sound stimuli are regarded as more startling than light stimuli.

At a slightly more complex level of definition the startle response may be operationally defined in terms of the subject's behaviour. We may be able to observe several aspects of this and to grade the aspects. For instance, we may consider the following phenomena: widening of the palpebral fissure, muscular jerking and movement of the body or head towards or away from the source of the stimulus. The startle response is then defined as the observation of one or more of these phenomena. Its intensity is measured by summing the scores obtained on each observation. These scores may have differing ranges, for example widening of the palpebral fissure may be scored from 0 to 2, muscular jerking from 0 to 4, movement of the head from 0 to 3 and movement of the body from 0 to 3. Each subject may then obtain a score ranging from 0 to 12 for each exposure to a stimulus. These scores may well be distributed in a fairly normal way and some may argue that parametric statistics can be used with little error. It is more appropriate though to regard the scores as a device for giving an ordinal distribution so that scores can be given to each subject and a suitable test, for instance the Mann–Whitney U-test, can be applied to determine whether there is a significant difference between the responses to the two stimuli. Again the direction of the difference is determined from the original data.

Our third operational definition of 'startle' may be even more restricted and removed from the psychological concept, yet more precisely measurable. We may consider the involuntary motor movement which occurs in association with a sudden stimulus. This can be measured easily, as by connecting the hand to a recording device. Perhaps the response to be measured will be the first deviation of the device in any direction occurring after the presentation of the stimulus. (In practice it would probably be necessary to frame the definition more precisely to exclude physiological tremor and other possible factors.) Measurement would then be in units of length, probably millimetres. All scores would be be regarded as positive. This would give us a ratio scale, susceptible to analysis using parametric techniques. Theoretically it might be established that the whole population from which our sample is drawn would give normally distributed results on this measurement but the assumption that this is so seems to be safe, or at least acceptable, in biological and psychological experiments. The scores which we derive from an experiment using this measure will be examined for statistical significance using the t-test (p. 198). The size of the two means will indicate the direction of any difference found.

If we are using a method of measurement which is amenable to parametric techniques we may extend the area of our original experiment. For instance, we may consider that it is possible that the startle response varies between the sexes as well as with the type of stimulus and further that it differs as between normal, neurotic and psychotic subjects. Hypotheses of this type can be examined using an analysis of variance technique. If the factors mentioned above are to be considered we shall also be able to consider the possibility of significant interactions between any pair of these factors. It will be necessary to obtain scores on twelve groups of subjects, thus:

Male						Female					
Normal		*Neurotic*		*Psychotic*		*Normal*		*Neurotic*		*Psychotic*	
Sound	Light	Sound	Light	Sound	Light	Sound	Light	Sound	Light	Sound	Light
scores ↓	scores ↓	scores ↓	scores ↓	scores ↓	scores ↓	scores ↓	scores ↓	scores ↓	scores ↓	scores ↓	scores ↓

Ideally, the numbers of subjects in each column will be the same, but it is not essential. From the raw data, means and variances are calculated according to one of the various techniques available and eventually a table like the following will be obtained:

Source of Variance	Source of Squares	Degrees of Freedom	Variance Estimate
Sex	S	1	S
Diagnosis	D	2	D/2
Stimulus	St	1	St
Sex × diagnosis	SD	2	SD/2
Sex × stimulus	SSt	1	SSt
Diagnosis × stimulus	DSt	2	DSt/2
Residual (This is the 2nd-order interaction: Sex × diagnosis × Stimulus + variance due to random factors	R	2	R/2

The significance of the various factors is determined by the ratio of the variance estimate of each factor to that of the residual and by checking the significance level for the appropriate degrees of freedom in tables of the various ratio F. When scores are clearly not significant, i.e. $F \leqslant 1$ the variance estimate associated with that factor may be pooled with that due to the residual, the number of degrees of freedom increased by summation and the sensitivity of the test increased.

If the relationship of the startle response to other measurable characteristics is to be examined correlational techniques may be used. In the first instance it may be that, although the two stimuli differ quantitatively in their effect, those who respond most to one stimulus also respond more than others to the other stimulus. Computation of the correlation coefficient (p. 199) between the scores of subjects subjected to both stimuli will give an indication of whether this is the case. It is possible that subjects may vary in their response to the two types of stimuli and that this variability may be associated with other physiological or psychological characteristics. Where these can be measured further correlation coefficients can be computed. The techniques used will vary according to the standard of measurement obtained. If it is required to use the same coefficient for all comparisons the scores obtained on higher scales can always be degraded. Thus ratio scores can always be used as the basis of a rank order and a rank correlation coefficient computed. An array of correlation coefficients may then be set up, for instance those between the results with the two types of stimulus and scores on tests of intelligence, pain threshold, pain reaction point, extraversion–introversion, neuroticism and perhaps some other stimulus–response tests, say increase in heart rate after exertion and increase in physiological tremor under load. Such an array may be subjected to factor-analysis, which may reveal whether any groups of findings are significantly associated and if so in what way. It may be found, for instance, that the variance is effectively accounted for by one factor and that the scores of physiological reactivity correlate with the introversion–extraversion dimensions of personality. On the other hand two or more factors may be necessary to account for the variance (in our example this should be the case, anyway, as extraversion and neuroticism are held to be orthogonal, i.e. independent, factors while intelligence is not thought to be particularly closely related to them). Further, the experimenter should not accept his statistical results uncritically no matter how impressive. Again we can illustrate this from our example as a correlation will always be found between pain thresh-hold and pain reaction point due to the fact that the second is by definition above the first. This correlation may have no other significance.

We hope that this discussion of some imaginary experiments will have served to suggest some of the ways in which the statistical techniques described in theearly part of this chapter can be used. We should emphasize that for the majority of people working in psychology and in medicine the best way to learn statistics and experimental design is to do experiments.

References and further reading

An introductory text of this nature is better not overburdened with references. The books selected here will take the reader deeper into the various aspects of the subject and will themselves provide reference to original work. The *Penguin Modern Psychology* series provides a useful and varied collection of original papers.

General references
WRIGHT, D. S., TAYLOR, A., DAVIES, D. ROY, SLUCKIN, W. G., LEE, S. G. M. & REASON, J. T. (1970) *Introducing Psychology—An Experimental Approach.* Harmondsworth: Penguin. A good inexpensive introduction to general psychology which will give the framework of the subject. It has an extensive list of further references.

EYSENCK, H. J. (ed.) (1961) *Handbook of Abnormal Psychology.* London: Pitman Medical. A collection of experimental and review articles, now somewhat outdated, on standard areas of abnormal psychology.

MITTLER, P. J. (ed.) (1970) *Psychological Assessment of Mental and Physical Handicaps.* London: Methuen. An up-to-date survey of practical assessment problems.

Chapter 1. Intelligence
BUTCHER, H. J. (1968) *Human Intelligence—Its Nature and Assessment.* London: Methuen. An up-to-date survey of this field, which includes discussion of Piaget's contribution and of the controversial areas of creativity and ability.

VERNON, P. E. (1960) *Intelligence and Attainment Tests.* London: University of London Press.
WECHSLER, D. (1958) *The Measurement and Appraisal of Adult Intelligence.* Baltimore: Williams & Wilkins.
Both the above can now be regarded as classic texts in this branch of psychology.

Chapter 3. Intellectual Deficit
The books by Wechsler and Mittler mentioned above both provide extensive discussion and further references in the subject.

WILLIAMS, M. (1970) *Brain Damage and the Mind.* Harmondsworth: Penguin. A concise introduction to the assessment of brain damage.

Chapter 4. Perception
VERNON, M. D. (1970) *Perception through Experience.* London: Methuen. The standard textbook on perception. It will provide a full account and a source of further reading.

MERSKEY, H. M. & SPEAR, F. G. (1967) *Pain: Psychological and Psychiatric Aspects.* London: Baillière, Tindall & Cassell. Still an up-to-date and comprehensive review of this medically important aspect of sensation and perception.

Chapter 4. Personality, personality assessment and differential diagnosis
VERNON, P. E. (1964) *Personality Assessment*. London: Methuen. A general introduction.

CATTELL, R. B. (1965) *Scientific Analysis of Personality*. Harmondsworth: Penguin.

EYSENCK, H. J. (1970) *The Structure of Human Personality*, 3rd ed. London: Methuen. Although essentially accounts of the authors' own theories, these two books provide excellent illustrations of the factorial method of personality research.

Chapter 5. Emotion
HARLOW, H. F. (1962) 'The development of affectional patterns in infant monkeys' in *Determinants of Infant Behaviour* (ed. Foss, B. M.). London: Wiley. An experimental study of the influence of parental behaviour on subsequent emotional development.

LORENZ, K. (1966) *On Aggression*. London: Methuen. A classic ethological study.

MORRIS, D. (1967) *The Naked Ape*. London: McGraw-Hill. A rather general and speculative account of human behaviour, based on the ethological approach.

ARNOLD, M. (1960) *Emotions and Personality*. London: Cassell. A rather old but sound basic account.

Chapter 6. Motivation
Much work and writing on motivation overlaps with that on personality and emotion. General texts on psychology invariably include a discussion of the subject, including the general text recommended above (Wright *et al.* 1970).

BINDRA, D. & STEWART, J. (ed.) (1966) *Motivation*. Harmondsworth: Penguin.

COFER, C. N. & APPLEY, M. H. (1964) *Motivation*. New York: Wiley.

Chapter 7. The varieties of psychotherapy
FREUD, S. (1949) *An Outline of Psychotherapy*. London: Hogarth. Freud's own summary of his own approach. There is no substitute for the first-hand account.

FREUD, S. (1971) *The Complete Introductory Lectures on Psychoanalysis*, trans. Strachey, J. London: Allen & Unwin. A more extensive discussion.

BROWN, J. A. C. (1961) *Freud and the Post-Freudians*. Harmondsworth: Penguin. An excellent discussion of the Freudian school and its evolution.

Chapter 8. Psychoanalytic therapy and its derivatives
FROMM REICHMAN, F. (1950) *Principles of Intensive Psychotherapy*. Chicago: University of Chicago Press. One of the many books dealing with technique, generally helpful and straightforward.

Chapter 9. Behaviour therapy and behaviour modifications
MEYER, V. & CHESSER, E. S. (1970) *Behaviour Therapy in Clinical Psychiatry*. Harmondsworth: Penguin. A full and inexpensive account of theory and technique, giving further references.

ALLYON, T. & AZRIN, W. H. (1968) *The Token Economy*. New York: Appleton Century Croft. An account, by active workers, of approaches using operant conditioning methods.

HILGARD, E. R. & BOWER, G. H. (1966) *Theories of Learning*, 3rd ed. New York: Appleton Century Croft. A standard academic account.

Chapter 10. Some other psychotherapies
BALINT, M. (1957) *The Doctor, His Patient and His Illness*. London: Pitman. An interesting account of the use of psychotherapy, based on analytic theory, in general practice.

BERNE, E. (1968) *Games People Play*. Harmondsworth: Penguin. Originally intended as an illustration of the practical application of transactional game analysis, this book achieved great popular success.

LAING, R. D. (1967) *The Divided Self*. Harmondsworth: Penguin. The first of the author's series of original and provocative discussions of schizophrenia and alienation.

LIFTON, R. J. (1961) *Thought Reform*. London: Gollancz (1967, Harmondsworth: Penguin). An account of brainwashing techniques, based on original investigations.

BARBER, T. X. (1969) *Hypnosis: A Scientific Approach*. London: Van Nostrand. Most books on hypnosis are unsatisfactory. This is one of the few which attempts a scientific approach of acceptable standard.

Chapter 11. Physical therapies
KALINKOWSKI, L. B. & HOCH, P. H. (1969) *Physical Treatment in Psychiatry*. New York: Grune & Stratton. A comprehensive review with an extensive list of references.

Chapter 12. Small groups
FOULKES, S. H. & ANTHONY, E. J. (1957) *Group Psychotherapy*. Harmondsworth: Penguin. A rather discursive account, but by pioneers of the method.

CARTWRIGHT, D. & ZANDER, A. (1968) *Group Dynamics: Research and Theory*. 3rd ed· London: Tavistock. A general review, not limited to therapeutic groups.

ARGYLE, M. (1967) *The Psychology of Interpersonal Behaviour*. Harmondsworth: Penguin. A brief introduction to interactional behaviour with reference to non-verbal communicative behaviour.

Chapter 13. Large groups
STANTON, A. H. & SCHWARTZ, M. S. (1954) *The Mental Hospital*. New York: Basic Books. The classic early text.

CLARK, D. H. (1964) *Administrative Therapy*. London: Tavistock. A description of the application of change based on the therapeutic community approach to an English mental hospital.

KATZ, D. & KAHN, R. L. (1966) *The Social Psychology of Organisations*. New York: Wiley. An extensive discussion of organizational behaviour, mainly related to industry, using open system theory as a framework.

Appendix 1. Statistical methods and experimental design
MAXWELL, A. E. (1970) *Basic Statistics in Behavioural Research*. Harmondsworth: Penguin. A cheap but sound account of experimental design.

McNEMAR, Q. (1962) *Psychological Statistics*, 3rd ed. New York: Wiley. A basic and intelligible account of general statistical methods.

SIEGEL, S. (1956) *Non-parametric Statistics for the Behavioural Sciences*. New York: McGraw-Hill. Non-parametric statistics are the only ones applicable to many experiments. Siegel provides a clear and practical discussion of these methods.

Index